THE POPULARITY OF MIDDLE ENGLISH ROMANCE

Velma Bourgeois Richmond

The Popularity of Middle English Romance

by

Velma Bourgeois Richmond

Bowling Green University Popular Press
Bowling Green, Ohio 43403

Copyright © 1975 by the Bowling Green University Popular Press, Ray B. Browne, Editor.

The Bowling Green University Popular Press is the publishing division of the Center for the Study of Popular Culture, Ray B. Browne, Director.

Library of Congress Catalogue Card Number: 75-21516

ISBN: 0-87972-114-6 Clothbound

Printed in the United States of America.

For Hugh

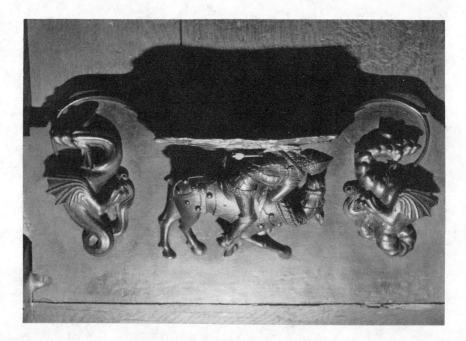

The Falling Knight   Courtesy of Lincoln Cathedral

The carving on this misericord has the clearest representation in England of plate armour of the later fourteenth-century. The subject has sometimes been identified as the 'Fall of Pride' from the Psychomachia.

CONTENTS

PREFACE

Probably it is never possible to express fully one's indebtedness for the various kinds of assistance which help to shape a study like this. Many I have indicated in the text and notes, but here I would like to single out a few particular individuals. First, I want to thank the Administration of Holy Names College for the generous granting of a sabbatical leave to begin this study. I am very grateful to my colleague and friend Sister M. Claire Madeleine Carlin with whom I have spent countless hours talking about literature. My deepest appreciation, as the dedication indicates, is of my husband, whose personal encouragement and professional advice have been consistently and immediately available.

V.E.B.R.

LIST OF ILLUSTRATION

CHAPTER I

THE POPULARITY OF MIDDLE ENGLISH ROMANCE

The Middle English romance has elicited throughout the centuries a curious mixture of indifference, hostile apprehension, and contempt that perhaps no other literature—except its most likely offspring, modern best-sellers—has provoked. Philologists, historians, and folklorists have written copiously about the romance, and recent attempts have been made to describe its structure, style, and oral tradition.[1] Yet many of these narratives lack both readers and admirers, even among medievalists; and no satisfactory explanation of their undenied early and sustained popularity but subsequent lack of reputation has been offered. Some reasons for this historical phenomenon may emerge from a rather unconventional approach which deliberately seeks to define that "popularity," for as I. A. Richards, writing about 'badness in poetry,' noted: "Best-sellers in all the arts, exemplifying as they do the most general levels of attitude development, are worthy of very close study. No theory of criticism is satisfactory which is not able to explain their wide appeal."[2]

The general problem was precisely stated by William Matthews in his discussion of "Inherited Impediments in Medieval Literary History": "Many once-pleasing things there must be in their themes, ideas, styles, presentation which now escape us. We have very few analyses of medieval aesthetics, of the medieval criteria relating to literary content and form which could help us to understand why this work or that was aesthetically a failure, a mediocrity, or a success in its own day."[3] As Matthews intends, the scope of the challenge implied in such a statement is enormous. Much of his hope for future medieval study lies in overcoming "some unexamined traditional idea or attitudes."[4]

Perhaps these rather formidable challenges can never be satisfactorily answered, but they do make clear the dangers of literary criticism which is too exclusive and thus suggest a need for alternatives. An informed awareness can result from a knowledge of increasingly diverse and precise scholarship about the 'medieval period' to prevent grotesque improprieties of forcing a 'modern interpretation' or misunderstanding essential elements of style. But these esoteric particularities should not obscure the universality that is characteristic of all successful literature, nor should today's critic assume that he can 'become a medieval mind' so that he displaces his twentieth-century sensibility, with its concerns and knowledge. Traditional approaches to medieval literature may, then, helpfully be modified so that they do not get in the way of a fuller appreciation. Perhaps nowhere is the need greater than with the medieval romance. Even the use of this generic designation has been challenged,[5] in "the most elusive of literary forms,"[6] so that the supposedly elementary detail of definition has occasioned much divergence of opinion. Thus "All critics apparently concur that . . . there will emerge only hazy borderlines where epic, saga, *chanson de geste,* romance, historical romance, *lai,* saint's life, pious legend, fabliau meet and blend."[7] Further, much of the material is yet to receive more than cursory treatment in general studies or fragmentary elucidation of very precise particularities.

The so-called "gems" of this genre, like *Sir Gawain and the Green Knight,* the *Morte Arthure, Troilus and Criseyde,* Malory, have obviously not been neglected. They have been written about and judged as have the works of Shakespeare or Dickens or Faulkner. And although enthusiasts have from time to time asserted the claims for other individual romances, Matthews' comment on *Morte Arthure,* "No one has written an extended critical study of the poem,"[8] would describe most of the narratives. The conventional view has been that most Middle English romances are tedious and uninspired. The genre which originated in French and German was long thought to have gained little in its English manifestations; however, more recent critics have argued that the later derivations, though undeniably different, are not necessarily inferior.[9] Actually discussions of French and German romances do not strikingly contrast with those of English romances, for they also tend to emphasize and praise a few unusual examples, like the works of Chrétien de Troyes or Gottfried von Strassburg's *Tristan,* while deprecating most romances as uninspired.[10]

The genre as a whole, then, supposedly lacks literary finesse and distinction of ideas. Typically there are few attempts at incisive characterization, lively dialogue, fine dramatic or narrative scenes, and a controlling intellectual idea or sense of moral purpose. Written to amuse an audience with somewhat limited entertainments, the medieval romance seems to many of its modern readers long and repetitive, abounding in undistinguished detail which somehow was tolerated by the less critical men and women of the Middle Ages who had no better resources. Even many students of literature do not read the romances, apart from the "gems"—and these often in translation. Yet the popularity of the Middle English romance is clear over a period of several hundred years: through the survival of more than one hundred romances, often in several manuscript versions; in the choice of many such narratives for early printing, and the enthusiastic work of printers like Caxton, de Worde, and Pynson, who made personal, vital contributions to the genre; and by the sustained reprinting of certain favorites into the seventeenth century and the enthusiastic praise of many of England's great poets as well as critics like Sidney, Puttenham and Dr. Johnson.[11] Surely we have here a cogent argument for the validity of a reconsideration of the Middle English romance as something more than a dull corpus enlivened only by a few brilliant and untypical achievements (which, incidentally, have not all survived in more than one manuscript). Without ignoring the obvious attractions of Chaucer or exquisite lyrics which so instantly appeal, without denying the historical and traditional interest and values of the Arthurian material, we may read these narratives very much more sympathetically—particularly if we can find an approach which explains their appeal in more universal terms. In short, we need to understand what there was in the medieval romance which made it so popular with its immediate audience and with later readers for more than a century—but has not characteristically elicited the admiration of subsequent readers.

The popularity of the Middle English romance cannot be statistically charted in the ways used by Q. D. Leavis in *Fiction and the Reading Public* and James Hart in *The Popular Book*[12] to define modern tastes and influences. The amount of material that has survived simply is not adequate. H. S. Bennett's comprehensive study of early books makes the point in a discussion of fifteenth-century tastes (for old romances among other things): "For us today it is impossible to do much more than to record these things in summary fashion, and to make what deductions we will on very general grounds. So much has perished, and in any case the number of manuscripts of any work was so comparatively small that statistics are useless."[13] Or as Lillian Herlands Hornstein notes: "Yet, sensible and seductive as are the theories which this bibliography [revised *Manual*] records about why, where, and how the romance came into being and flourished, the latitude of our speculation is circumscribed almost exclusively by the internal evidence of the romances themselves."[14] Thus she gives a page summary of what we do not know, the "abyss of ignorance" that confronts us. Nevertheless, some general points can be made about the survival and diffusion of romances that provide a helpful background for analysis of the popularity of the texts themselves.

A brief study of where Middle English romances appear in manuscripts is very illuminating.[15] There are few purely 'secular' collections comparable to the French and German. Dieter Mehl summarizes: "Nearly all romances have survived in large collections containing for the most part religious and didactic literature. In many cases the close relationship between the romances and other items is also suggested by the language and style of the poems."[16] His helpful appendix calls attention to key characteristics of some of the most important collections such as the Auchinleck MS., B. M. Egerton 2862, and the two Thornton MSS. Obviously many of the romances exist in unique copies. Although Mehl expresses a hope for much more extensive study of manuscripts, his chief conclusion is very helpfully suggestive when he adds that hardly any romances survived in the 'Aureate Collections,' with the works of Chaucer, Gower, and Lydgate. Rather they appear in unpretentious collections and are often with didactic and religious works, so that the exemplary quality is immediately suggested.[17] In short, much of the argument of this excellent study suggests the importance of moral and religious elements in Middle English romances, one of the commonplace bases of their popularity, and the inadequacy of previous views of the material which stress sources or 'matters' or prosody or genres. Nevertheless, Mehl, reflecting modern preoccupation with form, emphasizes length, its relation to oral recitation, rather than the meaning of the texts.

The profession of letters in the Middle Ages has been briefly described by H. S. Bennett in the introductory part of his study of *English*

Books and Readers 1475 to 1557.[18] Clearly authors did not depend upon writing to earn their livings, so that selection of materials would rarely have been merely an expression of personal tastes. An overwhelming number of authors were ecclesiastics, and many others were private retainers in noble families, so that these anonymous authors were writing characteristically, to order.[19] The inclusiveness of this generalization is clear from references to Chrétien and Gower, or chroniclers like Froissart and Trevisa, but many anonymous works, especially in the later period, seem more modest in their anonymity and increasing popular audience.

In Anglo-Norman literature a particularly strong case for the influence of patrons upon writers has been made by M. D. Legge, who designates many of the most popular as "Ancestral Romances."[20] She argues that after the Conquest a new type of romance, a kind of 'family chronicle' was invented to deal with English legends and characters. Two of the most popular Middle English romances, *Bevis of Hampton* and *Guy of Warwick* are, of course, in the group. The authors were "quite possibly members of the regular clergy, inmates of houses founded or patronized by the family for whom these stories were concocted. Perhaps the most surprising thing is the widespread popularity of most of them. Although created for a specific and local purpose, they had sufficient topical interest to become part of universal literature. Nevertheless, today it is difficult to understand the fortunes of some. The fame of Roland and Tristram can be understood much more easily than the reputation of Bevis of Hampton or Guy of Warwick. But it is just a matter of taste, the hardest thing in the world to understand."[21]

This characteristic bafflement about the popularity of certain romances is the occasion for the present study, particularly the selection of the narratives included, and the issues will be dealt with more fully. Here I want to emphasize Legge's singling out the unanimity of taste: that romances commissioned by the nobility and written by the clergy should also have generated enthusiastic response from a much wider audience. Laura H. Loomis' definitive article about the Auchinleck Manuscript makes very clear the early association of the romances with a popular reading public in England.[22] The evidence of a lay bookshop in London before 1350 that produced this substantial, but not 'luxurious,' manuscript of writings in English, indicates an alternative to the splendid books written in Latin or French which typically filled libraries of the time. The "natural reading public" for the book, "wholly English in character,"[23] clearly had a taste for romance. Of the forty-four items that remain (thirteen of the original have been lost) in 334 leaves, eighteen are romances, and "both in number and individual length make up by far the largest section of the book."[24] The works have been described as the efforts of "literary hacks," particularly for their pedestrian style and verbal indebtedness, especially in formulaic utterances that suggest borrowings analogous to those due to oral tradition and similarly used as aids to facilitate comprehension.[25] The last significant detail to be emphasized about the Auchinleck Manuscript is that it was produced in London, for as J. W. Thompson notes: "The English book trade developed not around the Universities, as on the Continent, but in London, where the stationers formed a guild as early as 1403."[26] The relationship between non-academic and popular will become increasingly clear. Here it is worth noting that the Auchinleck Manuscript provides the earliest known text for both *Guy of Warwick* (which has been most popular with readers through the centuries and contemptuously regarded by scholars) and *Amis and Amiloun* (which is central to critical discussions of the nature of romance, especially in the last ten years), as well as *Kyng Alisaunder* (which is most highly esteemed of the English versions and whose author is praised as "very learned") and *Otuel* (which is 'idiosyncratic' and 'banal').

The same broad interests and diversity in romance can be more fully documented by an investigation of the early history of printing. A larger public had been created through the centuries. By Chaucer's time, though the magnificent illuminated manuscripts were in Latin and French, English was clearly going to prevail, and in the fifteenth century the vernacular was in control. Thus a larger group of readers, not merely ecclesiastical and noble, were eager for materials, and the new demand was filled by an increased output of writers and scribes. Indeed it was the existence of such a demanding reading public, already being served in the fourteenth century and clearly established in the fifteenth century, which made possible the early success of printing in England.[27]

The publication and dissemination of books has always been closely related to their popular acceptance. Fifteenth-century producers of manuscripts offered materials for which there was a demand; for example, works of a specifically religious, moral, or didactic nature, chronicles, and some pure literature; and William Caxton's work is of

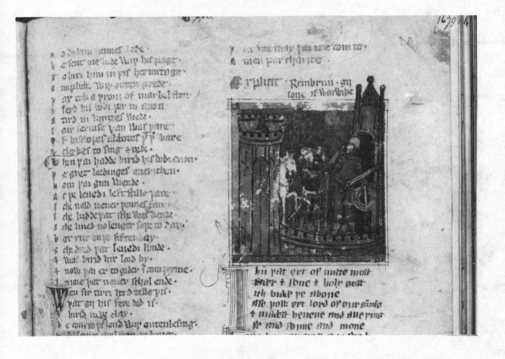

The Auchinleck Manuscript (Adv. MS. 19.2.1.)

This half page shows the conclusion of Guy of Warwick's story and illumination introducing the story of his son Reinbroun, which is a separate romance here. This page indicates how the Auchinleck editor divided the work between various translators.

the same variety. Indeed Caxton explains that he undertook to learn the art of printing because he was too old to make enough copies to supply the demand for his translation of *The Recuyell of the Historyes of Troye.* [28]

Studies of this first English printer amply document Caxton's careful understanding of his audience's taste and his cautious business sense. His selection of texts involved very little risk. Nearly half of his publications (35 out of the 77 original editions, or 56 out of 103 published items) were of a religious or didactic nature. Of these, nine ran into two or more editions, an indication of the accuracy of Caxton's view of the market. Popular poets, works of instruction, and romances make up the rest of his list. Of the seventy-seven original works published, twenty-three had the favor of powerful patrons and some assured financial support. Bennett summarizes: "He makes little attempt to educate or lead public taste, but prints what it was easy for him to know was popular by inquiry of the scriveners concerning manuscript circulation, or what the prevailing predilection for religious writings made a certain success." [29]

So unpretentious a view of the fifteenth-century Englishman whose name is most familiar (apart from those of monarchs) is basic to N. F. Blake's recent definitive study of William Caxton. [30] This biography and evaluation of Caxton stresses the merchant quality which is pronounced throughout his lifetime, for Blake refutes the idea of Caxton the businessman who turned into a pious scholar when he devoted himself to printing and translating. The significance of Caxton's business skill in the history of English printing is that it gave a unique continuity, for if his successor Wynkyn de Worde is included, the business survived for nearly sixty years, rather than for the few years which most early continental presses managed. A virtual monopoly was assured by the desire for English books (Caxton's almost exclusive choice of vernacular is unusual), and Caxton's sure sense of the public tastes, many parts of which he may well have solidified.

The genuine passion for romance that has long been attributed to Caxton is more strongly urged by Blake, who argues not only that most of Caxton's career was devoted "to providing the upper classes with moral tales of chivalry," but also that Caxton would have published nothing else had political conditions been sufficiently stable, since religious books were printed during periods of civil strife. [31] More medieval than modern in outlook, Caxton expresses his deep moral concern and religious fervor—which detailed comparisons of his translations with original texts often make clear—through the romances that he had become acquainted with while associated with the Burgundian court. His lack of interest in the humanistic thought, the New Learning, developing at the end of the fifteenth century, is clear from his not publishing the classics and his distinctively 'medieval' translation of Virgil, so objected to by Gawin Douglas for its French basis, additions and cutting (of the last six books). Such criticism is typical of that leveled at Caxton specifically and the medieval romance generally for its lack of literary finesse and integrity according to the criteria of humanistic thought.

The conclusion of Blake's study is that Caxton's "individual contribution to English letters is not so important as the evidence he gives of the taste and culture of the fifteenth century."[32] From my point of view this is crucial, since the popularity of the romance is the key element. As a businessman Caxton may have been too keen to curry favor with the aristocracy, though the smaller quartos suggest the broadening of his audience as the printing house continued. The richly documented vogue of chivalric romance through several centuries undercuts Blake's argument against the fashionable nature of Caxton's enterprise: "the books Caxton published, while purporting to be serious moral works, were essentially ephemeral. They appealed to his buyers because they believed them to be what others were reading at the time; but they had to be convinced that this was so by the inclusion of a patron's name."[33] Perhaps this is yet another example of the humanist preconceptions which have doggedly condemned medieval romance since Erasmus and Vives made this the fashionable attitude. His argument that such books are not necessary for "the functions of everyday life" is given the lie by the sustained popularity of these narratives and their successors—bestsellers, thrillers, magazine short fiction.

Caxton's close connections with Margaret of Burgundy, and his many prefatory comments about patrons, give the impression of writing for a noble audience. But his publishing output is only part of the romance's story, for de Worde and Copland must also be taken into account. Further, it might be worth noting Q. D. Leavis' observation that tastes in fiction gradually filter down from the intelligentsia to the next classes,[34] which is particularly appropriate in a period of expanding literacy. In addition, there is the previously noted enthusiasm expressed for Anglo-Norman romances by varied readers. Such popularity can be more fully documented by a consideration of romances produced in the first hundred years of printing, when readers again were apparently not restricted to a single group.

The basic circumstances were defined in Ronald S. Crane's pioneer study of *The Vogue of Medieval Chivalric Romance during the English Renaissance*. He says that paucity of documents make precise descriptions of the reading public difficult, but the surviving evidence suggests two groups who read romances during the first hundred years after printing was introduced. The aristocrats, relatively few in number, preferred translations of French prose romances; and there was a small market for expensive and elegant folios of romances like *Le Morte Darthur, The Recuyell,* and *The Four Sons of Aymon*. A larger group, socially less clearly defined, delighted in fourteenth and fifteenth century metrical romances; and they bought the simply printed quartos—for example, *Sir Bevis, Sir Guy, Sir Degare, Sir Eglamour, Richard Coer de Lion*—that sold cheaply. This humbler audience was reached in the country by traveling booksellers.[35] For example, John Rush bought from Pynson twenty copies of *Bevis* and sold them in the country for ten pence apiece, in contrast with a price of two shillings for "bocas off the falle of prynces" and five shillings for the "canterbery Talys." And in 1520 the Oxford bookseller John Dorn sold *Bevis* (with a small tract) for sixpence, *Sir Eglamour* and *Robert the Devil* for threepence, and *Sir Isumbras* for twopence. Prose romances were dearer; a quarto *King Ponthus* sold for eight pence and a folio *Four Sons of Aymon* for one shilling eight pence. These prices, particularly when compared with costs of three shillings and four pence for a massive volume of *The Golden Legend* or six shillings and eight pence for a leather-bound version of Lyndewode's *Constitutions,* indicate that the purchasing power of the reading public had a wide range.

The less pretentious printings of the romance were particularly fostered by Wynkyn de Worde to whom we owe at least ten or eleven first editions: "No one else showed so keen an interest in this field."[36] Copland, of course, printed editions of more than a dozen romances in the middle of the sixteenth century. The significance of these surviving materials is eloquently attested by Bennett: "At least fifty editions of the romances exist, but this only partly tells of their popularity. Few forms of literature have been thumbed to pieces more completely than these slender quartos. When we speak of fifty editions we are not speaking of present copies, but of those remains which enable us to say that once an edition existed."[37] The random survival of a page or two merely suggests the popularity of romances. Such modest editions were not carefully tended or preserved, and undoubtedly many were read until they fell apart and were discarded as paperbacks are today.

Although there is a more diversified fiction available in England after the 1570's, with the enthusiasm for continental and especially Italian tales, as well as native writers like Deloney, Nashe, and Forde, the medieval chivalric romance continued to be popular. Metrical versions disappeared, and there were losses of some prose romances; but into the seventeenth century the material held its own, particularly *Guy* and *Bevis,* and prose romances like *Valentine and Orson* from the Caxton house enjoyed reprintings and new versions. Finally, the Spanish chivalric romances, which are very similar, attest the sustained popularity of the form.[38] As might be expected, the American reading public showed the same preference for romances. The invoices of John Usher, Boston's leading bookseller, show that between 1682 and 1685 these narratives made up the fourth largest category of titles (after Religious, School Texts, Bibles and Psalm Books), nearly five per cent. And the selections included *Guy of Warwick* as well as Renaissance favorites like Nashe, Deloney, Sidney, Quarles.[39]

With such evidence of the popularity of the Middle English romances, the mixture of contempt, indifference, and apprehension they have generated seems remarkable. Throughout much modern critical commentary there is an uneasiness about making any claim for these narratives,[40] and the reasons are fairly clear. The differences in the reading public observed by Q. D. Leavis in the history of modern fiction, that is, a polarization between popular novels and significant literature, simply are not evidenced in the Middle Ages, when aristocrats, clerics, and populace all enjoyed romances. The discrepancy between the 'bestseller' and quality is not true in the eighteenth or even the nineteenth century when the well educated and the man in the street read the same novels.[41] The loss of Dr. Johnson's "common reader," in short, is a modern development with the advent of tabloid journalism, but this loss is presaged by humanistic responses to the medieval romance. The intellectual processes of the New Learning, based upon enthusiasm for the classics, were not compatible with much medieval thought and literary modes that had developed in their own distinctive ways.

This is particularly ironic since one strong argument for the origin of romance is its association with the revival of classical studies in the schools of twelfth-century France. Faral's basic work shows that the romancers were formed by study of the trivium and quadrivium with emphasis on the great classical authors. These clerics, seeking a more popular and broader audience for their knowledge of classical literature, used a vernacular form in seeking to repeat the success of *chansons de geste* which had been so effective with Carolingean legends. For the *romans bretons* the Celtic sources and influences must be recognized, but the *romans d'antiquité,* it is generally agreed, precede these. In short, there seems to have been no great conflict between academic and popular or classical and medieval during the Middle Ages. The charge of "vayne carpynge" at the beginning of *Speculum Vitae* is unusual, and it is less characteristic than the beginning of the English biblical omnibus *Cursor Mundi* which, before explaining that its subject matter is the Christian story, lists many popular romances without denouncing them as base and immoral. Furthermore, there are few such references; positive values in romances are more typically expected.[42]

To Erasmus and Juan Luis Vives may be attributed the origins of the hostility that has determined present estimate of the medieval romance. As a classical-minded pedagogue, Erasmus objected to stories of Arthur and Lancelot—"fablae stultae et aniles"—because they distracted the student from his proper concern with classical poetry and history. Vives' opposition took a moral tone, and his injunctions appear—not without significance—in a treatise dealing with the conduct of women, who are not to defile their minds with such books. *De Institutione feminae christianae* (1523) contains a list of forbidden romances, which is quietly expanded in the 1540 (reprinted in 1541, 1557, and 1592) translation of Richard Hyrde to include English examples. As might be expected, the titles are among the most popular—Parthonope, Generydes, Ipomedon, Lybaeus Desconus, Arthur, Guy, and Bevis. Vives' *De Officio Mariti* also contains warnings in the section "De Disciplina Feminae," and the translation of Thomas Paynell (1546) shows the tone:

. . . and many other which are written in the vulgar tonge, as of Trystram, Launcelot, Ogier, Amasus and of Arthur the which were written and made by suche as were ydle & knewe nothinge. These books do hurte both man and woman, for they make them wylye & craftye, they kyndle and styr up covetousnes, inflame angre, & all beastly and filthy desyre.[43]

Montaigne's first book of *Essays* (1580) contains a comparable denunciation, admittedly based on prejudiced ignorance rather than actual reading of the texts. Florio's translation (which adds Arthur) was widely read:

For of King *Arthur*, of *Lancelot du Lake*, of *Amadis*, of *Huon of Burdeaux* and such idle time consuming, and wit-besotting trash of bookes wherein youth doth commonly ammuse it self, I was not so much as acquainted with their names, and to this day know not their bodies, nor what they containe: So exact was my discipline.[44]

An extra hostility developed after the Reformation, for the romances were clearly seen as the work of Papists. The best known objector is, of course, Roger Ascham. In *Toxophilus* (1545) he wrote:

In our fathers tyme nothing was red, but books of fayned chivalrie, wherein a man by redinge, shuld be led to none other ends, but only to manslaughter and baudrye. Yf any man suppose they were good ynough to passe the time with al, he is deceyved. For surelye vayne woordes doo worke no smal thinge in vayne, ignoraunt, and younge mindes, specially yf they be gyven any thynge therunto of theyr owne nature. These bokes (as I have heard say) were made the moste parte in Abbayes, and Monasteries, a very lickely and fit fruite of suche an ydle and blynde kinde of lyvying.[45]

And there is the better known revision in *The Scholemaster* (1570):

In our forefathers tyme, whan Papistrie, as a standyng poole, couuered and ouerflowed all England, fewe bookes were read in our tong, sauying certaine bookes Cheualrie, as they sayd, for pastime and pleasure, which, as some say, were made in Monasteries, by idle Monkes or wanton Chanons: as one for example, *Morte Arthure*: the whole pleasure of which booke standeth in two speciall poyntes, in open mans slaughter, and bold bawdrye:[46]

It should perhaps be recalled that the passage concludes with Ascham's estimate that bad though *Morte Arthure* is, a translation of a book made in Italy was ten times worse!

Two years later a Puritanical clergyman, Edward Dering, prefaced his *Bryfe and Necessary Catechisme or instruction* with a lament over contemporary taste for books "full of synne and abominations" which was like the "wickedness" of their forefathers who "had their spiritual enchantments, in which they were bewytched, Bevis of Hampton, Guy of Warwicke, Arthur of the round table, Huon of Burdeaux, Oliver of the Castle, the foure sonnes of Amond, and a great many other such childish follye."[47] The eccentricity of such attacks is particularly striking when we recall that less than a hundred years previously Caxton had not only alternated medieval romances with books of religious instruction, but also expressed his own moral and religious sensibility in his translations. What this means to the fundamental English moral point of view is cogently expressed by G. R. Owst in his defense of another area of 'popular literature': "And that strange Providence that often delights to order the ways of men so differently from the history-books and the wise conceits of *Littérateurs* ordained for its 'primers' of study, not the learned tomes of the Classical Revival, but these same little works of devotion and moral instruction. The fact that they and kindred trivialities figure so largely in Caxton's list only goes to prove, of course, how far they had already become the true literature of a people, for whom Reformation was to mean more than Renaissance, and character more than wit."[48]

Literary, as well as ethical, hostility developed in the sixteenth century as standards of classicism and rationalism were applied to the romances. "Their remoteness from reality, their improbability, their extravagant idealism were bound to offend tastes formed on the literature of antiquity."[49] In The *Anatomie of Absurditie* (1589) Thomas Nashe objected to "the fantasticall dreames of those exiled Abbielubbers, from whose idle pens proceeded those worne out impressions of the feyned no where acts" of heroes like Arthur, Tristram, Huon, and the four sons of Aymon; and he also ridiculed rimes in metrical romances like *Bevis*. The humanists' exaltation of the classics is explicit in Sir William Cornwallis' Essay 15 (1600) when he asks:

If in *Arthur of Britaine, Huon of Burdeaux* and such supposed chivalrie, a man may better himselfe, shall he not become excellent with conversing with *Tacitus, Plutarch, Sallust,* and fellowes of that ranke?[50]

Not surprisingly, then, the seventeenth-century audience for romances was not academics but rather tradesmen, servants, women, country gentry, children—in short, the less fashionable and pretentious, the basic popular readers who preserved the old-fashioned tastes and morality of the Middle Ages.

The ridicule of such tastes in Beaumont and Fletcher's *Knight of the Burning Pestle* (1610-1611) has delighted scholars with its burlesque of romances and romantic dramas. However, the publisher of the first quarto edition (1613) frankly admits that the play's first audience at Blackfriars, where it was produced by the Children of the Queen's Revels, promptly rejected it. It is tempting to feel that this 'popular' audience was not convinced by the new humanist prejudices. A contrast is afforded by the much earlier work of Nicholas Udall; *Ralph Roister Doister* (1538?) happily blends classical and native English material. Specifically, Merrygreek names (I.ii.118-26) some of the most popular romance heroes—Lancelot, Guy, Alexander, Hector, Colbrand (Guy's opponent), as well as Biblical and classical figures in his inflation of the braggart, who is so obviously unworthy to be included in such company. And Shakespeare's use of the Nine Worthies in *Love's Labor's Lost* has an impressive mixture of playful exaggeration but ultimate recognition of the values of medieval romance. The dazzling, sophisticated courtiers are silenced when Armado (as Hector, exalted in *Lydgate's Troy Book,* for example) stops their witty badinage: "The sweet war-man is dead and rotten. / Sweet chucks, beat not the bones of the buried: / When he breathed, he was a man" (V.ii.652-54). The play's exposition of poetic and intellectual values makes very clear Shakespeare's early partiality for what can only be described as the mundane, popular values. The virtues of romance to a writer with this vision are demonstrated not only in *As You Like it,* but in the choice of the romance as the form for his final, most mature presentation of human experience.

Significantly, it is in the theatre that the romance had greatest influence. The last thirty years of the sixteenth century saw produced many plays derived from chivalric romance, like *Paris and Vienne* and *Valentine and Orson.* Although the Jacobean taste did not share this Elizabethan enthusiasm, *Guy* appeared in several plays between 1618 and 1639, and the *Tragical History Admirable Achievements & various events of Guy Earl of Warwick* even survived the closing of the theatres to be reissued in 1661.[51] Nevertheless, by the eighteenth century, when humanism reinforced by rationalism had won, *Guy* was described in the *Tatler* as a tale for a boy under eight years old. The same changes in taste are clear in the history of *Valentine and Orson.*[52]

This survey of the popularity of Middle English romance has neglected so far two important groups, the poets and the antiquarians. The antiquarians of the eighteenth century were interested in recovering lost texts, establishing historicity of a figure like Guy, praising the achievement of Caxton, for example, as the first English printer.[53] And in the nineteenth century the focus is still historical with the mere printing of texts, many of which are now being revised by the Early English Text Society. There were detractors among poets, from Chaucer's parody in *The Tale of Sir Thopas* onwards, but a large roster can be assembled of those who praised, while the humanists damned. Sidney's *Apology* (1595) admits that *Amadis* stirred men "to the exercise of courtesie, liberalitie, and especially courage," and William Drummond of Hawthorndon mentions his eager reading of this romance, the most popular of the newer vogue. Puttenham's *Arte of English Poesie* (1589) is not hostile. For all that Nashe condemned the romances, his contemporary Greene perpetuates the form in his *Pandosto*. Lodge not only produced *Rosalynde,* but also a version of the older, very popular *Robert the Devil.* Spenser's enthusiasm need hardly be mentioned, but Drayton's use of legends of Guy and Bevis in *Polyolbion* (Songs XII and XIII) is less familiar. The poet who most completely embodies humanistic enthusiasm for classical learning is, of course, Milton. For him, however, there was no incompatibility with medieval romance. The original plan for his great work was to have Arthur as hero, and the abandonment of this idea came with his evolving sense of the Christian hero. Milton's sympathetic response to the romance and its ethical worth is expressed in the *Apology for Smectymnus:*

I betook me among those lofty fables and romances which recount in solemn cantoes the deeds of knighthood founded by our victorious kings, and from hence had in renown over all christendom.[54]

Such praise and enthusiasm are perfectly in keeping with the judgment of England's first great literary critic, John Dryden, when he writes:

They wholly mistake the nature of criticism who think its business is principally to find fault. Criticism, as it was first instituted by Aristotle, was meant a standard of judging well; the chiefest part of which is, to observe those excellencies which should delight a reasonable reader.[55]

An aesthetic for Middle English literature has, as noted earlier, by no means been defined. But there is no doubt that the dominance of form and style over meaning that characterizes much modern literary criticism[56] is not possible from a medieval point of view. St. Augustine's *De doctrina Christiana* (IV.12-13) defines *eloquentia* as "to teach, in order to instruct; to please, in order to hold; and also assuredly, to move, in order to convince." Following Cicero, Augustine sees *docere, delectare, flectare* or alternately *probare, delectare, movere* as the proper concerns of Christian art, which in the Middle Ages involved an *imitatio Dei.*[57] The anxieties of many humanists indicate recognition of the power of romances to influence, but their expositions of certain Christian values which form the basis of centuries of popularity are not compatible with enthusiasm for the classics where, for example, strong emphasis upon formal structure (unities and meter) prevails.[58] The lessening of the demands of literary conventions which Ian Watt[59] associates with the novel's realism, does not exactly apply to the romance; they are characteristically rich in authentic detail.[60] But its corollary, the authors' carelessness about style, since their concern is exhaustive rather than elegant presentation, is certainly evident and the occasion of much hostility. As has been argued for *Piers Plowman* (another very popular work that has only recently been praised by scholar-critics), very long works inevitably contain some patches of poor writing.[61] Thus undue emphasis upon style rather than the poet's vision is particularly damaging to many romances; this is true of shorter narratives like *Amis and Amiloun* or the stanzaic *Le Morte Arthur* occasionally, but even more so of the most popular long works like *Guy of Warwick.* Finally it should be noted that popular readers are delighted by greater length in their entertainments. The extraordinary success of *Ben-Hur* and *Gone with the Wind,* which are a kind of latter-day romance as well as many other things, is among the most vivid recent illustrations.[62]

Perhaps the greatest advantage of fiction is its freedom, its admittance of variety in subject matter and techniques. Certainly the medieval romance exploits this resource; and the opportunity for investigation of experience without the constraints of hierarchal patterns so characteristic of medieval thought, is especially important. The resulting diversity, however, is a chief obstacle to criticism, for it makes stereotypes even less valid than they are in describing other kinds of literature.

Thus although romances contain endless lists and precise descriptions, they also admit a multiplicity of bizarre creatures and circumstances. Magic and the supernatural are combined with the mundane; and the use of disguise, mistaken identity, and coincidence is often fundamental. Like the modern thriller or science fiction, the romance presents a world which is highly conventional, but not the expected 'normal' and 'real' world of the reader. In fact, it is very easy to demonstrate how conservative expectations are frequently given the lie by actual experience. However flamboyant we may think the exploits of James Bond as 007, the real experiences of Richard Sorge, a German who was Russia's key director of espionage in the Far East just before and during the Second World War, are much more dazzling and daring. The feat of Apollo 11 makes it a little more difficult to regard as frivolous the work of Jules Verne and H. G. Wells. And certainly the appearance of Arthur Clarke as a commentator for the TV coverage of the moon landing offers great satisfaction in a public, international fusion of scientific technology and literary finesse. Acceptance is repeatedly given to the view of John Le Carré that the necessity for invention in his spy stories stems from a knowledge that to write about the extraordinary real experiences of today's world would provoke disbelief in the veracity of the story he is writing. Many contemporary novelists, like Lessing, Pynchon, Barth, Sinclair, and other lesser writers, reflect dissatisfaction with that 'realistic' quality of fiction which has prevailed since the eighteenth century and which was perhaps stimulated by humanist antipathy to romance.

The great popularity today of thrillers and science fiction is analogous to that of the romance in the Middle Ages. The precision with which their various worlds are described both entertains and gives credence to what is imagined. And this technical virtuosity, this characteristic handling of form, is ancillary to the more serious writers' real concerns. There is no fundamental conflict between the 'medieval sense of order' and the multiplicity of the romance world, just as there are no incongruities in the worlds created by a Bradbury, Wyndham, Asimov, MacInnes, or Deighton. The characteristic knightly hero is a man whose attitudes and ideas are well defined and constant. Whatever the circumstances, he behaves in accordance with a set of values which is both clearly established at the onset and continually reiterated and refined through many trials and adventures. Typically his point of view is not that of the world in which he must live; most frequently it comes from a heightened perception, a sense of value that gives the human being a dignity and significance which are denied or rejected by the world which challenges him.

Perhaps the simplest statement of the relation between contemporary fiction and medieval romance is a reference to the works of Tolkien, editor of the most esteemed example of the Middle English romance and author of the most successful 'modern romances.' The worlds and adventures of Hobbits and the Ring provide many of the same satisfactions as the romances which inspired their scholarly creator. Particularly notable is that they appeal to men and women of professedly sophisticated and modern tastes and interests, though academics became less approving as the Ring gained greater popularity. There is, of course, a startling absence of any 'feminine' interest (which is true in only some science fiction and almost never in thrillers). This lack is more severe in Tolkien than in narratives written hundreds of years ago, perhaps indicating a wistful longing for a relatively uncomplicated situation in which behavior can be more simply and absolutely decided upon. Certainly Tolkien's anxieties about the political and social circumstances of Europe in the thirties inform much of the writing, giving it an intellectual dimension that is analogous to the moral concerns of earlier narratives, and demonstrating that scholar and critic alike introduce their own concerns into what they write.

This kind of fiction has, then, a surface appeal and fascination; it introduces a variety of the familiar and strange—persons, creatures, places—that excite, surprise, amuse, and reassure us. When it is most successful, however, such fiction provides much more than the suspense entertainment of 'What will happen next?' and 'What strange creature, what curious behavior, will next be encountered?' or the reassurance of the familiar in evocative descriptions of clothing, landscape, or everyday activities. It offers exposition of a system of value. This is not necessarily a humanly realizable way of living; in fact, it usually offers a means of behavior which requires an excellence, a perfection that is far from attainable—by the worthy protagonist, let alone the humble listener or reader. What is memorable, and indeed inspiring, is the capacity of the human personality to strive, and in some ways to cope with and endure the manifold stresses and challenges of existence. Giants and dragons and paynims are the nominal opponents, but the knights of romances are really combating their own limited humanity—and thus providing the reader with an exposition of his own nature and some indications of how he too may survive. This positive quality is basic to the romance's popularity, and the occasion, I suspect, for its lack of appeal to modern readers who have been conditioned to think optimism a sign of lack of intelligence and/or sensitivity.

A brilliant exposition of the philosophical implications of such

narratives is to be found in Ralph Harper's *The World of the Thriller,*[63] which begins with John Buchan, sees the tradition developing with Eric Ambler, Dashiell Hammett, and Graham Greene, and flourishing today with Ian Fleming, Len Deighton, and John Le Carré. This fascinating study of existential themes and the psychology of the reader's involvement provides a phenomenology of reading thrillers. Content, not form, gives the genre definition; and it is the hero's own peril which provides suspense beyond what is characteristic in detective stories and gives an important philosophical dimension. Many of Harper's observations apply aptly to the Middle English romance as it has just been described. For example, the thriller typically shows concern with moral implications and the resolutions provide satisfactions; quest and self-discovery are crucial.[64] The language itself suggests connections;[65] Marlowe says in Raymond Chandler's *The Big Sleep* that there are "no knights in the game." But Harper's conclusion about the thriller's hero (and this is true of Chandler's Marlowe) is: "Never mind plausibility, it is virtue that really counts, the stability and honesty of the basic self."[66] Few devices occur more frequently in Middle English romances than hidden identity. Using the proper designation, Harper dicusses "cover" at length; and he concludes: "On his use of identity everything depends. This is the true sense of the crisis in the thriller. Not the nature of tension, or of the danger, or violence, not the quality of isolation, but the search for a new life through a new identity. The way of the thriller i not the way of the moralist; it is secret, not open. The hero employ ruses and disguises."[67] Other nationals have certainly written thriller but that it is preeminently an English genre makes the analogy wi Middle English romance the more cogent.

This twentieth-century genre, like all forms of literature, reflects spirit of the times which produce it. R. W. Southern has eloque climaxed his description of *The Making of the Middle Ages* by refer to literary forms. He argues that romance emerges because of the changes that were taking place in religious and secular life o twelfth century. Social, intellectual, and spiritual changes are focu a view "of life as a seeking and a journeying" when men see them "more as pilgrims and seekers" and "the imagery of journeying b a popular expression of spiritual quest."[68] Specifically, St. Anse St. Bernard exemplify the shift from static endurance to movem growth, which is reflected in the demise of the epic. The C

searching of the soul, a systematic program rooted in logic, and yet building upon compassion and tenderness, led to the popularizing of piety that results in emotional intensity which characterizes the later Middle Ages. A close connection between thought and feeling pervades, as the art vividly indicates, particularly with the acceptability of popular forms. *Miracles of the Virgin* are the most influential popular literary expression of these materials in the twelfth century; and Peter Damian, Abbot Hugh of Cluny, and the younger Anselm are among their distinguished exponents. In the succeeding centuries many romances were written, and a variety of historical events made them a popular literature.

One of these is particularly significant, the Fourth Lateran Council (1215-16), deliberately used by Pope Innocent III to reform the Church from within in response to severe strictures. With a frank admission of dangers, ignorance, and corruption of the clergy, the Council advocated an intensive program of instruction to reform these evils. The result was increasing use of the vernacular in order to reach more people, and the moral arguments emphasized sin, death, and punishment as never before. Just as the visual arts show this emphasis, so the vernacular romance narratives often have a strong, didactic, purpose. Although pleasing entertainment, they urge religious behavior, the availability of redemption, the necessity for repentance, and the bliss of eternity.[69]

Middle English romances belong to a later period than their continental counterparts. A glance at the historical context makes clear that English knighthood was not so exclusive nor courtly life so important as in France, and the romances reflect this. "This is why, from the beginning, the English romances were fairy-tales, stories from a distant past, 'of eldirs, þat byfore vs were' (*Sir Ysumbras,* 1. 2). With very few exceptions, they were not an immediate confrontation with the present. They did not aim at a faithful representation of present-day reality, but, as will be seen, at the illustration of moral truths by way of an exemplary story. They are, for the most part, homiletic in intention rather than courtly and topical."[70] And they are, unlike Gottfried von Strassburg's *Tristan und Isolde,* addressed to a much wider audience,[71] so that their appeal has always been as a more popular literature.

The everyday reality of fourteenth-century England has been epitomized by Charles Muscatine as an age of "crisis."[72] This is clear from even the briefest references to historical events like the long

economic depression which gripped Europe from the late thirteenth to the middle of the fifteenth century, famine and the Black Death (perhaps one-third of England's population died in the eighteen months, 1348-50) in the fourteenth century, the Peasants' Revolt of 1381, the deposing and murdering of Edward II and Richard II, futile struggles with France, political vagaries of pardons and revenges, a Church with two popes and a Great Schism and clerical corruption that is legion. Human responses to such realities vary, and the literature chronicles the most sensitive of these. The increased enthusiasm for romance is clear from the many texts that were produced in the fourteenth century and their avoidance of the extremes of artificiality (in light of contemporary circumstances) in their French models. The seeking and journeying which crystalize in twelfth-century romance could handly find an age in which they would exercise more popular appeal than one which was so difficult and threatening.

The fifteenth century[73] was hardly a more reassuring time, for England was constantly engaged in both foreign wars in France and the civil Wars of the Roses at home. Lawlessness and violence were legion. Not only were lords of the realm at strife, but even flourishing commercial trade was hampered. Men like the Pastons, nevertheless, worked constantly for advancement of family fortunes, and many important educational foundations were established. The dreadful circumstances of living are reflected in soberness of thought epitomized by the Danse Macabre and increased concentration on the hereafter. Perhaps nowhere is the search for escape from the temporal more vividly illustrated than in the combined precision of line and upward reaching of the English Perpendicular Style. This architecture is, of course, best known in King's College, Cambridge, but also appears in countless parish churches in towns like Gedney and Walpole St. Peter. It is not surprising that romances which offer heroes who similarly seek and achieve an alternative to this world, found an enthusiastic audience. Just as the thriller and science fiction have today an irresistible appeal because they provide a sense of personal possibility and other worlds, so the Middle English romance offered relief to fourteenth- and fifteenth-century readers and listeners.

Perhaps the most appropriate evidence of the characteristic medieval blend of an aspiration toward the eternal and a practical coping with the pains of the temporal, is to be found in the least pretentious decorations of cathedrals and parish churches—the carved misericords. Largely work of the fourteenth and fifteenth centuries in England, the misericords are even precisely associated with popular Middle English romances, for included in the diversified subjects of the carvings are some of their favorite heroes—Alexander, Ywain, Chevalier au Cygne, Tristan and Iseult, and many similar knights of uncertain identity. Because religious services were so long, they made great physical demands of priests, particularly those who were old and weak, and some relief had to be provided. The misericord (Mercy Seat) was an appropriate resolution of the dilemna. The corbel, which projected from the underside of the seat, gave a support to rest upon when the seat was tipped back. With so utilitarian a purpose and so inconspicuous a position, the misericords were not suitable for decoration of a highly schematic or doctrinaire argument. They have aesthetic appeal and formal interest, but subjects are more important than techniques. Thus misericords are an exuberant and diversified expression of medieval interests, including grotesque and fantastic creatures (especially from Bestiaries), some Scriptural themes, everyday activities of music, drama, dance, sport, domestic life, knights often of uncertain identity—and heroes and episodes from popular romances.[74] Earlier Roland had been placed on the facade at Lucca and Cremona, and Arthur appeared in a Romanesque archivolt at Modena; the later popular heroes of romance are less conspicuous, but nearer the altar, in the choirstalls.

This suggests the medieval church's tolerance of the marvelous in inspiring popular romances even when popular players and minstrels were generally denounced. At any rate, misericords of cathedral and parish stalls have subjects from secular literature, and they combine utility and delight with edification. Like medieval drama, they blend vital artistic expression with popular interest in ways less favored in the Renaissance when the romances they illustrate become unacceptable to the new classical sophistication.[75]

A predisposition to similar denigration of these medieval achievements has been evident in much modern criticism, which has been shaped by the enormous influence of Matthew Arnold's *The Study of Poetry* (1890). When the *Chanson de Roland* is inferior to Homer and Chaucer lacks 'high seriousness,' it is not surprising that the popular Middle English romances, lacking the obvious distinction of these highmarks of medieval literature, have not been thought of as 'touchstones' of excellence, or even worth serious consideration. Yet theirs is not an insignificant achievement. Arnold's cautionary injunctions against personal and historical estimates are helpful, but his own judgments (like those of any critic) show the same kinds of prejudices. These have contributed to the peculiar confusions in critical evaluations of Middle English romance that alternate approaches might mitigate.

Northrup Frye has argued that in all ages "the romance is nearest of all literary forms to the wish-fulfillment dream."[76] Q. D. Leavis notes: "It is wish-fulfillment in various forms that the modern best seller and magazine story provide";[77] and she is hostile and disapproving of this fiction's satisfaction in 'likeable' people, its expression of a sensibility that is more cheerful than that found in 'highbrow' literature and that aims to uplift the reader's spirits and persuade him that life is fun.[78] Similarities between romances and best-sellers are, then, very clear. Obviously, no broad generalization is without exceptions that show distinction; some best-sellers are acceptable to the humanistic academic, and not every Middle English romance is of the same quality. But my contention is that the attitude epitomized by Leavis' study is analogous to the humanist rejection of the romance, and the exceptional argument—*Troilus and Criseyde, Sir Gawain and the Green Knight,* alliterative *Morte Arthure*— is not an adequate commentary for the hundred narratives which constituted one of the most popular literatures of the Middle Ages. While examining the nature of this popularity in a long tradition, this chapter has suggested many bases for the appeal of the romances. Now we must turn to the evidence of the individual narratives themselves—hopefully with fewer prejudiced preconceptions.

Regretfully not all of the important romances can be included; it seems preferable to select a few widely representative illustrations for full analysis to support my basic theme. *Guy of Warwick,* for example, is used as an epitome of what was most popular. The briefer and widely read *Sir Eglamour* has much of the same subject matter and demonstrations of the triumph of good, but somewhat cruder moralizing. Another favorite, *Ipomadon* also tells of valorous deeds undertaken to win a lady; and, in addition, it exploits the disguise of a fool (like *Robert the Devil*) and family combat (as in *Valentine and Orson*). I recognize that some romances more clearly support my argument than others, but the specific selections chosen are not deliberately sought to force the argument, nor are they the only texts which would support such analysis.

Thus while I have used several romances from the Auchinleck MS, the popular collection, I have also included examples without so distinctive a manuscript survival to broaden the reference. Similarly, an attempt has been made to include illustrations of various matters, a wide chronological period, and prose as well as verse. A remarkable proportion of romances can be described by a popular aesthetic in which exploitation of the exotic and exciting, often forbidden and heinous human behavior, is juxtaposed with the ultimate triumph of firm moral purpose. Those chosen provide an opportunity to convey my delight and appreciation both of them and their absent analogues, and thus testify to their continuing popularity.

CHAPTER II

FORTUNE'S HEROES

The attacks on medieval romance which originated with and were sustained by the humanists of the Renaissance emphasized the inferiority of this material to classical texts and the falsity of their moral/religious values. Thus it is appropriate to examine in some detail representative medieval romances whose subject matter is classical. Here the medieval adapters, obviously regarding the classical view as inadequate, have transformed their material through the introduction of Christian attitudes. The older ideals of human importance, the seeking of fame and glory without the mitigation of humility and charity, contradict much that is essential in the teaching of the Gospels and in the preaching of the established Church.[1] Such classical tales, then, are modified to provide inspiration by a firm exposition of behavior that is pleasing to God because of self-discipline and denial of excessive pagan pleasures. Truly extraordinary romance heroes thrill by their accomplishments, but they also reassure a popular audience because through their errors and ultimate awareness of the limitations of their successes, they are revealed as humanly fallible. Belief in Heaven, which is available to all through God's grace, provides encouragement of a blissful existence beyond the cares of the world.

Although there are many changes in taste through the centuries, such consolations are reiterated in the popular novels of both Britain and America, especially in times of great stress, as the thorough analysis of best-sellers (which are possible with publishing records) of Q. D. Leavis and James Hart have so eloquently shown.[2] Both of these critics argue a decline in the quality of the reading public of the nineteenth century which so obviously preferred high sentiment, vigorous but virtuous action, and a hopeful attitude about human possibilities to most of the less optimistic and reassuring views of 'significant' writers. Two studies of the 'popular' fiction of the eighteenth century make something of the same case.[3] Medieval taste, as we noted in the previous chapter, seems to be much less sharply divided; the romances which pleased aristocratic audiences were also admired by others, and clerics may well have written as well as enjoyed the same materials. This unity in taste comes from a much more consistent scheme of value that is rooted in the Christian belief which is central to all experience in the earlier period, lessens with the advent of Reason (which was in the eighteenth century even crowned in Notre Dame de Paris), and, interestingly, remains today crucial to those readers whom critics usually describe as 'unsophisticated, naive, provincial' and who often determine which books are popular.

Belief in eternity as a more important part of man's existence than temporality, is perhaps the salient difference between classical and Christian thought. Knowledge of this infinite possibility, readily available to man because of God's gift of Christ, transforms the value systems which in pagan times stressed primarily man's achievements in the temporal world. Worldly accomplishments, then, are viewed as a preliminary and subsidiary feature of human life, if not totally eschewed. Thus the heroic warrior, the noble king, the worthy knight, can no longer simply be esteemed for his feats of prowess, either physical or mental. Rather the limitations of fame and glory become clear because of the limitless possibilities of an after-life with God.

The rich body of varied literatures which deals with the theme *de contemptu mundi* indicates how widespread and significant this idea was in the Middle Ages.[4] Complete eschewal of the world is, of course, an ideal to which the mass of humanity is not readily adaptable, and the Gospels make clear that this kind of life is not enjoined to all. Nevertheless, there is a great need to establish that worldly pursuits which are sustained must not be falsely esteemed. Perhaps no man can more dramatically realize this essential Christian truth than the eminent hero. Thus the Middle English romances often center upon classic figures noted for their humanly temporal accomplishments, but rather than merely repeating their exploits and altering the descriptive details to medieval taste, these narratives also provide a firm moral judgment about the felicity of such personages. They thereby offer a system of value which differs markedly from a simple praise of Fortune's heroes and their accomplishments.

An ambivalence of judgment appears repeatedly in the many accounts of the Trojan War which so appealed to the Middle Ages.[5] The full accounts of this material include a vast number of episodes and the chronicle-like quality somewhat limits the possibility for a tightly sustained thematic argument and literary excellence. Nevertheless, a work like *The Gest Hystoriale of the Destruction of Troy* argues the importance of eternity, advocates man's humility (especially in figures like Hector and Ulysses), and challenges a simple view of Fortune. In addition, there are many sections which show genuine artistic distinction. Thus a conventional view that the poem is merely a plodding translation of Guido delle Colonne—enlivened only by occasional brilliance, for example, in nautical descriptions[6]—can be shown as unduly negative and sweeping. Inevitably so massive a work is uneven, but there is strong evidence of an attempt to unify the whole through a Christian viewing of the most famous stories of classical mythology.

Of all the diverse personages in medieval literature none, save Christ and Mary, is mentioned more often than Alexander the Great, who is an archetype of worldly success in the classical ethos and thus presents a challenge to Christian values.[7] As William Matthews has so eloquently argued, Alexander elicited a duality of response in the Middle Ages. He is, on the one hand, an exemplar of victory, possessed of attractive verve, strength, and ambition. Because of his magnanimity he is a model for the good king, and he pleases also with his wisdom and respect for learning. Further, he offers reassurance to a western, European point of view which is at once fascinated by the exotic quality and impressive cultural achievement of the East and also frightened by the military might and religious fervor of Islam. Yet there is an alternative tradition in which Alexander is the archetype of pagan worldliness and the vainglorious conqueror. To this tradition most English writers, especially notably John Gower, make their contributions. Thus Alexander is viewed at the very least in the perspective of *de contemptu mundi* and more typically as a sinful man whose vanity leads to his destruction.

Alexander's popularity and fascination resulted in several Middle English romances, so that there is ample documentation of these generalizations. Almost all readers of these narratives would agree that *Kyng Alisaunder* has greatest literary excellence, a subtlety in plan and execution of stylistic control that make it one of the rare masterpieces. Thus it is a particularly important illustration of the Christianizing of pagan values. The later *Prose Life of Alexander,* although a less brilliant achievement, is an able work which more explicitly makes the argument, especially through the exhanges of letters between not only Alexander and Dindimus,[8] but also between Alexander and Darius. The similarities between Christianity and certain Brahman attitudes were used not simply to Alexander's disadvantage but as an explicit attack on espousing worldly achievement.

Not surprisingly, Alexander is frequently the subject of visual art. Splendid manuscript illuminations are to be found throughout Europe; for example, Bodley MS 264, which has such rich illumination of sports and pastimes in the borders, is a particularly important and justly famous document, where romance and popular activities are memorably combined. Two very distinctive and different representations are worth mentioning here. Richard of Haldingham's Mappa Mundi of Hereford Cathedral (c. 1300) includes, as well as theological and symbolic cartography, cryptic illustration of Alexander's adventures. These are shown in the context of a world picture surmounted by the scene of the Day of Judgment and centered in Jerusalem and Calvary, the focal point of human history.

The carvers of misericords included this most challenging pagan hero in their representations, and he appears throughout England (at Hereford, Gloucester, Wells, Chester, Whalley, Darlington, Lincoln, and Beverly). The episode selected from the romances is appropriately the Flight of Alexander, an epitome of the wondrous possibilities of man's achievement and his dangerous aspirations. The conqueror, having arrived at the end of the world, wants to explore the heavens, somewhat like Icarus. He thus arranged to be lifted in a basket/cage/chair to which have been attached griffons that have been starved so that they will fly upward toward the meat that Alexander holds as bait on the spears in his hands. This triumphant scene is captured on the misericords with a suggestion that an extraordinary view was possible, but it was also fleeting. For in the familiar romance narratives, the chair must soon come down, and Alexander become mortally ill. The misericords, especially that at Wells, are very beautiful and exciting in their combination of an impressive kingly figure with exotic griffons, those half-eagle and half-lion creatures so exciting to the medieval imagination, which reveled in the grotesque. The thrill of daring and achievement are momentarily enjoyed, but Alexander's aspirations and exploits are also evidence for a way of life not to be espoused by those who know the dangers of pagan vainglory. Similarly, there is perhaps an illustration from the Alexander story on a misericord at Exeter which shows a strange crowned man placed on all fours with a horse's hind legs and wearing a saddle. Aristotle's infatuation with the courtesan against whom he warned Alexander but to whom he himself succumbed, is a frequent identification. Again peculiar effects compel attention, and moral awareness is heightened through a contemplation of man's achievements and limitation.

The universality of this theme is neatly demonstrated by the close relationship of the alliterative *Morte Arthure* to the medieval view of Alexander.[9] There are few narratives in Middle English of comparable literary quality, and its distinctive handling of the relationship of a single protagonist to Fortune, the world, and God is a significant expression of Christian values. Arthur's battle against the Roman Emperor is clearly a reflection of the militant Christianity of the Middle Ages, but the poet subtly and firmly rejects the commonplace satisfactions taken in warfare. He does this by careful ordering and selection of episodes, by comparisons of Arthur with Alexander and Christ, by the pivotal dream sequence of the Duchess-of-Fortune, and by the eloquence of his lyric devotions to God.

The Gest Hystoriale of the Destruction of Troy

Probably the earliest full account of the Trojan material in Middle English, *The Gest Hystoriale* is a compendium of stories from Jason's seeking of the Golden Fleece to the killing of Odysseus. Thus, like the *Laud Troy Book,* it is often thought of as a chronicle.[10] Yet these two 'genres' have many similarities in their intention, and the generic distinctions are not clear and consistent.[11] Even in a narrative so vast and mixed as the *Gest* we find indications that the author is trying to view the multiplicity of events of classical story in a Christian frame of reference.

The narrative begins with the conventional invocation to the everlasting "Maistur in Magesté" to aid the poet ("of þi grace") in his task of providing "sothe stories" which characteristically do not survive in men's memories as do those "Breuyt into bokes for boldying of hertes" (14).[12] This plea of historicity is, of course, typical of the attitude toward the Trojan material in the Middle Ages as is the poet's vigorous objection to Homer. Predisposed to the Greek side and untruthful, Homer is specifically accused of inventing entertainment.

> How goddes foght in the filde, folke as þai were,
> And other errours vnable þat after were knowen, (45-46)

This explicit attack on pagan belief is sustained throughout much of the narrative, so that we have not simply a recounting of the many episodes— and the often justly praised splendid descriptive passages, especially of the sea—but also a criterion for evaluating them.

In the first episode emphasis is placed on the skills of Medea, whose knowledge of necromancy produces extraordinary results. But the poet makes very clear the dubious and unreliable nature of her accomplishments through his assertion of a belief in God and the gift of Christ to man.

> Hit ys lelly not like, ne oure belefe askys,
> þat suche ferlies shuld fall in a frale woman;
> But only gouernaunse of God þat þe ground wroght.
> And ilke a planet hase put in a plaine course,
> þat turnys as þere tyme comys, trist ye non other.
> As he formed hom first flitton þai neuer;
> Ne the clere Sune neuer clippit out of course yet,
> But whan Criste on the crosse for our care deghit;
> Than it lost hade the light as our lord wold,
> Erthe dymmed by dene, ded men Roose,
> The gret tempull top terned to ground. (420-30)

Here the attack on Medea is not simply anti-feminism but rather a firm and early indication of the author's point of view. Man should trust only in God, Whose governance of the universe is absolute and Whose gift of His Son assures man's possibility of salvation. The Crucifixion was significantly accompanied by disturbances in the natural world controlled by God. Would-be necromancers are ineffectual, and their blatant temporal limitations are dramatized in the picture of "the soden hote love of Medea." Seen in the throes of primitive passion, she is hardly a reliable power. Her aid to Jason is specifically described in terms of idolatry, for she gives him, among other things, a charmed image (775 ff.). Paris, when he sees Helen, notably has no thoughts of the Gods (3016-19 and 3087-88). And the Trojans are finally destroyed by their idolatry of the horse (11846 ff.). There is, then, ample evidence of a kind of sloth in the medieval sense.[13]

These commonplaces, although inherent in the story, can thus be placed very precisely in a Christian context. Endless references to the "Goddes" and to particular deities like Jupiter, Juno, Venus, Pallas, and Apollo suggest the pagan world; but they are balanced by many references to "God," the sacraments, bishops, saints, evensong, and so on. Similarly, the seven deadly sins are abundantly documented in this story that originates in pride and lechery and is sustained by endless outbursts of anger which produce violent deeds. Envy and avarice, as in *Piers Plowman*, are particularly emphasized, though gluttony is less crucial. Not only do we have frequently the naming of the failings as well as their enactment, but also the poet notes their insidious effects.

After the Trojans reject Hector's sensible counsel and the warnings of Cassandra to proudly rush to their "destyny," the poet proceeds to relate how Paris went into Greece for Helen. Book Seven begins with these lines:

Envy, þat Euermore ertis to skathe,
Ryxles full Ryfe in her ranke hertes.
This forward was festynit with a felle wille,
And all the purpose plainly with pouer to wende. (2725-28)

Thus the entire action is evaluated as a moral failing. The passage is placed strategically to precede the conventional seasonal description of the month of May which leads into the actual description of the expedition. Like Hercules in the Jason episode (1002), Paris seeks war because of Envy.

It is significant that the Trojan defeat comes because of a failure of the priest who yields to Covetousness and sends the Palladium to Ulysses. The poet is moved to comment and evaluate the situation:

A! God of þis ground, who graidly may trist
Any lede on to leng, as for lele true,
Syn this prest þus priset the pepull to dissayue,
As a kaytiff, for couetoise to cumber his land?
This poynt is not prynted in proces þat are now:
Hit lenges not so long tho ledis within,
To be cumbrid with couetous, by custome of old,

> That rote is & rankist of all the rif syns.
> There is no greuaunce so grete vndur god one,
> As the glemyng of gold, þat glottes þere hertis:
> Hit puttes the pouer of pristhode abake,
> And forges to the fend a forslet with-in.
> Couetous men comynly are cald aftur right,
> A temple to the tyrand, þat tises to syn. (11768-81)

The crucial idea, as is typical with the *Gest*, is in Guido,[14] but the emotional tone of the poet's exclamation reveals his personal concern with the issue. Obviously the failure of the religious, a priest pledged to God, makes the deceitful betrayal doubly distressing, and the absolute emphasis upon immediate satisfactions is shocking. Gold is more important than God in this system which is diametrically opposed to Christian trust in eternity.

Passages like these provide reminders of the Christian world which is explicity delineated in relation to the pagan ethos in a crucial section that is central to the *Gest Hystoriale*. Just as Paris' departure is evaluated in terms of envy, and the Trojan betrayal as covetousness, so the entire pagan mythology is judged. The Greeks observe the religious convention of paying homage at Delos to Apollo:

> þof it defe were & doumbe, dede as a ston,
> The gentils hit aiugget as a iuste god,
> With errour vnable þat erst hom began,
> And worshippit hom wofully, for hom wit lacket
> Of þe Godhed giffen, . . . (4281-85)

How terribly inadequate is pagan idolatry, deeply rooted as it is in vast ignorance which cannot go beyond the natural world. Revelation is, then, crucial:

> ffor lacke of beleue þai light into errour,
> And fellen vnto fals goddes, (4287-88)

Thus Fiends deceive the people, and the poet is compelled to make a long digression so that he can explain the alternative values of God's glorious gift of His Son which makes possible the end of idolatry. Knowledge of Him will crush all evil power in the world. The gospel is cited as evidence for the collapse of idols when Christ entered Egypt. There is debate about who first made idols, but the poet argues that man seems to have an inherent proclivity for evil, so that he merely hastens to trace its existence without placing blame on anyone in particular (4295-4331).

The discussion, again following Guido but with skillful expansion and heightened religious concern, continues with an account of idolatry of Belus and others.

> Thus þurgh falshed of þe feudes þe folke was dissayuit,
> Vnder daunger of þe dule droupet full longe, (4391-92)

A description of God's creation concentrates upon Lucifer whose pride (4409) and envy (4413) led him to fall with many of his peers. The poet draws upon the Gospel, Isidore, and the Psalms, as well as a Life of St. Brandon, to describe this Leviathan who tempted Adam through envy (4447). This initial deceit of the devil involved a kind of idolatry and is archetypal. An easy transition is made, then, to the Greek consultation of Apollo, who is part of a long tradition of false gods.

Again we have an explicit exposition of traditional religious values which gives the whole of the Greek expedition a quality of falsity. Much care is expended to indicate at the onset that the honored gods are false. Thus the foretelling of a Greek victory is shown to be less meaningful, and the alliance of Achilles with the traitor Calchas illustrates further the ignobility of worldly concerns. Significantly, this note is repeated almost at the end of the narrative when Ulysses makes inquiries of an informative god during his journeys.

The restriction of pagan awareness to the things of this world and the inability to transcend through a knowledge of the eternal are succinctly noted. Ulysses observes of the island god:

> There answare hade all men after þere wille,
> Both certayn & sothe, þat soght for to wete.
> At þat orribill I asket angardly myche,
> Of dethe, & of deire, as destyny willes;
> And other ferlies full fele I fraynit of hit.
> There spird I full specially in spede for to here,
> When dethe hade vs drepit, & our day comyn,
> And we went of this world, what worthe of our saules.
> To all thing he answarit abilly me thoght,
> But of our sawles, for-sothe, said he me noght. (13258-69)

The last couplet, which particularly focuses our attention even by its rhyme, neatly makes the precise point: The non-Christian system of value is trapped in worldly experience and lacks a knowledge of the soul, of the limitless possibilities of an eternal existence, of life after death, that most reassuring alternative that always attracts popular response, especially in times of stress. Ulysses, then, must simply put out to sea again and again.

In yet another crucial episode the *Gest* makes the same point. Perhaps the anti-Greek sentiment of the Middle Ages has obscured the fact that the Trojans also elicit a critical evaluation. Even Hector is shown as a pagan with all the limitations of his non-Christian value system. Hector's failure to press his advantage to gain victory (Book XV) is thus recognized not only as a military blunder, a lapse in the carrying out of knighthood (7120-24), but also as a kind of religious idolatry. He allows himself to swerve from his purpose because of a rather trivial concern; he accedes to the request of his cousin Telamon-Ajax to desist fighting. A social amenity is allowed to determine crucial issues, and the advantageous opportunity is forfeited. The judgment of the poet is stringent:

> And he þat kepis not kyndly the course of his heale,
> But sodanly forsakes þat sent is of god,
> Hit shalbe gricchit hym þat grace in his grete nede. (7070-72)

The necessity for realizing God's proffered advantages is thus clear. Not to maintain safety is to behave unnaturally; to reject what God proffers is to relinquish "grace." For a Christian the implications are very clear, and Hector's ignoble end is both predictable and blameless. Like Ulysses, Hector is constrained by his exclusively worldly values, his decision to think and act only in immediate terms.

The not infrequent references to Fortune[15] in the *Gest Hystoriale* underscore this essential idea. The traditional medieval view of sharp contrast between prosperity and adversity is mentioned (note especially 13676-83) several times. This emphasis upon transiency in worldly matters is fundamental, for it suggests the corollary that man must, as Ulysses perceives, be concerned with his soul, for only in eternity will the vagaries of Fortune no longer be relevant. All man's attempts to circumvent this conclusion are futile, and the pagan gods and primitive sinful men who fill the chronicle of the Trojan War repeatedly illustrate the inadequacy of the non-Christian view.

Kyng Alisaunder

Much more elaborate and deliberately literary in style than most Middle English romances, *Kyng Alisaunder* at first glance might appear to provide ample evidence against my basic argument for the moral intention and significance of meaning in this popular kind of narrative. Detailed, convincing demonstration has been made of the extraordinary knowledge and control of rhetoric which the author of *Kyng Alisaunder* commanded. Thus it has been argued that only by reference to the French models can one understand the nature of the work, its reflection of learning and traditions, especially the rhetorical traditions of French epic similes, listings and catalogues.[16] Similarly, the Alexander material is often described as a collection of *mirabilia* which tend to obscure the basic biographical structure of the narrative as they provide a seemingly endless succession of exotic and bizarre circumstances. Without underestimating the validity of these arguments, I think that certain other observations can be accurately made.

As is not infrequently the case, this romance appears in its fullest and best version in a manuscript (Laud Misc. 622) which contains largely religious and didactic poetry,[17] so that an immediate association with these popular values is inevitably suggested. Further, the main source of the poem is the *Roman de Toute Cheualerie*, the Anglo-Norman work of Thomas of Kent, which is notable for its moral tone.[18] Although the Middle English handling is fairly independent, it is demonstrable that this fundamental quality has been sustained and indeed strengthened. Attention has frequently centered on the rather unusual opening, the author's frequent interruptions of his narrative for moral or didactic observation, and the distinctive 'head-pieces,' which were added by the Middle English adapter. A brief analysis shows how these portions of the narrative, which have consistently been singled out for praise, give further evidence of the poet's basic Christian viewpoint. Even though the hero is not a reflective individual who is concerned with his spiritual state and gains understanding to influence his less perceptive followers, nevertheless the author of *Kyng Alisaunder* shows himself in agreement with this elemental Christian system through comments which appear at crucial moments.[19]

By clearly stating the theme of the transitoriness of earthly life, the transience of worldly attainments, the justly famous opening lines direct our thoughts and attention to a series of episodes that, by detailing the progress of a King's ambitions and victories, and lack of cosmic awareness, relentlessly illustrate the basic theme that the pursuit of fame and glory are unwise:

> DJuers is þis myddellerde
> To lewed men and to lerede.
> Bysynesses, care and sorouȝ
> Js myd man vche morowȝer,
> Somme for sekenesse, for smert,
> Somme for defaut oiþer pouert,
> Somme for þe lyues drede
> þat glyt away so floure in mede.
> Ne is lyues man non so sleiȝe
> þat he no þoleþ ofte ennoyȝe
> Jn many cas, on many manere,
> Whiles he lyueþ in werlde here.
> Ac is þere non, fole ne wys,
> Kyng, ne duk, ne kniȝth of prys,
> þat ne desireþ sum solas
> Forto here of selcouþe cas;
> For Caton seiþ, þe gode techer,
> Oþere mannes lijf is oure shewer.
> Naþeles, wel fele and fulle
> Beeþ yfounde in herte—and shulle—
> þat hadden leuer a ribaudye
> þan here of God siþer Seint Marie,
> Oiþer to drynk a copful ale
> þan to heren any gode tale.
> Swiche Ich wolde weren out bishett,
> For certeynlich it were nett.
> For hij ne habbeþ wille, Ich woot wel,
> Bot in þe gut and in þe barel. (Laud, 1-28)

Eloquently and pecisely these opening lines establish a point of view and suggest a system of value. All men, whatever their awareness or station, are subject to vicissitudes, so that no one can avoid experiencing tribulations while he is in the world. The relevance of this generalization is made explicit when the author not only cites the familiar maxim that we learn from the lives of other men, but also strengthens its impact by precisely identifying its author Cato. He then adds to his source the crucial contrast between tales which are merely entertaining and those that are edifying,[20]and explicitly rejects the former. Surely such an introduction leads us to expect the author of *Kyng Alisaunder* to have a strong moral point of view, however much the nature of his subject matter impels him to *mirabilia* and rapid advancement of his hero's career. At very least, we have specific evidence of his moral awareness and

Courtesy of Wells Cathedral

Misericords: The Flight of Alexander (see p. 28)

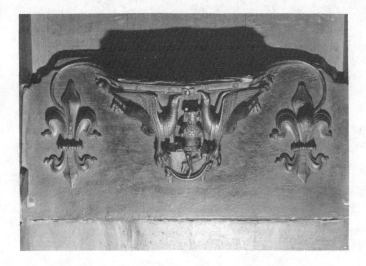

Courtesy of Lincoln Cathedral

responsibility, initially placed to guide us in our reading.

More succinctly, and vividly, the poet reiterates this concern with the limitations of worldly existence in a pointed comment upon the first personal relationship presented in the romance. Skilled in the art of astronomy, Neptanabus knows of impending disaster and plots revenge against Philip of Macedon, whose wife Olympias he admires for her beauty. This lady returns his interest, and thus begins the relationship which results in Alexander's birth. In a direct and explicit passage the poet makes definite his moral concern:

> GAmen is good whiles it wil last,
> Ac it fareþ so wyndes blast —
> þe werldelich man, and lesse and maast,
> Here leue þere-inne so wel waast.
> Whan it is beest to þee henne it wil haste.
> Me wondreþ men ne beeþ a-gaste,
> And þat somme hem by oþere ne chasteþ. (Laud, 235-41)

Certainly these lines may be read as a warning, a cynical traditional comment on love affairs,[21] but the universal view of transience is also present, so that the poet is refining his opening lines as well as making a particular comment. Neptanabus occupies only a small position in the narrative ("lesse"), but his fate is not unlike that of Alexander ("maast"). The hero receives more expansive treatment in both life and death; however, the terse comment upon Neptanabus' death would be just as applicable to Alexander.

> Sooþ it is, vpe al þing,
> Of yuel lijf yuel endyng. (Laud, 751-52)

By succinctly and summarily dealing with the first episode, the author of *Kyng Alisaunder* provides a reference point from which we view the larger complexity of his story.

Throughout the narrative, at frequent and fairly regular intervals, he sustains this commentary. Notable are the famous headpieces which typically refer to seasons and times of the day (often in comparison with a human activity) and introduce a new episode. Thus the Olympias episode is marked (Laud, 457-64) by a general comment which reiterates the judgment about Neptanabus' death we have just noted. The autumnal references—to ripening, to knights' hunting—are neatly repeated (Laud, 795-800), fixing in our minds the idea that evil is soon revealed. And the expansion of the theme to universal transitoriness comes in a passage about dawn:

> Many ben jolyf in þe morowenyng
> And þolen deþ in þe euenyng
> Nis in þis werlde non so siker þing,
> þe tyme neiȝeþ of her wendyng. (Laud, 916-19)

Continued repetition of this idea of change (e.g., Laud, 1239 ff., 1658 ff., 4056 ff., 6988 ff.) suggests a definite and deliberate intention of the poet to emphasize—indeed make central—an idea, not just to divide the narrative neatly into portions suitable for oral recitation.

Several passages are worth quotation and brief commentary to enforce the point. In the midst of the episode about Darius, among whose host "was pride and mychel bost," the poet utters a passionate prayer:

> MErcy, Jesu! þou vs socoure!
> Jt fareþ wiþ man so dooþ wiþ floure —
> Bot a stirte ne may it dure;
> He glyt away so dooþ þe[ss]ure.
> Fair is lefdy in boure,
> And also kniȝth in armoure. (Laud, 4313-18)

Specific references to Christ are not so frequent (but note Laud, 992, 3880) that one passes them over lightly in this tale set in pagan times.[22] Again the theme of inconstancy appears through a comparison between man's life and the natural world. Darius is Alexander's most distinguished and admired adversary; their manners are similar, and the Persian's fate prefigures that of the hero who both laments his death and punishes those who betrayed him. An epigrammatic comment, "Traisoun haþ yuel endyng" (4724), recalls the poet's initial evaluation of Neptanabus' end. Thus we are again aware of a kind of thematic unity in this episodically diversified romance.

A final summary comment, made before Alexander goes on to adventures in India, reinforces the poet's artistic and Christian view:

> FAire ben tales in compaignye;
> Mery in chirche is melodye.
> Yuel may þe slow hye,
> And wers may blynde blynde siweye.
> Who þat haþ trewe amye
> Joliflich may hym [disgy]e.
> Jch woot þe best is Marye —

She vs shilde from vilenye! (Laud, 4739-46)

The diversity of this world's pleasures is clearly recognized, but emphasis is placed upon man's predilection for choosing wrong directions, so that a reliance upon Mary is enjoined as the best safeguard. It is significant that this passage separates two of the most impressive portions of the Alexander story. Like the prayer to Jesus, it is explicitly Christian in reference and follows a discussion of the traitorous circumstance of Darius' death, which is a notable illustration of the failure of the ideal of chivalry.

"Chivalry" is referred to in the romance (e.g., Laud, 1505, 3776, 7196), but the ideas are nowhere more fully detailed than in the treatment of Darius, that tyrannical figure of Herod-like rages (N.B. Laud, 1805 ff.). The would-be assassin of Alexander pleads for clemency because he was loyally serving his Persian lord, who had enjoined such treachery, and he even offers trial by combat (Laud, 3962 ff.). With appropriate irony, then, Darius is himself slain by traitors among his followers. The poet makes clear his disapproval of such treachery (Laud, 4593-4600), and the cumulative effect of this material is to indicate that even with a worthy ideal of loyalty as it is required by chivalry, one is indeed vulnerable because of man's human failings. Thus a "trewe amye" (and the words have broad connotations, I think) is not likely in this world, and the wise man turns instead to God, specifically to the most sympathetic intercessor. This ultimate evaluation of knightly ideals, though it is not central as in *Sir Gawain* or *Guy of Warwick* is not unusual in medieval romance and is one basis of their popularity, for it offers reassurance to those who must live with limitations of the code.

As *Kyng Alisaunder* nears its end, this material receives more intense treatment. From the trees of the sun and moon, Alexander learns that he must expect death through treason in Babylon in the next year on March 20. With this certain knowledge the hero yet hopes "þei3 it be to hym yshape, / On sum manere forto a-skape" (6970-71). Perfectly in keeping with a pagan delight in this world, such an attitude is diametrically opposed to that Christian view held by Guy, Lancelot, or Amiloun, who rejoice in foreknowledge of death as a gift of God Whose presence they joyously seek and eagerly await. The poet clearly has little sympathy with Alexander's derisive ignoring of his fate.

> þoo þou mi3ttest on many wise
> Yseen solace and game aryse,
> Leigh3en, syngen, and daunces make,
> Dysoures talen and resouns crake.
> Swiche chaunce þe werlde kepeþ —
> Now man leig3eþ, now man wepeþ!
> Now man is hool, now man is seek;
> Nys no day oþer ylyk.
> Noman þat lyues haþ borowe
> From euene libbe forto amorowe. (Laud, 6978-87)

Once again the multiplicity of earthly possibilities is recognized, but their transitoriness is insisted upon. And the following headpiece reinforces the argument through its references to April rains, birds, flowers, and love which is changeable. Thus the poet provides an alternative system of value. Succinctly he offers two basic essential ideas of Christianity:

> Fair juel is gode nei3boure.
> þe best þing is God to honoure. (Laud, 6993-94)

We may recognize a hierarchy in earthly values, but God is beyond all these; He is man's only constant, the focus of his being.

Not surprisingly the actual death of Alexander is described in somewhat less specifically Christian terms, for the hero is relentless in his obsession with worldly glory. Nevertheless, this last episode is introduced with yet another reminder of the ease and inevitability of change:

> JN þis werlde falleþ many cas,
> Gydy blisse, short solas!
> Ypomodon, and Pallidamas,
> And Absolon, þat so fair was,
> Hij lyueden here a litel raas,
> Ac sone for3eten vchon was.
> þe leuedyes shene als þe glas,
> And þise maidens, wiþ rody faas,
> Passen sone als floure in gras;
> So strong, so fair, neuere non nas
> þat he ne shal passe wiþ 'allas!'
> Auenture haþ terned his paas,
> A3eins þe kyng and rered maas. (Laud, 7820-32)

The references to Biblical and classical figures provide a broad basis for the generalization; men are forgotten soon after their deaths, and no man's triumph is long-lasting. Very quickly we are told how Alexander is given poison, so that his death—like that of Darius which prefigures it most closely and that of Neptanabus which he perpetrated—comes through treason (Laud, 7862-63), a violation of the chivalric ethic and trust. Thus the dominant thematic material culminates in a final illustration of the vanity of most men's expectations. The poet's concern has been to show us how futile are the assumptions of man who trusts in and values anything but God and eternal life.

Alexander's failure to understand is absolute; even on his deathbed, this hero thinks of worldly dimensions, and the romance concludes with an expansive lamentation for himself that emphasizes the distribution of his kingdoms and wealth among those who survive. This somewhat unusual self-threnody is characteristic only of the most arrogant and dominant of heroes,[23] and it is the final statement of Alexander's values. As well as grief, there is a grotesque quarrel about where he should be buried; this reveals the adherence of most of his survivors to a system which has been consistently opposed by the poet's essential thematic material. Very immediately the romancer puts all into perspective by brief references which recall his basic argument. One gentle human being says:

> "Barouns, leteþ ȝoure strijf,
> And dooþ Goddes hest, blyf!" (Laud, 7992-93)

Quickly, the burial is accomplished, and a few terse lines end the poem. There is a single-line prayer, "God us lene wel to fyne!" (Laud, 8009), followed by the sad comment that the barons continued their factious quarreling with bloodshed. Next the opening lines of the poem are repeated:

> þus it fareþ in þe myddelerde,
> Amonge þe lew[ed] and þe lerde! (Laud, 8016-17)

In the context of such distress and distortion, then, the final prayer —"God vs graunte his blissyng! Amen." (Laud, 8021)—is much more than a conventional formula. Such lines characteristically conclude romances, but they also accurately convey the basic argument of man's relationship to God, the essential moral sense that informs so many narratives in Middle English and gives them their popular appeal. Much of the distinctive contribution, both thematically and stylistically, of the poet of *Kyng Alisaunder* lies in his addition and elaboration of many passages which express awareness of the transitoriness of temporal existence and man's ancillary longing for eternity with God. That much of the narrative recounts marvels should not destroy an awareness of this unifying material which is the core of the poem. A notable sense of moral, specifically Christian, value comes through its counterpointing of Alexander's absolute involvement with himself, and with his achievements, against those philosophic and lyric passages that make clear the futility of such obsessions. Here, then, an apparently unlikely subject is skillfully adapted, indeed given an admirable distinctive quality through the poet's introduction of his own moral sense, that awareness which is the basis of popular appeal.

The Prose Life of Alexander

Probably written a hundred years after *Kyng Alisaunder, The Prose Life of Alexander*[24] in the Thornton MS lacks much of the artistic finesse of the early fourteenth-century romance, yet it has its own distinction and much more obviously exploits popular qualities. As is typical with the Alexander material, the narrative is concerned with a presentation of a heroic figure in almost epic manner and with the *mirabilia* of the conquests. Very precisely, however, the author of *The Prose Life*, like several other fifteenth-century authors, adds many details which make explicit his concern with Christian values and thus assures a sympathetic response from an audience that delights in firm assertions about right behavior. The two chief means to this end are his introduction of exact references to religion, including Biblical echoes both in phrasing and episode, and the sustaining of thematic material which makes clear the concern with the temporal and the eternal. Where *Kyng Alisaunder* succeeds in a subtle presentation of the essential moral vision, *The Prose Life* relies upon a more direct expression of the key ideas.

The romance has many references which suggest a pagan world. Frequently the "gods" are acknowledged (pp. 13, 64, 83, etc.) and individual classical deities, like Diana, Mercury, Jupiter, are mentioned (pp. 31, 45, 81, 109). Similarly, Anectanabus is clearly a pagan figure: "he . . . taking down a brazen shell, which was full of rain-water, and holding in his hand a brazen rod, sought by magic spells to summon the devils" (p. 1). Alexander is upon several occasions thought to be a god (pp. 46, 62) and indeed he once chides the Persians for this error

(p. 59), but he remains as essentially un-Christian figure of dubious origin and acts.

Early in the romance Alexander's foreknowledge of his death is argued against with bold pagan logic, for it would destroy his joy in temporality (p. 15). The thoroughly Christian individual, like Guy or Lancelot, rejoices in such knowledge, for he eagerly anticipates and prepares for the transcendence of his union with God. Finally, when Alexander has drunk the fatal poison, he attempts suicide, which is the ultimate pagan solution. His behavior is hardly noble:

for he myghte noghte ga vprighte₃, he creped one hende & one fete doune to-warde Eufrate₃ for till hafe drownned hym selfe, þat þe strenth of þe water my₃th hafe borne hym away whare neuer man solde hafe fun hym. (p. 111)

Further, the administering of the poison has been provoked by a wantonly uncharitable act: "Bot so it be-felle apon a tyme þat Alexander smate Iobas on þe heued wit a warderere for na trespasse" (p. 110). Feeling the painful effects of the poison, Alexander "suffred a grete penance." With such religious details, the romancer suggests the conflict between pagan and Christian values. Forceful egotism, lack of concern for others, can only lead to destruction.

Perhaps even more striking, however, is the treatment of Alexander as a Moses figure. In the land of Israel Alexander observes the imprisonment of the tribes because they had forsaken the law of their God. Thus he prays to the God of Israel, for an intensification of their punishment, and he is answered by an avalanche of rocks which seal in the people of Gog and Magog. After forty days' travel Alexander comes to the Red Sea, and like Moses he goes up a mountain, and "hym thoghte þat he was nerre þe Firmament þan þe erthe" (p. 105). The Greek hero's vision, however, is of how to make a griffon bear him aloft! Such a direct adaptation of Biblical material makes the reader inevitably aware of a reference outside the pagan world. Alexander wants ever more comprehensive knowledge of worldly phenomena; indeed this is the salient feature of his career. The romance, then, provides endless *mirabilia*, a source of popular entertainment, which contrast sharply with a view of eternity that is central to Christianity.

Of Alexander's many opponents Darius is most notable, and a series of letters between the two heroes in *The Prose Life* provides an exposition of the dangers of pride which places all worth in worldly achievement. Darius' first letter argues that Alexander is "raysed in pride and vayne glorye" (p. 21) and asserts the wealth of his own Persians. In his reply Alexander makes clear his recognition of the limitations of such a view:

> If we graythely & sothefastly be-halde oure selfe þare es na thynge þat we here hafe þat we may bi righte calle ours, bot all it es lent vs for a tyme. For alle we þat ere whirlede aboute wit þe whele of fortune, now ere we broghte fra reches in-to pouerte: now fra myrthe & ioy in-to Sorowe & heuynesse; and agaynwarde₃: and now fra heghte, we are plungede in-to lawnesse. (p. 23)

This thematic material is extensively developed in the exchange that follows. Thus the vanquished Darius is forced to recognize his own failings, and he laments:

> "Allas, full wa es me, vnhappye wriche, þat euer I was borne, for þe ire & þe indignacion of heuen es fallen one mee. For I Darius þat lifte my seluen vp to þe sternes, Now am I broghte lawe to þe erthe. Now es Darius, þat conquerede all þe Este nacyons, & made þam subiecte & tributaries vn-till hym, fayne for to flee fra his enemys and submytte hym vn-to þam. And it ware knawen vn-to þe wreched man, what schulde falle till hym after-warde₃, he schulde hafe littill thoghte of þe tyme presentt, bot one þe tyme to come solde his tho₃te be. In a poynte of a daie it falles, þat þe meke es raysede vp to þe clowdde₃, and þe prowde es putt to no₃te." (pp. 49-50)

Wounded by traitors, the dying Darius speaks to Alexander, who is moved to great compassion for the fallen hero that provides an archetype for the limitations of the world and prefigures Alexander's own death. Darius' long speech to the young hero reiterates the falsity of temporal experience—its ever-changing quality; and he gives an orthodox theological explanation of the reasons for God's plan for man.

> . . . For if godd hadd ordeyned all thynge₃ esy to man and alwaye wit-owtten chaungynge sent hym prosperitee, man schulde be lyftede vp so hie in pryde & in vayne glorye, þat he solde no₃te arett alle his wele-fare & his welthe vn-to godd, bot till his awenn desert & his awenn vertu. And so schulde men gaa fra þaire makare. On þe toþer syde if þe heghe wyssedom of godd hadd made þe werlde on þat wyse þat all illes and infelicytes fell apon man wit-owtten any maner of gudenesse, so many freletese sulde folow þe kynde of man, þat we schulde all be drawen in-to þe gilder of disparacion, so þat we solde hafe na triste in þe gudnes of godd. And þarefore grete godd wolde so wisely skifte all thynges, þat, when a man full of felicitee, thurgh his heghe pride will no₃te knawe his makere, Fra þe heghte of pride in-to þe pitte of mekenes & lawnes he mon be plungede. So þat he þat thurgh pride & felicite forgatt his godd, thurgh fallynge in wrechidnesse & disesse hafe mynde of his godd. (p. 55)

Here, then, is an exact explanation of the principles which form the basis for the crucial concern with the relation between temporal and eternal experience. Alexander—and the popular reader—could hardly ask a clearer exposition of Christian values, and Darius continues with a personal application by confessing his own failure to live by these principles. He exhorts the youthful conqueror:

Bot alway thynke on thy laste ende. For þou ert a dedly man, and ilk a day if þou be-halde graythely þou may see thy dedd bi-fore thyn eghne. (p. 55)

Further when Alexander mounts the throne of Cyrus and assumes the crown of Darius, there is another reiteration of this value. Two of the seven steps recall Darius' explanation. The third step is of a bright topaz which shows man upside down; "And it be-takenes þat a kyng schulde alway take hede till his laste ende" (p. 57). The seventh step is of clay, so "þata man þat es raysed vp to þe dignyte of a kyng sulde alway vmbythynk hym þat he was made of erthe, & at þe laste to þe erthe he sall agayne" (pp. 57-58). Even the phrasing here indicates the deliberate attempt of *The Prose Life* to transform the pagan quality of its subject.

Just as the letters of Darius provide this reference in the first of the narrative, those of Dindimus[25] repeat the argument in the middle of the narrative. The life of the Brahmans is very close to that for which essential Christianity strives. A poised people who worship one god, the Brahmans have inward tranquility and are at peace with the outer world.

We desire þe life of þe werlde þat es to come, and vs liste no3te here þe þyng þat turne3 to na profett. (p. 79)

The description of their way of life includes an avoidance of the seven deadly sins, which are indulged in by the Greeks, but more essentially their lives have a basis in prayer and the performance of good works. Thus they place no value in material wealth, or animal sacrifices, as do the Greeks.

Bot for gude werkes þe whilke Godd lufes, and thurgh þe wordes of deuote prayere. Godd will here a man for þe worde. For thurgh worde we ere lyke to Godd. For Goddes worde, and þat worde made all þe werlde and thurgh þat worde all thynge3 hase beyng, Mouyng & lyfe. That worde wirchipe wee and luffes & honowres. Goddes a spirite. (p. 82)

Eloquently Alexander argues for the pagan ethos. He enumerates and extols the delights of the world and eschews the rigorous Brahman code with its otherworldly orientations and pleasurable sensations. Not to enjoy this world, he insists, is an assertion of pride or envy. Dindimus' reply is a further declaration of Christian values:

We er noȝte lordeȝ of this werlde, as we sulde euermare lyffe þare in. But we ere pilgrymes in þis werlde, and when dede commeȝ we wende till oper habytacions. (p. 87)

Here, then, is a general statement of the theme of pilgrimage which occurs so frequently in the Middle English romances. The argument is extended to include the idea of free will in choosing a way of life, and the key point is epitomized in the question "what profit does þis [worldly attainments] ȝow" (p. 87). Thus the endless dissatisfactions which come from worldly seeking are again noted. The episode of the Brahmans concludes with a final letter from Alexander, who once again asserts his pagan values.

Although his early experience with Darius made clear the issues and indeed convinced Alexander of the validity of the view that man must rely upon eternal, not temporal, values, he remains too much a glory-seeking Greek. He is heedless of the Christian truth and erects another pillar to commemorate his achievements. Alexander does not learn from the wisdom available to him, but clearly the author of *The Prose Life* hopes that his readers will be more responsive. The inevitable death of the hero comes, then, with conventional lamentation, and flamboyant ceremonials follow. But Alexander, like Darius, is betrayed by a traitor and his own lack of the elemental virtues of Christian charity and humility, so that the traditional epic modes are mingled with an ethos that distinctly challenges the earlier pagan values. The romance determinedly makes this explicit through continuous reiteration of the ascendancy of eternity over temporality; even the feats of the greatest conqueror of the Greek world and the *mirabilia* of the Near and Far East pale when shown against transcendence.

This moral stance, subtly introduced by the Middle English author of *Kyng Alisaunder* and boldly articulated by *The Prose Life of Alexander,* challenges the worth of classical experience by making clear its limitations. Not surprisingly humanists like Erasmus, Vives, and Ascham, who were keen to foster classical study and ideas, found romances antipathetic to their goals, and that Renaissance humanistic approach has prevailed in subsequent critical evaluations of narrative fiction, both medieval and modern. The response of less academic readers, the popular audience which for centuries has supported romances and novels, has been quite different. The combination of firm moral principle, in the conventional Christian code, with exotic and bizarre adventures is unfailingly appealing. And the universality of this appeal is clear from the way in which the original aristocratic audience of the twelfth century has expanded to include middle-class and working-class readers as well, though unfortunately the academic critics have largely eschewed this popular tradition.

Morte Arthure

One of the most brilliant achievements of medieval romance both in technique and meaning is the fourteenth-century alliterative *Morte Arthure*. Unlike many later versions of the Arthurian legend, it is focused upon the character of the king and thus looks forward to Malory's most interesting concern. King Arthur himself, not a chief knight such as Gawain or Lancelot, is central to the argument and story, and this focus governs many details.[26] This romance, like most of the Middle English narratives about Charlemagne, pictures a society in which many primitive values still influence men although the ideas and attitudes of Christianity triumphantly prevail.[27] Men who behave courageously, not subtle and complex courtly intrigues, provide the basic thematic material.[28] The richness and brilliance of descriptive detail (as in *Sir Gawain and the Green Knight*) celebrate vividly the attractions of this world, but the basic argument of the poem is the triumph of death which a Christian joyfully welcomes.

Superficially several pagan attitudes are potent in the *Morte Arthure*. Notable are the ideas of vengeance and Fortune. The code of revenge was retained in much of Europe for centuries, posing grave difficulties to the essential Christian virtues of charity and humility.[29] Certainly Arthur and his nobles frequently utter cries for revenge and ruthlessly attack those who have done them injury, but the romance is less aggressive than many and the placing of actions into a Christian context is sustained throughout. The classical concept of Fortune undergoes change in the Middle Ages, and the poet here makes it crucial to his argument.[30] God is frequently mentioned, prayers and references to the liturgical year occur often, and the Christian point of view continually informs the poem.[31] Thus both incidental and larger details make clear the essential meaning of the poem: man's acceptance of his death is reflected in his attempt to use his temporal existence in the most meaningful and worthy manner.

As is so frequent in medieval romance, the poet's invocation is not simply a token prayer but a means of establishing the perspective, the raison d'être, for the narrative to come.[32]

> Now grett glorious Godde, thurgh grace of hym seluene,
> And the precyous prayere of hys prys modyr
> Schelde vs ffor schamesdede and synfulle werkes,
> And gyffe vs grace to gye, and gouerne vs here,
> In this wrechyde werlde thorowe vertous lywynge,
> That we may kayre til hys courte, the kyngdome of hevyne,
> Whene oure saules schalle parte and sundyre ffra the body,
> Ewyre to belde and to byde in blysse wyth hyme seluene;
> And wysse me to werpe owte some worde at this tyme,
> That nothyre voyde be ne vayne, bot wyrchip tille hyme selvyne,
> Plesande *and* profitabille to the popule that theme heres. (1-11)

This explicit statement is crucial. Accepting the inevitability of death and rejoicing in the prospect of heavenly union with God, the poet prays for grace to live well. Specifically he wants to write, so that he can convey his understanding of man's nature. This sense of vocation is evident in many writers of romance. Its importance here is reinforced by the repetition of the idea when the philosopher explains Arthur's dream of Fortune. The King will be one of the Nine Worthies, whose deeds will long be recorded in chronicles and romances (3440-45). Thus although his temporal existence will be an inspiration, the need for repentance and a concern for the afterlife are still crucial.

> I rede thow rekkyne and reherse vn-resonable dedis,
> Ore the repenttes fulle rathe alle thi rewthe werkes!
> Mane, amende thy mode, or thow myshappene,
> And mekely aske mercy for mede of thy saule! (3452-55)

Arthur is not a perfect being, as his vain, human response to this exhortation makes clear. He arrays himself in marvelous robes, which contrast sharply with the modest appearance of the pilgrim (Sir Cradok).[33] Arthur uses Biblical language—"Whedire wilnez thowe, wye, walkande thyne onne?" (3479)—but his concern is the threat of death in the temporal world. Sir Cradok's Christian understanding is exemplary: with God's help he will forgive any injury done to him, and no worldly activities will deter him from his essential purpose of attaining salvation:

Bot I wille passe in pilgremage this pas vn-to Rome,
To purchese me pardonne of the pape selfene;
And of paynes of purgatorie be plenerly assoyllede;
Thane salle I seke sekirly my souerayne lorde, (3496-99)

Thus his spiritual, not his bodily, well-being is given primacy. The knight's recitation of the ills which characterize Arthur's kingdom perhaps explains accurate rejection of temporal value. Significantly, many of the enemy are pagans who ravish nuns and rob the religious so that they blatantly oppose established Christianity. For the popular audience there is evoked, then, a conservative response, a sympathy for the threatened establishment.

In contrast to this other-worldliness Arthur maintains a kingly attitude and that elemental commitment to fame and glory which makes him desire revenge and leads him to organize his knights for battle when the cause is right. There is perhaps more justice than mercy in Arthur's attitude, but he does exercise extraordinary discretion in fighting. Modred is typically characterized as the "fende" or devil, and his knights are "heythene tykes." They are definitely a threat to Arthur's worldly superiority, and also to his essential values—as the evil and immoral nature of Modred's crimes makes clear.

The anti-Christian quality of Arthur's antagonists is yet more evident when Gawain leads an attack against them. This hero wills the souls of the enemy to the devil (3739, 3776), and he promises his knights an eternal bliss—not temporal fame or wealth—if they are valorous:

"We are with Sarazenes be-sett appone sere halfes!
I syghe noghte for my selfe, sa helpe oure Lorde;
Bot for to [see] vs supprysede, my sorowe es the more.
Bes dowghtty to-daye, ȝone dukes schalle be ȝoures!
ffor dere Dryghttyne this daye, dredys no wapyne.
We salle ende this daye alls excellent knyghttes,
Ayere to endelesse joye with angelles vnwemmyde.
Thofe we hafe vnwittyly wastede oure selfene,
We salle wirke alle wele in the wirchipe of Cryste.
We salle for ȝone Sarazenes, I sekire ȝow my trowhe,
Souppe with oure Saueoure solemply in heuene,
In presence of that precious, prynce of alle other
With prophetes, and patriarkes, and apostlys fulle nobille,
Be-fore his freliche face that fourmede vs alle!
ȝondire toȝone ȝaldsones, he that ȝeldes hyme euer,
Qwhylles he es qwykke and in qwerte vnquellyde with handis,
Be he neuer mo sauede, ne socourede with Cryste,
Bot Satanase his sawle mowe synke in-to helle!" (3795-3812)

Significantly the enemy are pagans, the opponents of medieval Christianity, and their destruction is sought in God's name. Certainly there is vehemence and violence in attacking pagans in *Morte Arthure*, but this is mitigated by its careful juxtaposition with Christian belief and the muting of sheer delight in violence that occurs in narratives like the militant Charlemagne romances[34]—which, of course, are not very popular in English versions. Here, then, we find a more controlled blending of primitive aggressiveness and simple justice with notable Christian forbearance and a yearning for eternity. Later, when Gawain has been slain by Modred, Arthur expresses the basic idea most succinctly as he leads the army onward, exhorting the nobles to kill Saracens:

> "Sett one theme sadlye, for sake of oure Lorde!
> 3if vs be destaynede to dy to-daye one this erthe,
> We salle be hewede vn-to heuene, or we be halfe colde!" (4089-91)

Undeniably Arthur shows little Christian charity in the vehemence of his reaction to the traitor Modred, whose very death he regards as too noble for such a traitor. However, Arthur sees his victory as the accomplishment of the will of God Whose instrument he is in the destruction of the devil, and this is the rationale of his vindictiveness and his limitation.

The poet's casting of Modred as a devil, the enemy of Christian values, is but the culmination of his attitude throughout the romance. The first threat to the Round Table is that posed by the Roman Emperor Sir Lucius Iberius. This arrogant man of the classical world gains military support from the pagan East (570 ff.), whose "hathene kinges" (1284) join in opposition to Arthur, the "knyghtlyeste creatoure in Cristyndome" (534) and a descendant of Constantine who gained the Cross on which Christ was crucified (282 ff.). Sir Lucius' other allies are giants "engenderide with fendez" (2111). The poet also emphasizes the heathen nature of those slain by Arthur (2274 ff.), and he hopes these will "martyre hys knyghtes" (560). Arthur is very precise in his thanks to God and his recognition that victory is due not to his own prowess but to the will of God (1559 ff.). The last sacrament is given to Arthur's fallen knights on the battlefield (2193 ff.). In contrast, Sir Lucius exhorts his men to fight by exulting that Romans "Encrochede alle Cristyndome be craftes of armes" (2036). Thus the poet makes abundantly clear that Arthur fights for Christianity.

Not all of those who oppose the Round Table are irredeemable.

Sir Priamus agrees to tell Gawain how to staunch the wound he has just received if he will provide for his Christian end:

> "With-thy that thowe suffre me, for sake of thy Cryste,
> To schewe schortly my schrifte, and schape for myne ende." (2587-88)

Thus Priamus is granted the sacraments, and he confesses that his pride and vanity led to his participating in war. Naturally, the shriven knight desires to know the identity of his benefactor, and Gawain at first hedges. However, once Priamus asks his question in Christian terms— "Now fore the krisome that thou kaghte that day thou was crystenede" (2636)—Gawain immediately complies. This trust leads to Priamus' warning of an ambush in a neighboring wood against the Arthurian forces. Further, he gives them his heavenly balms (2704 ff.). And when they are hard-pressed by hundreds of Saracens, Priamus offers aid "for sake of thi Criste" (2817), and ultimately leads his men to desert from the Duke of Lorraine who has failed in largesse. So complete a conversion to the Christian forces of the righteous king bears comparison with that memorable change of faith by Firumbras in the Charlemagne romances, or the inspiration of Guy of Warwick in turning many to truly Christian values.

Arthur's dedication to Christian forms is perhaps most explicitly stated in his promise to spare from vengeance that part of the Roman world which is Christian.

> "I gyffe my protteccione to alle the pope landez,
> My ryche penselle of pes my pople to schewe.
> It es a foly to offende oure fadyr vndire Gode,
> Owther Peter ȝr Paule, tha postles of Rome.
> ȝif we spare the spirituelle, we spede bot the bettire;
> Whills we haue for to speke, spille salle it neuer!" (2410-15)

And when victory is Arthur's, he agrees to have his sovereignty formally established by having the Pope "crowne hyme kyndly with krysomede hondes" (3185). This careful respect for the Papacy, the temporal representative of God, contrasts sharply with the militant response that Arthur makes when attacked by heathen opposition. A twentieth-century view, informed by a spirit of ecumenism, may well see the justification of revenge as less than truly Christian. However, the poet of *Morte Arthure* is, by medieval standards, moderate in his characterization of Arthur and his nobles who, though they oppose the paynims, yet maintain courtesy and hospitality and indeed are never agressors. Further, an appeal for mercy like that made by the ladies of a besieged city, "for sake of ȝoure Criste!" (3051) is answered, and ravage forbidden by Arthur (3078 ff.).

Arthur's antagonists are thus forces of evil, devil-figures, who threaten Christianity, not randomly chosen knights challenged in order to enhance prowess and reputation. The deliberateness of this judgment is revealed in Arthur's restraint. Sir Cador rejoices in the opportunity and is gleeful to return to fighting (249 ff.), and Lancelot is delighted to resume combat (368 ff.) as is Sir Lottez (383 ff.). It is, then, noteworthy that Arthur has kept the Knights of the Round Table from their natural, primitive bent toward warfare. The King is grateful for their strength and loyalty, but clearly he allows violence only in an approved cause. Even though he is confident that as an anointed king he will not receive injury (2446-47), he does not wantonly display and exploit his superiority.

Moreover, Gawain is slain by Modred when he has fought so fiercely as to become mad:

> And for wondsome and wille alle his wit failede,
> That wode alls a wylde beste he wente at the gayneste;
> Alle walewede one blode, thare he a-waye passede;
> Iche a wy may be warre, be wreke of an-other! (3836-39)

The death blow is appropriately received in Gawain's head. Indeed the point is neatly made; unthinking violence leads to temporal destruction, for it renders even an accomplished knight ineffectual.

Gawain's physical death is not, however, a negative achievement, for it leads to Modred's temporary remorse. The traitorous nephew "remyd and repent hyme of alle his rewthe werkes" (3894); he retreats from the battlefield and warns Guinevere, whom he has married, to flee. The Christian point of view of the poet of *Morte Arthure* is consistent, for he has the Queen flee to Caerlon and take the veil, "And alle for falsede, and frawde, and fere of hir louerde!" (3918). She is influenced by complex motivations, but the distress at her failing is paramount, and her refuge lies in established Christianity. As with Arthur's loyalty to Rome, we see a reliance upon this authority in the temporal state. Gawain, presumably, gains the eternity he sought. His burial is celebrated by monks with many dirges and masses. His virtue is recognized by all kinds of people in the world. An enemy (Modred), an observer who does not know his identity (King Frederick), and his loyal friend and king (Arthur)—each laments his dying.[35]

The Gawain material provides a statement of the poem's theme in a minor key, but Arthur is the hero-protagonist of *Morte Arthure*. The first major combat is Arthur's slaying of the giant who ravished the Duchess of Brittany. Like Arthur's death, this event is foretold in a dream, and victory is promised to him "thurghe helpe of oure Lorde" (827). When the British land in Normandy, a Templar informs Arthur that "A grett geaunte of geene, engenderde of fendez" (843) has, like a latter-day Herod, slain all the male children and thus "marters made" (1065-66). He has also ravished the Duchess. Arthur answers the plea "As thow arte ryghtwise kynge rewe on thy pople, / And fande for to venge theme" (866-67). The sanctity of Arthur's mission is symbolized by his assuming the guise of a pilgrim to Mont St. Michel, and he ascends the mountain alone to attack the fiend. Here, then, we have a suggestion of the apartness of the hero, his individual striving for self-realization and the necessity for facing evil with only his own resources. The thriller hero of modern popular fiction is his heir in this solitary confrontation with evil. When Arthur confronts the giant, he asks God's help and accuses his foe of horribly murdering Christian children and defiling a lady. It is "thurghe the crafte of Cryste" (1107) that Arthur is able to defeat his extraordinary foe. The rightness of Arthur's cause is testified to by natural phenomena. Even the birds kneel and pray for his success:

> "Criste comforthe ȝone knyghte, and kepe hym fro sorowe,
> And latte neuer ȝone fende felle hyme olyfe!" (1138-39)

The Christian context is further emphasized by Bedever's ironic play on the word "seyntez" when the giant is felled. Arthur is enthusiastically greeted by the people, who hail him as

> "Gouernour vndyr Gode, graytheste and noble,
> To whame grace es graunted, and gyffene at his wille!
> Now thy comly come has comforthede vs alle!
> Thow has in thy realtee reuengyde thy pople!" (1201-4)

The poet leaves no doubt of the explicitly Christian nature of his hero.

> Thane the conquerour cristenly carpez to his pople,
> "Thankes Gode," quod he, "of this grace, and no gome elles,
> ffor it was neuer manns dede, bot myghte of Hym selfene,
> Or myracle of hys modyre, that mylde es tille alle!" (1208-11)

In a spirit of charity Arthur distributes the giant's treasure to the clergy and people, and he also builds a church and convent. Clearly, Arthur is motivated here not by a wish for worldly repute and wealth, but by a belief in Christian values. He is prompted by the urgency of destroying a force of evil, and he generously gives the wealth incidentally acquired by this action to both the formal ecclesiastical authorities and to the people. The character thus clearly established in this first major episode in *Morte Arthure* is consistent throughout the poem. Arthur's dedication never falters, and he behaves always with a sense of his inevitable achievement of eternal existence.

The last scenes of the romance are, then, climatic. The poet repeats the earlier pattern by having Arthur dream of his approaching death as he had earlier known of his victory. The importance of understanding the relation between this world and the next is boldly shown by the poet's ordering of events. Arthur's greatest worldly triumph is the victory over Rome, and he exults:

> "Now may we reuelle and riste, fore Rome es oure awene!
> Make oure ostage at ese, thise auenaunt childyrene,
> And luk ȝe hondene theme alle that in myne oste lengez,
> The emperour of Almayne, and alle theis este marches;
> We salle be ouerlynge of alle that one the erthe lengez!
> We wille by the Crosse dayes encroche theis londez,
> And at the Crystynmesse daye be crowned ther-aftyre;
> Ryngne in my ryalltés, and holde my Rownde Table,
> Withe the rentes of Rome, as me beste lykes;
> Syne graythe ouer the grette see with gud mene of armes,
> To reuenge the renke that one the rode dyede!" (3207-17)

Here we see the complexity of Arthur's character. He has an understandable pride in his accomplishment, he practices courtesy and hospitality to enemy and ally alike, and he looks forward to his power on earth. Yet even at this time he sees his behavior in comprehensive terms; thus he will act "by the Crosse," and he has plans for a crusade against enemies of Christ to achieve a just revenge.

Soon after he goes to bed "with a blythe herte," Arthur sleeps and he dreams of Fortune, whose description suggests the Virgin Mary.[36] She leads him to hear the sad stories of six fallen kings and then explains that he has been chosen to achieve the chair and provides symbols to show that Arthur "sothely was souerayne in erthe" (3357). The delights of this world are equisitely suggested by the interlude in the woods, but Fortune quickly places them in perspective.

> "Kyng, thow karpes for noghte, be Criste that me made!
> ffor thow salle lose this layke, and thi lyfe aftyre,
> Thow has lyffede in delytte and lordchippes inewe!" (3385-87)

The Wheel whirls and Arthur is crushed down. The philosopher's exposition of the meaning of the dream experience is explicit and relentlessly honest. Arthur is now at the highest point, and further great achievements will not be his. (The victory over Modred, of course, is but a holding action, and fatal.) To secure such glory he has killed many, some innocent; and this was done "in cirquytrie" (3399). The only remedy for such pride, as popular didactic writings and pulpit oratory constantly asserted, is repentance: "Schryfe the of thy shame, and schape for thyne ende!" (3400). This injunction is that which every man must heed if he is to gain salvation, to enjoy the blessings of heaven. Arthur, as a champion of Christianity, is given the privilege of knowing rather precisely the time of his death "with-in fyve wynters." This, of course, is less exact than knowing the hour of death as do Guy of Warwick and Lancelot in *Le Morte Arthur*. Perhaps the poet thus indicates that, although a worthy champion, Arthur yet preserves too much of the primitive hero's delight in vengeance and self-satisfaction. He has not completely subjugated himself to God's will.[37] Although Arthur is one of the Nine Worthies, he is again exhorted to think of his end:

> "Mane, amende thy mode, or thow myshappene,
> And mekely aske mercy for mede of thy saule!" (3454-55)

Such tutoring is vital to all men, and the audience would be reassured by observing the lesson for so worthy a protagonist whom they might emulate.

The narrative develops with amazing rapidity, for as Arthur rises and dresses he sees approaching a pilgrim, Sir Cradok, who brings news of Modred's treachery. And the remainder of *Morte Arthure* is devoted to Arthur's return to Britain and the fight against Modred, the sea battle, Gawain's attack, and then Arthur's. Just as in the fight against the giant in Britanny, here Arthur is willing to fight alone (4034 ff.), and he thus swears to Christ and Mary ever to "pursue the payganys that my pople distroyede" (4046). Thus his consistent role as the champion against enemies of Christianity is maintained. Hard-pressed in battle, Arthur yet urges Sir Idrus to rescue his father Sir Ewaine. But the young man's loyalty to Arthur is in keeping with his father's command, and he accepts the inevitability of death:

> "3iffe hyme be destaynede to dy to-daye one this erthe,
> Criste comly with crowne take kepe to hys saule!" (4153-54)

Thus a true perspective of the relation between the temporal and the eternal is held even by the younger members of the Round Table.

Arthur's last combat is vigorously undertaken, for he is unstinting in his fight against Modred and his men. The King's grief over the loss of his men is heartfelt, as his lament eloquently attests. But he properly thanks God for their victory, and joyfully accepts his fast approaching death:

> "Of this dere day werke, the Dryghttene be louede,
> That vs has destaynede and demyd to dye in oure awene." (4305-6)

Certainly this hero has achieved that delicate balance sought by medieval man—and present-day Christians. He has steadily striven for excellence and accomplished much in this world but he eagerly awaits eternity. True to his traditional belief, Arthur makes a last request for the Sacraments:

> "Doo calle me a confessour, with Criste in his armes;
> I wille be howselde in haste, whate happe so be-tyddys" (4314-15)

He provides for rule of the Kingdom after his death, and he makes the ultimate human expression of charity, "I fore-gyffe alle greffe, for Cristez lufe of heuene!" (4324). Thus he can joyfully speak the last words *In manus*. Quickly the poet concludes with a brief noting of the traditional religious observances of death and a final placing of Arthur in the epic tradition as a descendant of Hector of Troy. Unlike many other heroes of romance, Arthur is not shown combining his own self-knowledge with the inspiring of followers. The poet chooses to emphasize his individual greatness and achievement of salvation; the universal applicability of Arthur's experience is left to the hearers and readers of his story.

The medieval romances that treat fortune's heroes, those men whose lives are still governed by classical values, show a remarkable success in transforming pagan attitudes. The fundamental seeking of glory is not eschewed, for as myths of Prometheus and Lucifer/Adam make clear, striving and struggle are inherent in the human condition. However, worldly ambition is placed in the context of Christian values which make clear its limitations. Pagan heroes like Hector, Ulysses, and Alexander are shown as extraordinarily powerful and successful in their pursuit and achievement of fame, but this is restricted to time in the world. Their exploits delight an audience which relishes the exotic excitement of strange adventures and creatures in faraway places and times. But the romancers counterpoint these exploits with other alternatives, often presented in lyrical and symbolic passages or the words of the heroes' opponents, that are crucial in the lives of those listening to the stories. The result is epitomized in Chaucer's conclusion of *Troilus and Criseyde,* when Troilus in the eighth sphere laughs at worldly struggles which he took so earnestly while alive, when he lacked the medieval capacity for "game." Troilus' last perspective is that of the medieval Christian, who is the audience for the romance. Thus we see a successful transformation of pagan ideas; the thrills of human endeavor are maintained, but very comfortably accommodated through a recognition that these are not the totality of man's being. Explicitly classical heroes of Fortune like Alexander do not themselves achieve this knowledge, but Arthur, an early hero of medieval Christianity who continues this pagan ancestry, finally realizes that the older values are inadequate. Physical prowess and rationality, dual pagan ideals for man, are seen as not all-encompassing, and the supernatural has new dimensions for man's exploration.

CHAPTER III

FIENDISH ORIGINS TRANSFORMED

A fascination with strange creatures is perhaps most obviously documented in medieval romance by the frequency and elaborateness with which giants and dragons appear. Like the grotesque gargoyles of so many French cathedrals, or indeed like the splendid griffons of medieval Indian sculpture, these strange beings express a basic sensibility which involves simultaneous attraction and aversion. Perhaps nothing illustrates this more vividly than the tympani of French cathedrals like Conques, Bourges, Autun or Amiens, and the remaining bits of frieze at Lincoln, where scenes of the Last Judgment and Hell exploit the monstrosity of the damned.[1] As any modern tourist knows, these tortured, grotesque figures always seize the imagination of the beholders more emphatically than the sublime repose of the blessed. Precisely the same comment can be made about devils and angels in the Corpus Christi and morality plays. The many vigorous representations of evil suggest similar enthusiasm in their creators, and the same fascination has drawn readers to Milton's Satan in *Paradise Lost*.

In each instance the artistic intention is not to encourage imitation, yet dynamically to exploit man's potential for monstrosity. This is possible when the artist works with a sure confidence in the acceptance of a moral view which will ultimately lead to a choice of harmonious order. Thus it is feasible for audience and artist to enjoy both possibilities. The undeniable fascination of evil, as Shakespeare's deformed Richard III so eloquently demonstrates, is allowable because of a belief in a God-controlled universe where evil will not finally prevail. Any monstrosity may be allowed because it can be reconciled within the moral framework. This is very obvious in the physical structure of sculptured tympani, where space is carefully controlled. The gaze may first fall on a gaping devil's head with open hell-mouth, but inevitably it moves to and rests upon the central apex where a judging Christ dominates, while the damned figures shrink into comparative insignificance. Just as the bestial qualities of damned mankind often predominate, so the concrete representation of the animal is often curiously humanized by an expression or pose that suggests a rational awareness. Thus the beholder often has a startling revelation of the coexistence of his physical and spiritual natures, which are analogous to his temporal and eternal existence.

It is not very difficult to move from this awareness to the representation of a human being whose qualities are such that he ceases to function as a human being and, in Christian terms, is identified as a devil. For as the angels violated their nature, through pride and self-indulgence, to become devils, so men repeat the pattern when they eschew the essential human qualities of charity and humility. Investigation of the supernatural is one of man's most exciting challenges, and its possibilities were perhaps more fully exploited by medieval artists than any others because belief in a God-centered universe legitimatized its existence. The great popularity of marvels seen in Alexander stories reflects this interest, and human monstrosity provides further evidence. Medieval visual art abounds with devils, and such references are a commonplace in the romances. There is, however, one kind of romance which uses the human-devil[2] very exactly to demonstrate the necessity for penance and its importance in man's salvation. Here an individual, who not infrequently has a physical deformity as well as moral insensitivity, is shown first as behaving in a totally un-Christian and appalling way. Then he miraculously comes to a recognition that he is evil and must repent and do penance to regain his humanity and so rid the world of a fiend. Often he is presented as a child of the devil, either in his begetting or in his parents' deliberate disavowal of his (or their) humanity. The narratives then recount a life of penance which is exemplary and characteristically lived in great joy and hope because the penitent has recognized his own particular evil, his devil nature. He knows, then, how futile are worldly blandishments and how destructive is the relentless pursuit of self-satisfaction. Usually he continues to live in the world, but this typically involves restitution for his evils and then a life of goodness. All is accomplished within the context of God so that worldly and otherworldly existence are reconciled.

Again the popularity of such thematic material is attested by the many illustrations of it in a wide variety of Middle English romance. Breton lays, as they are defined in the openings of the *Lay le Freine* and *Sir Orfeo,* are "of other diverse thyngs" but "Most off luffe." This preferred subject matter and the brevity of the form (usually only about one thousand lines and often less) make the lay a less likely narrative for the exposition of fundamental moral points of view than the longer Middle English romances. Nevertheless, the presence of such thematic material, which is the basis of the popularity of medieval fiction, is boldly evident even here.

Most of the lays contain incidental, traditional Christian materials —prayers of thanksgiving to God, references to His power, precise ecclesiastical details, and so on—that are the commonplaces of medieval literature. In addition, however, two of the eight Breton lays in Middle English are clearly written to convey an essential morality, as well as to entertain. *Emaré,* which is one of the most popular stories of the period, describes how evil tries to overcome good and strongly emphasizes the role of penance in Christian life. The charge of fiend is false and only part of the many difficulties which Emaré, who is in the tradition of Constance, must undergo. However, the poem provides an excellent introduction to the idea of penance.

Sir Gowther is a rich exposition of the questing individual's seeking of God in spite of his fiendish antecedents (he is actually begotten by the devil) and winning temporal peace through penance, so that eternal salvation is assured as earthly miracles attest. The brief narrative is admirably controlled; its even tone and brevity give great impact to the basic argument, and its seriousness is recognizably inspiring. Indeed the basic legend has been described as "the preeminent expression of monkish meditation over the problem of extreme sin and the possibility of atonement."[3] Gowther's story, like that of Robert of Sicily, is related to the legend of Robert the Devil, which is widely known throughout Europe and appears in a variety of forms. In England both metrical and prose versions of the romance have survived and perhaps enjoyed most popularity at the beginning of the sixteenth century when they were printed by Wynkyn de Worde; at the end of the century another prose version was produced by Thomas Lodge. The earlier prose version is in many ways most venturesome, for it richly expands the idea of the fool—who is, of course, the penitent Christian in an uncomprehending though not directly malicious world—as well as the device of making the dumb speak and other miraculous occurrences. Thus it has been chosen for full discussion here.

Finally, the romances of Lusignan provide not only a larger and more comprehensive expression of the relation of penance to man's seeking of eternity with God, but also a richly varied exposition of the fiend motif in the many sons of the fairy lady. Each of these has some physical mark or peculiar feature which suggests inhuman quality. Indeed "Melusine" means "not lacking marvels." Such descriptive characterization is very popular in modern thrillers from the deformed finger in *The Thirty-Nine Steps* to the more obvious *Dr. No* and *Goldfinger*.

The sons' modes of conduct reflect varying degrees of humanity and inhumanity. As his name indicates, Horrible is too evil to risk, but Thierry performs good deeds. Most interesting are the paralleling accounts of the repentance of Raymond and his son Geoffrey, whose behavior bears close resemblance in many ways to that of Sir Gowther and Robert the Devil. Both prose (*Melusine*) and verse (*Partenay*) versions have survived, and the following discussion will be based on *Partenay* because of its superior literary excellence and its explicit use of Fortune in advancing the argument. Thus it has qualities which suggest comparisons with the romances discussed in the previous chapter.

Emaré

The poet of *Emaré* begins with an invocation that is very like that of the longer romances.

> Ihesu, þat ys kyng in trone,
> As þou shoope boþe sonne *and* mone,
> And alle þat shalle dele *and* dyghte,
> Now lene vs grace such dedus to done,
> In þy blys þat we may wone,
> Men calle hyt heuen lyghte;
> And þy modur Mary, heuyn qwene,
> Bere our arunde so bytwene,
> That semely ys of syght,
> To þy sone þat ys so fre,
> In heuen wyth hym þat we may be,
> That lord ys most of myght.

Menstrelles þat walken fer and wyde,
Her and þer in euery a syde,
    In mony a dyuerse londe,
Sholde, at her bygynnyng,
Speke of þat ryghtwes kyng
    That made both see and sonde. (1-18)[4]

The opening stanza is a prayer to Christ for the bliss of eternity; the poet accepts humbly the nature of grace and views Mary as man's most helpful intercessor. Thus from the outset the reader (hearer) of this lay is predisposed to approach the narrative with a clear sense of man's total existence. Specifically the author of *Emaré* notes that minstrels should begin their work with an awareness and an acknowledgment of their place in the scheme of the universe. And the last three lines of the poem are another prayer to Jesus for joyful union in eternity. It is the argument of the lay itself, however, which makes abundantly clear that the author is not simply repeating an expected formula.[5]

Like the Constance of Chaucer and Gower,[6] Emaré is a worthy young woman much oppressed and tried by difficulties. However, her faith and prayers triumph in many trials, and through God's grace all is set right (314, 332, 670 ff., 680 f., 836, 943). Tranquilly and with faith unshaken, Emaré survives her father's attempt at incest, his setting her adrift without earthly resources, the wicked mother-in-law's accusations that she is "a fende" (446) and her child "a deuylle" (536), her husband's belief in this latter charge (556 ff.) which leads to a second banishment at sea, residence in yet another set of circumstances. Finally, Emaré effects a neat reconciliation with both father and husband after each has done penance. The lay is, then, a varied study of penitence, not just an innocent's capacity to endure which shows symbolically the way of patience.

Most frequently the medieval writer of narrative presents a reconciliation of temporality and eternity through the self-discovery of a knightly protagonist whose increasing self-awareness leads to his choice of explicitly Christian values. Thus his own life is transformed, and he also becomes an example of transcendence to less gifted human beings. In *Emaré* these roles are divided among several characters. Never unbalanced by the vagaries of her fortunes, Emaré herself is more symbol than person. Very specifically she is identified as a being who "semed non erþely wommon" (245, 396, 701), and she is recognized as

> ... þe konnyngest wommon,
> I trowe, þat be yn Crystendom,
> Of werk þat y haue sene. (427-29)

She accepts her husband's decision, but notes that

> So gentylle of blo[l]de yn Cristyante,
> Gete he neuur more! (635-36)

She is thus an embodiment of Christian ideas, and through their knowing her the two men realize their own transcendence.

The Emperor incestuously desires Emaré and tries to make her his wife, even securing a papal dispensation to that end. This blatant failure of the temporal representative of God serves to emphasize the elemental responsibility of the Christian conscience. Emaré is not intimidated by temporal authority. Steadfast in her own belief, she asserts that incest would lead to damnation and repulses her father's advances. Very quickly the Emperor is inspired by Emaré's values:

> The emperour hym be-þowght
> That he hadde alle myswrowht,
>   And was a sory knyȝte. (280-82)

Swooning and lamenting, he publicly admits his sin:

> "I wrowght a-ȝeyn Goddes lay,
> To her þat was so trewe of fay." (295-96)

Years later he still "þowȝt on hys synne" (951); and

> He þowȝt[e] that he wolde go,
> For hys penance to þe Pope þo,
>   And heuen for to wynne. (955-57)

This is not the last seeking of assurance by a dying man, but the public expression of humility by one who is recognized as the greatest lord in Christendom (968-69). Thus the principals are reunited for a worldly reconciliation which prefigures union with God in heaven. The monstrous nature of incest makes an exciting topic, as is attested by the many analogues and continued success of versions of the Latin romance of Apollonius of Tyre, best known in English through Gower's *Confessio Amantis* and Shakespeare's *Pericles,* which begins the vogue of romance in the Jacobean theatre.[7]

The king of Galys serves as yet a further illustration of the necessity for repentance. Where Emaré's father had been obviously guilty (first of attempted incest and then of attempted murder), her husband is not guilty of ill feelings or actions. He is himself the victim of his mother's evil in changing the letters that led to Emaré's banishment. As is characteristic in human behavior, he is not, however, totally blameless. He has experienced his mother's hatred and animosity to his marriage (445-56). Although he rejects her false charge that Emaré is a devil, he does not suspect that his mother may be responsible for the charge that his child is a fiend. In short, his sin is not of commission but of omission, for he fails to protect himself and his family against the evil forces which seek to destroy Christian truth. After a first primitive wish for revenge against his mother, his basic charity prevails (793 ff.). Then after a long period of grief, he actively accepts his responsibility for his lady's drowning and resolves:

> "Thorow þe grace of God yn trone,
> I wolle to þe pope of Rome,
> My penans for to take!" (820-22)

He also performs good works. Further, he accepts his earthly responsibility when he tries to adopt a son (actually his own Segramoures) who will be able to carry on his heritage. Thus we see a man who is inspired to behave well, exercising both his spiritual and physical resources to seek salvation.

Like the Emperor, the King of Galys is led to his greatest realization of Christian values through his relation to Emaré, who embodies charity and is sustained always by faith. Her unblemished robe is the outward symbol of her inner worth.[8] The narrative tells us that

> She was dryuen toward Rome,
> Thorow þe grace of God yn trone,
> That alle þyng may fulfylle. (679-81).

On the surface level the principals are thus neatly reunited in Rome. This is, however, not a mere coincidence of plotting; Rome, whatever the Pope's vagary in granting an outrageous dispensation, is the best temporal resource for the medieval Christian. The individual acceptances of responsibility and the attempts to behave with charity, not just a formal declaration of penance, lead the two knights to a realization of that earthly bliss which prefigures union with God in heaven.

Although the chief emphasis in *Emaré* is upon temporal existence, there is a clear argument of its relation to eternity. A rather lifeless heroine becomes dynamic and understandable if she is viewed in almost symbolic terms, and the significance of penance is reiterated. Combined with extravagant adventures, the poem's firm moral control—the reassurance that innocence will not be destroyed and that disastrous error can be redeemed through penance—provides the inspiration and optimism that are the mainstays of popular fiction.

Sir Gowther

Another Breton lay, *Sir Gowther*, is in effect a microcosm of the medieval preoccupation with the thematic material of the temporal and the eternal. In less than seven hundred lines the author presents a model for Christian behavior.[9] Like *Guy of Warwick*, the poem shows a mode of earthly behavior which leads to heaven. However, this hero's difficulties are far greater than those of the usual questing knight who is the protagonist of the Middle English romance.

Gowther is not simply a fallible human being who must achieve the self-knowledge that leads to transcendence. He is a devil figure, an incarnation of evil, for he is begotten by a "fowle fend" (74) and "Marylyng's half brother" (98).[10] The minstrel's invocation is more specific than many we have encountered; he asks God to

> Shilde us from the fowle fende
> That is about mannys sowle to shende
> All tymes of the yere! (4-6)

The exact relevance of this prayer becomes very clear as the lay develops with descriptions of Gowther's prodigious violence; as an infant he slays nine wet-nurses, and as a youth he willfully destroys both religious houses and churches and ecclesiastical and devout persons. Thus an old earl neatly summarizes:

> "Sir, whi doest thow so?
> Thow comest never of Criste strene;
> Thou are sum fendes sone, Y wene;
> Bi thi werkis it semeth so.
> Thou doest no good, but ever ill;

Thou art bisibbe the devel of hell!" (201-6)

This explicit charge leads Gowther to a confrontation with his mother, who admits that his father was a "fend" who came to her in the likeness of her husband. The mother's admission of her culpability climaxes the narrative's exploitation, in several dramatic exchanges, of the widely used folk-motif of the Wish-Child.[11] Gowther has, of course, been baptized (107) and lived in a Christian atmosphere, so that this explanation of his evil impulses results in immediate prayers and desire for penance.

"Now wol I to Rome, to that appostell,
To be shreven, and after asoyled; " (238-39)

Significantly he goes alone, without man or horse to ease his journey, and he hurries eagerly to fall on his knees to ask "Cryst and absolucion" (257).

Sir Gowther's development, his humble and uncomplaining self-mortification and achievement of sanctity, occupies the bulk of the narrative. The Pope defines Gowther's penance:

"Thow shalt walk north and sowthe,
And gete thi mete owt of houndis mouth;
This penaunce shalt thow gynne.
And speke no word, even ne odde,
Til thow have very wetyng of Godde
Foryevyn be all thy synne." (283-88)

As a penitent Gowther abides exactly by these conditions of the beast penance which is used in Eastern and Western tales,[12] and he shows no pride or self-pity. In the castle of the Emperor of Almayn he mutely takes only the food brought him by dogs, and soon has an established role:

And Hobbe the Fool thei gan hym calle;
To Criste he gan him yelde. (359-60)

The contrast between this situation and his previous dominance is notable; we observe Gowther in the midst of earthly wealth abiding by the exacting terms of the Pope's penance, and through this self-discipline acquiring great strength just as Ipomadon assumes the role of fool to further his achievements to win the temporal love of his lady.

Thus when the kingdom is threatened by Saracen invaders, the former devil becomes a champion of Christianity. He fights for the Emperor who has rejected the Sowdan of Persia's demand for his mute daughter as wife. Gowther is clearly an agent of God; he prays for armor, and it is sent by God. His modest self-effacement is maintained, for only the mute lady knows his identity. As the attacks of Saracens continue, three battles are fought—in black, red, and white armor sent by God.[13] In the midst of triumph Gowther is constantly the penitent.

> His thowght was moch uppon his synne—
> How he myght his sowle wynne
> To blysse above the skye. (514-16)

> Yet durst he never in anger ne tene
> Speke no word, withouten wene,
> For dred of Goddes wreche;
> And thow him houngerd, he durst not ete
> But such as from houndes he myght gete:
> He did as the pope gan teche. (571-76)

Such dedication and humility are appropriately rewarded by miraculous happenings. After appearing to be dead, the Emperor's daughter speaks, and her first words are God's message to Gowther:

> "My Lord of Hevyn greteth the well;
> Foryeve ben thi synnes, every dell,
> And graunteth the His blysse;
> He byddeth the speke boldely,
> To ete and drynk, and make the mery;
> Thowe shalt ben on of His!" (613-18)

The Pope himself is immediately impressed so that he observes that the conditions for Gowther's redemption have been recognized:

> "Now art thow bycome Godes child;
> The dare not dred of thi workys wyld;
> Forsothe, I tell it the." (625-27)

Gowther is, then, extraordinarily honored by receiving explicit assurances of his salvation from God and His chief temporal representative.

Such honor serves, however, only to increase the knight's sanctity. Rather than lessening his humility and efforts to behave well, Gowther continues to do good works. Having secured victory over the pagan enemies of Christians, he now turns to the task of building abbeys as a continued expression of repentance for his youthful destruction of the religious. In short,

Of all Cristendome he bare the flowre,
Above the sarezyns hede. (665-66)

That which is asked in God's name, he so renders, and his charity is boundless. "Thus cawght he better rede" (672) for many years, and after his death miracles take place at the shrine where he is buried.

Here, then, in a very short and pointed narrative we have a career which in broad outline is like that of heroes such as Guy or Lancelot. Gowther's ancestry makes his development more startling, but the essential argument is the same. The evolution from devil to saint is a heightened exposition of the Christian belief in Redemption. However grievous his sins, any man may secure the blessings of heaven; he must simply choose God and so conduct his temporal life that he looks always to eternity. An active earthly existence is not thus forsworn but lived more meaningfully and creatively. Many knightly protagonists in romances must rid themselves of pride in trying to secure renown. This is a more subtle problem, for it involves doing many of the same things (achieving excellence as a knight) but for different reasons. Gowther is driven to evil destruction by his devil's nature, but his Christian heritage makes him reject this quality. Further, he becomes worthier than his peers by ridding himself of pride, trusting absolutely in God, and following the directions of the Pope, God's temporal seat of authority. Again we observe a virtue which is not cloistered, but tried by the rigors of temporal being, so that this lai is more exciting than romances like the *King of Tars* which share the theme of miraculous conversion. Such examples may well inspire less distinguished human beings, both those who encounter them in life and those who experience miracles after death, and their popular appeal is clear from the many versions sought by admirers for several centuries.

Robert the Deuyll

The selection of the story of Robert the Devil by Wynkyn de Worde for printing in not one but two editions at the start of the sixteenth century, its use at the court of Henry VIII as material for a disguising, and Lodge's prose version in 1591 suggest the popularity of romances in general and also a continuing interest in the idea of a devil who repents

Robert the Deuyll　　　　　　　　　　Wynkyn de Worde, 1502?
Courtesy of The British Library

Devils attend at Robert's conception.

Valentine and Orson　　　　　　　　　　Copland, 1565

The Beinecke Rare Book and Manuscript Library, Yale University

A knight fighting a dragon.

to become an admirable Christian. The legend is one of the most famous in Europe, recorded in 106 texts according to Breul,[14] found in France, Spain, Portugal, the Netherlands, England, and Germany. Laura Hibbard (Loomis) has observed: "The modern popularity of this typically medieval story is one of its most amazing features, and is best explained by the universal love for melodramatic story that combines excitement with unforgettable 'doctrine.' "[15]

The parents of Robert provide a necessary context in which we view the hero. His father the Duke of Normandy is, in spite of his reputation for pacticing charity and chivalry, a failure because he has not married and produced an heir. Urged by his people and a sense of devotion he weds, but after eighteen years of marriage the couple remain childless. The author does not presume to question God's will in such matters (p. 5),[16] but the frustrated parents are sad and despairing. At first the Duchess shows an admirable Christian virtue when she says, "Good lorde, we must thanke God of that whiche he sendeth us, and take it pacyently of what so euer it be" (p. 6). But she is then moved to speak foolishly:

"In the deuyle's name be it, in so muche as God hath not the power that I conceyue; and yf I be conceyued with chylde in this houre, I gyve it to the devyll, body and soule." (p. 7)

Such a rash vow is literally carried out, and the romance deals with the life of the son who at conception is deliberately given over to the devil. Here, then, is a more conscious initiation of events than in Sir Gowther, where the otherworldly creature is attractively shown in the orchard, or in Lodge's *Robert Duke of Normandy*, which omits the Devil's part, and thus loses one dimension of the spectacular.

Even at his birth Robert is inhuman; his mother is in labor for a month, and her life is saved only because of prayers, alms and good works, and penance done for her. A very blackness and storm in the heavens signal the unnatural birth, and at the christening the baby (who has a one-year-old's stature at birth) "neuer ceased cryenge and houlynge" (p. 8). He successively injures his nurses, is unruly to adults, and breaks the bones of all children who come into his presence. Very quickly, then, he is described as "wode Robert," "madde Robert," and named "Robert the Deuyll." At the age of seven he is given a schoolmaster, whom he promptly murders. His particular delight, however, is blasphemy, for he "mocked both God and holy chyrche" (p. 10) and injures any worshippers.

His father's explicit injunction to behave better leads only to Robert's adamant declaration that he will persist in evil. Thus the Duke prays to God for some relief from the pain of his parentage (p. 14), but his further attempts to discipline his devilish son lead only to threatened patricide. Robert vigorously pursues a life which embraces many deadly sins. The romancer particularly emphasizes his violence against anything that is religious; he and his band of outlaws kill pilgrims and Robert deliberately fails to keep any religious observances, such as fasting.

Not accidentally the climax of Robert's evil is the wanton slaying of "vii hooly heremytes" who suffer martyrdom for the love of God. He is described as attacking "lyke a man oute of his mynde" (p. 18), and he rides from the wood "lyke a deuyll out of helle," covered with blood which he smears over the countryside.[17] Thus Robert approaches a castle, and all the people flee from him in fear. This dramatic expression of his isolation, the conventional plight so exploited in modern thrillers, has a startling effect upon Robert, for he suddenly sees himself as he is, a most cursed wretch, 'more than a Jew or a Saracen,' "worthy to be hated of God and the worlde." Already chastened, he approaches his mother, who is so terrified by his wild appearance and drawn sword that she flees. He calls upon her in the name of Christ's passion to stop and begs her to explain how he can be so vicious.

Thus Robert is already prayerfully using God and Christ, against Whom he had earlier blasphemed. His most distinctive expression of Christianity comes, however, when he rejects his distressed mother's request that he kill her. "O! dere moder, why sholde I do so, that so moche myschefe have done, and this sholde be the worste dede that euer I dyde" (p. 21). Essentially this is the basic Christian belief that no man should judge another because he himself has sinned.[18] Even when the Duchess explains how she gave her son to the devil, Robert remains strong: he forsakes the devil and his evil and commits himself to a life of penance, specifically to a pilgrimage for confession to the Pope in Rome, Here, then, is the classic development from diabolic evil to devout good, an irresistibly popular theme.

If the sudden change in Robert seems arbitrary, it is well to note that the romance is by no means a simple account of miraculous conversion from devilish behavior. Very carefully the romancer has the Duke explain the complexity of repentance:

"Alas it is all in vayne, that Robert thynketh to do, for I here he shall neuer have power to make restytycyon of the hurtes and harmes the whiche he hathe doone in his lyfe, but I beseche Almyghty God to prolonge his lyfe, and sende hym a respyte that he may amende his lyfe, and do penaunce for his synnes." (pp. 22-23)

In short, there is no simple setting right of grave injuries and sins, but the offender need not despair, since with God's mercy he may live long enough to do penance and thus realize happiness with God. The unrepentant former companions of Robert provide clear evidence of evil. Just as Robert deliberately chose to renounce the devil and turn to God, so others can make the opposite choice. Urging repentance, he pleads:

"Gentyll felawes I praye you for goddes sake leue your condycyons, and thynke on our soule, and do penaunce for your moost fellest stynkynge synnes, and crye upon oure lorde for mercy and forgeueness, and he wyl forgeue you." (p. 24)

Man, then, need only want God's mercy to receive it. Vividly Robert's life illustrates the Christian choice that others reject. Indeed his Christianity becomes militant when he kills those who refuse to be converted! He does, however, show greater sensitivity than do the Christians in Charlemagne romances or *Richard Coer de Lyon:* the evil men are killed, but the house is saved for the poor and stolen goods returned. Similarly he personally seeks forgiveness of the Abbot and restores the goods he has stolen from the Abbey.

There is, then, a mixture of prayer and good works in Robert's Christian life, a theological view that perhaps contributed to its popularity in sixteenth-century England. But the central part of the narrative concentrates upon the idea of penance. It is as though the devil must not only be exorcised, but also a resource of Christian virtues developed in the person of the man who would truly escape soul-destroying worldliness and selfishness to find the loving peace of God. Going to Rome, Robert begins as impetuously as he behaves when a fiendish figure, so that there is consistency in characterization. His eagerness in seeking the Pope's absolution is disturbing so that attendants want to send him away. The romancer's respect for ecclesiastical authority is shown when the Pope recognizes Robert's devotion and orders him admitted.

Although the Pope is frightened by Robert's declaration of his sinfulness and knows his reputation as devil, nevertheless he gently proposes confession to a holy hermit. Thus the penitent is helped by a religious man like those he so wantonly murdered. And the narrative comments:

Robert that was so curst and myscheuous, ferful cruel, and proude as a lyon, is now as gentyll and curteys, and swete of wordes, and wyse in his dedes, as euer was ony duke or prynce lyuynge. (p. 30)

Somewhat in the tradition of knighthood Robert is told to spend a night in chapel. His prayer invokes God's endless mercy and asks protection "from the fendes temptacyon and deceyte." Rest, then, comes first to Robert and afterwards to the hermit who prays for him. This sleep prepares for the initial appearance of the angel who conveys God's command and sets Robert's penance: to behave as a fool, dumb and eating no meat except that given to dogs. Following years of behaving with exemplary devotion to God's command, Robert is released only after the hermit has another visit from the angel who orders Robert to cease his life as dumb fool. An angel also appeared to Robert in the midst of his life of penance to give God's command that he fight as a knight for the Romans "ayenst the Ethen dogges the Sarasyns" (p. 39). The life of the willing Christian is thus shown to be directed and controlled by God.

The extraordinary quality of Robert's experience is noted by the romancer, who comments about the acceptance of penance:

... goth to do his sharpe penaunce, whiche he helde but lyghte, remembrynge his grete abhomynable stynkynge synnes that he hath done all the dayes of his lyfe; this was a fayre myracle, for he that was so vycyous and so furyous a rebell, and proude a synner, is now so full of uertues and fayre condycyons and tame as a lambe. (p. 32)

Here, then, is yet another precise indication that Robert the Devil's conversion is a "miracle," and his joyous acceptance is both ample testimony of the value system and inspiration for the popular audience to seek virtue. The combination of elements is crucial for a success like that enjoyed by *Robert the Deuyll.* The supernatural can be accommodated because it is coupled with a full exposition of Robert's regeneration. Expiation is, then, provided to reassure and warn those who read Robert's (Gowther's) story.[19] The appeal of these qualities is also clear in the stories of other well-known penitents: St. Alexis, a fifth-century Roman who dies as a beggar under his parents' staircase before he was recognized, and Count Simon de Crépy, whose death was similar.[20] Such abnegation is always impressive, but its presentation in *Robert the Deuyll* is particularly compelling because of the dynamic account of the role assumed by the hero.

The life of the fool is one of the most startling and traditional metaphors for the man who is separated from worldly values. The fool is at once an occasion for hearty merriment and nervous awe from the conventional human beings whose lives reflect a commitment to worldly success. *Robert the Deuyll* exploits most fully this motif that is subordinated in *Sir Gowther*. Not only is the hero shown in friendship with dogs, but also deliberately eliciting laughter from the Emperor and his retainers by outrageous physical horseplay.[21] They observe great charity by feeding good meat to the 'dogs,' but they have no sense of Robert as a human being. The Emperor is not only incredulous but also angry at an argument for the fool's true worth when his daughter, who is also dumb, identifies him as the protector of the Romans. Only she has seen the angel bring him horse and harness, but she is judged to lack wisdom, and her own physical defect elicits impatience from an efficient world. Indeed she does not have the wisdom of the world, but a much greater insight beyond its confines. Further, she accepts a futility in trying to convey her vision of the angel to those whose temporal values are so deeply rooted that they cannot recognize an alternative, yet her own love for Robert increases steadily (p. 44). Robert as fool elicits condescending generosity; he cannot even be imagined as a force for positive good, a knightly champion against Saracen enemies and the wicked, traitorous seneschal.

Robert's seven years of penance as a fool are an eloquent testimony of his own resolution, and the romancer stops his narrative for an injunction against man's pride and great praise of the penitent's rejection of the worldly. He notes the contrast in Robert's fortunes, from the high estate of a nobleman to the position of dog; "how wyllyngly he hathe all forsaken for the saluacyon of his soule" (p. 35). Specifically he is identified as the savior of the Christians through the grace of God (pp. 38, 40). Not surprisingly Robert shuns fame, the hallmark of knightly achievement in the world and the basis for ill fortune in figures like Alexander.[22] In marked contrast, the wicked seneschal eagerly practices deceit for fame and power. Robert not only hides his identity, but indeed flees from the praise and thanks of the Romans, who accidentally wound him in their enthusiasm. Again he conceals injury, thus continuing his self-abasement. The role of the fool provides him with a means of living in and yet apart from the world; his valorous deeds, like those of Guy of Warwick, are performed in God's service, not in vainglorious seeking of fame or with a wish for thanks. Like Edgar in *King Lear,* he creatively uses his role as fool both to gain self-awareness and to help others as well as to perform his penance.[23]

The integrity of Robert is thus assured. The narrative is again dramatic in its argument, for when the end of Robert's penance is neared, other miracles take place. The daughter of the Emperor is able to speak and reveal Robert's true nature. Convinced by the miracle of the dumb being made to speak, the Emperor wishes to lavish praise. Once again Robert shows his sense of value, for he refuses to speak until the hermit tells him that God's angel has declared his penance complete. No longer will he be called "Devil" but "Servant of God," and a full Christian life lies before him:

"for it is Goddes wyll and commaundement, for he hath forgyuen you all your synnes, for by caus ye haue made satysfacyon and full done your penaunce." (p. 50)

The world's judgment, as Robert's mother later expresses it (p. 53), would regard the penance as hard, but the person most suffering remains as joyous as he was at the outset. His first words are:

"I gyue laude and thankes to God creature of Heuen and erthe, that it hath pleased the to forgyue me myne abhomynable and grete synnes thrughe so lytell and lyght penanunce that I haue done." (p. 51)

The sense of the rightness of man's devotion to God, his contrition for his sins and cheerful repentance and his confidence in God's infinite mercy, is the essential basis of Christianity.

Since the focus of *Robert the Deuyll* is upon the theme of penance, the narrative concludes quickly with a brief and optimistic forecast of his family's fortunes that balances the opening section on his parentage. Unlike the Duke and Duchess of Normandy, Robert and the Emperor's daughter soon after their marriage have a son who is to become a follower of Charlemagne to continue to strengthen the Christian faith. The English versions conclude with the marriage, not the further penances and solitudes of the original French *Robert le Diable* and the versions in the *Croniques de Normandie* and German prose redaction. This suggests that enthusiasm for marriage that is so clear in Caxton's *Paris and Vienne.* Concern for the continuity of the family, as well as personal delight, is indicated along with the final reiteration of the main argument to live a devout and virtuous life. The popularity of such romances lies in their encouraging optimistic view of man's redemption and strong moral argument for sturdy self-discipline. These high purposes are realized in the exciting account of an extraordinary creature: a monster who perpetrates shocking and distressing evils but who becomes a noble and attractive champion of right. The effects are melodramatic but their significance is clear. Few men are willed to the devil by their mothers, but effectively many men are 'fiends' in their corruption of their basic human dignity. The frequency and validity of their experience produced many romances that tell of men who lack the genetics of humanity.

Partenay

The relations between a mortal and an otherworld creature have provided continuous fascination in literatures as diverse as the classical Cupid and Psyche myth and modern science fiction.[24] Quite often stress is upon the sentimental and exotic details, as in the very popular *Partonope of Blois,* one of the late composites of courtly elements, magic, tournaments, and frustrated love. The characteristic English heightening of moral tone is evident here; for example, in the author's insistence upon the purity of woman and philosophical reflections, but the narrative focus is upon the single love relationship and the many complications involved in its achievement. *Chevalere Assigne* provides other appeal; it is sharply focussed to make the religious point of God's providence while exploiting sensational elements, but it is brief and the children are not individualized.

A more comprehensive treatment of the complications of children of otherworldly marriages and a subtler handling of moral issues combine in a romance that traces an entire family with a stress upon bizarre and grotesque possibilities. The medieval French narratives about Lusignan appear in both prose and verse Middle English translations, *Melusine*[25] and *Partenay,*[26] and continued to have currency in modern German versions.[27] The story has attracted extensive studies of origins and analogues, especially relations with folk tales, but not much critical attention. It contains an extraordinary range of incidents and exotic details, as well as an explicitly avowed concern with Christian meaning, that gives a firm moral argument. This latter lends a particular distinction to *Partenay,* which will be the basis for discussion here since it has some literary excellences—brevity and clearer structure—as well as thematic interest. Translated ca. 1500 into rime royal, *Partenay* illustrates late metrical romance, and the author's choice of La Coudrette's version, which reduces and clarifies Jean d'Arras, reflects a concern for accessibility to a popular audience.

The poet's opening declaration of his inadequacy to the task of telling the story is, of course, a commonplace, but he investigates the implications of the aspiring poet rather more thoroughly than is typical in such formulae, and the prologue contains notable additions (77 lines) to the original which immediately establish a point of view that is sustained in the original version. Thus he notes that pagan classical figures invoke gods who are not of value and indeed only figments of the imagination.

> Suche fayned goddys noght is to cal on,
>   Thing Agayne our feith And but fantisie;
> No help ne socour to cal thaim vppon;
>   I lay theim Apart And fully denye,
> Requiring that lord whych is Almightye
>   That of hys highnesse he be my trew gide,
>   The weyes of trouth me vn-to prouide;
>
> That in thys mater my penne conueid be
>   As plesaunce may be vn-to the highnesse
> Off our sacred lord, sitting in trinite;
>   Now be he myn ayde in thys besinesse;
> To hym only I trust in thys forth progresse,
>   That throgh his mercy he me send such grace,
>   For frensh tyll english that it may purchase. (57-70)

This Christian reliance upon God's assistance and direction is coupled with a favorable reference to Aristotle, who in the *Metaphysics* declares that the human intellect naturally wants to learn and to know. The romance, then, is introduced with the popular idea of instruction, and the poet, unlike Renaissance humanists, expresses respect for the learning that is to be derived from stories of Lancelot and Arthur. Histories of good knights and men bring benefit to all. Thus the story of Lusignan is a family chronicle—not unlike the earlier Anglo-Norman romances—undertaken with a deliberate reliance upon God,[28] Who is carefully thanked for its completion (6406-33). Indeed there is an elaborate litany of thanksgiving to the Trinity, Virgin Mary, and many saints (6434-6545) before the concluding apology for inadequacy in the translation. This extensive formal devotion is coupled with development of a basic Christian theme.

Not surprisingly *Partenay* in its narrative details shows a strong belief in the essential Christian view of temporal existence as a time when man must gain self-knowledge and through repentance approach the felicity of eternity. The stories of three generations make this clear, and the shifting time sequences of the poem not only add excitement by gradually unfolding the plot, but also emphasize the Christian belief. The prose *Melusine,* which follows a chronological arrangement, lacks such underscoring of the meaning.

Partenay is one of the few Middle English romances which contain mentions of Fortune, but as in *Le Morte Arthur* this idea is crucial. In the opening episode when Raymond accidentally kills his uncle Amery, there are several references. The poet specifically notes "fortune fals glotenous cruelte" (116), and Amery observes the strangeness in Fortune's sometimes allowing man to prosper from an evil deed (196 ff.). Raymond's lament[29] repeats this idea but asserts that Christ's mercy can triumph over Fortune (269 ff.). Later in his first startled reaction to the discovery of Melusine's serpentine quality, he complains against Fortune (3459-3500). Again Christianity is seen as the stronger force when Raymond prayerfully concludes,

> "God me ward and kepe fro werk diabolike,
> And stedfaste me hold in feith catholike!" (3499-3500)

Yet he must admit when he has lost Melusine,

> "But the Fals fortune, by cruel enuy,
> Me hath brought to thys full sharpe & hard port," (3986-87)

There is, then, a precise opposition between a pagan and a Christian force that Raymond recognizes, and his story is of a gradual gaining of wisdom that is expressed by his acceptance of his own failings and his surrender of self to God's will.

Raymond's furious anger when he learns that his son Geoffrey with Great Tooth has slain his brother Fromont and destroyed the abbey at Maillezais, results in a primitive wish for revenge (3441-44). This finds immediate expression in Raymond's rejecting Melusine as "Serpent"

(3548) and thus losing all the good that she has brought to him. Such a deliberate renouncing of good is not, Melusine indicates, simply pardonable: "Hit please ne wold the king celestiall" (3795). Raymond must undergo a thorough repentance. First, he admits totally his own guilt (3911-20, 3970 ff.), not only in his falsity to his lady but also in his slaying of his uncle and in his giving way to envy when tempted against his wife. This sense of responsibility is followed by Raymond's forswearing the world to make a pilgrimage to Rome to confess to the Pope.

> "Iesu crist, my soull warde and kepe to the,
> Fro thys worle me will put by good auice,
> Neuer seke no-thyng to conquere franchise." (4959-61)

Like Gowther and Robert, Raymond readily accepts the penance, and he becomes a hermit:

> And that thens wold go in-to som desert,
> So in wild exile all hys lif . . . (5131-32)

Thus

> The worle all forsoke at that houred stound,
> And full deuoutly liued ther Raymound
> TIll ende approched, to mortall deth went. (5179-81)

In a final comment on Raymond's death the poet observes the universal and inevitable nature of the experience;

> . . . when to ende nyhed he,
> That the soule moste yelde being spirituall,
> (As well lordes gret as tho being small),
> RAymounde to our lorde his soule ther yilding, (5290-93)

Raymond's life thus reflects a developing Christian awareness. He regrets his accidental murder of his uncle Amery, but he takes advantage of the happiness offered by Melusine. Even this largesse, however, is inadequate to man's inordinate demands for earthly bliss. Thus man must suffer a serious loss so that he recognizes how limited his world view has been and can focus his being in dedication to spiritual values. The actual pilgrimage to Rome is symbolic of his temporal existence, and the life of the hermit indicates man's essential apartness. Melusine, who is not of this world, is his mentor in the gaining of this Christian realization.

Although Melusine is an otherworldly creature who recalls details about mermaids, lamias, and Celtic banshees, her most striking quality is her preference for Christian values. At her first meeting with Raymond she predicts his good fortune, but she is more concerned to establish her relationship to God (435-36), after Whom she is Raymond's best friend (456). Indeed she declares her orthodoxy—"Euery Article beleue I and hold / Of the holy feith catholike named" (463-64)—and even summarizes some key points of doctrine. At their marriage, Melusine is described not as human, "But more better semed a thyng angell-lyke" (938), which contrasts with Raymond's later rejection of her as "diabolike" (3499). Such Othello-like extremes in the husband's evaluation of his wife are striking. Her bounty includes the building of churches (1677-87), and formal prayer is part of their lives (1670-73, 2696-2716). Further, Melusine recognizes sympathetically human repentance and behaves compassionately even when Raymond has broken his troth (2906 ff.). Similarly, she foresees the good that will come from Geoffrey's ultimate repentance and counsels mercy.

> "Yut may he his pees Full wel do to make
> Towardes our lord by grete repentance,
> And for his trespas pennaunce may he take,
> Therfor suffer pain in bodyly substaunce.
> For goddis marce is redy ech instance,
> So in hym he haue good contrecion,
> And efter veray pure confession.
>
> Off verray trouth my beleue is soo
> That our lord god on hym will haue mercy,
> For of the synner wold not deth shold go,
> But louith better that lif shold truly,
> To haue time And space, being here wordly,
> To effecte And end that he shold repent
> And to All goodnesse also to Assent." (3522-35)

Repentance, then, is the key idea. Man need only do penance and want God's mercy to receive eternal happiness. Geoffrey's failure, like his father's initial fault, is viewed as a possible starting point for greater good in the rebuilding of a better abbey with worthier monks (3669 ff.).

Melusine's own life is a working out of this experience. When Raymond has betrayed her, she explains her condition of trial. Full humanity would have been hers had her husband kept the covenant; she could have lived out a successful temporal existence and been united with

God after her death instead of having to suffer pain until Judgment.

> "yf truly ye had the couenaunt hold,
> Vnto Mortall deth me to haue ye shold,
>
> Ryght As A woman born here naturall,
> A feminine thyng, woman at al houres,
> To end of my days here terrestriall. " (3618-22)

Raymond's failure stems from two basic misunderstandings: he wants perfection in the way humans behave, and he cannot accept what is beyond obvious reason—like Melusine's nonhuman quality, though she is clearly a source of good in the world. Christian charity is most eloquently expressed when Melusine asks pardon for Raymond's offense against her, thus repaying injury with solicitude.

> "your misdedis god perdon euerydell,
> Whereof Agayne me ye haue so mysdo,
> For by you shall suffer torment And woo,
> vnto the dredfull day of Iugement; -
> And by the I was fro sorow ex[e]mpte,
>
> And into yoy entred!—Alas! wo I Am,
> For now Am I caste into dolorous woo,
> Fro-whens that I issewed and came!" (3755-62)

Here Melusine is a model for Raymond, showing that man must accept without recriminations the penance which is imposed. Her solicitude is expressed again through mother's love for her son Thierry as well as concern for her husband (4019 ff.).

Thus we have another narrative line which conveys the essential hopefulness of Christianity, its acceptance of man's incompetence, and even evil, with a happy confidence in God's unfailing mercy and generosity. The author of *Partenay* repeats again the basic concept which underlies Raymond's initial response to his first failing; man must not despair and commit suicide, but instead surrender himself to God (298-310). This belief in repentance as the means of man's salvation is perhaps most dramatically articulated in the life of Geoffrey, which in several ways parallels that of his parents Melusine and Partenay, but also argues a more startling realization of Christianity.

Geoffrey, like many heroes of romance, expresses the tension between ideals of knighthood and religion.[30] He is a great warrior, whose early conquest of the Saracen giant Guedon, establishes his reputation.

When Raymond sends a messenger to acknowledge this good news, he also explains that Fromont has become a monk at the abbey of Maillezais. Militant expression of Christianity in the fighting of paynims is a worthy activity, but a religious life in Christianity is viewed by Geoffrey with violent hatred. Indeed the poet tells us that he loses his wits, turns vermilion with rage, roams and sweats like a swine and terrifies all who are near him (3210-17). Geoffrey argues that Fromont must have been enchanted by the vile monks, so that he delays his expedition into Northumberland and resolves to burn the abbey.

In a direct confrontation with the Lord Abbot, Geoffrey with Great Tooth demands:

> "Ha! dan Abbot," toke hym to say an hy,
> "Abbot, forwhy haue ye made folyly
> My brother A monke in thys said Abbay
> To leue chiualry, takyng your ordre Ay?" (3259-62)

The valorous knight's angry indignation is not dispelled by the Abbot's assurance that Fromont has acted of his own free will, or by Fromont's confirmation of this with the added insistence that only a life of prayer will please him

> "To other dedes atteende wil no day,
> But only to god, to whom I am yild." (3283-84)

Thus "Almost in wode rage" Geoffrey quickly closes up the Abbey and sets it and its one hundred inhabitants afire. This wanton destruction, clearly seen as an act of madness, is the occasion for the dissolution of Raymond and Melusine's marriage, since the aggressive child's act frightens and angers the father so that he doubts and investigates his otherworldly wife and thus betrays their goodness. The poet's sense of the dramatic in the burning episode is suggested by his repetition of it (3291 ff., 3403 ff.).

Geoffrey himself almost immediately realizes his sin (3316) and laments, "Alas, caitife!" saide, "don haste folily, / Which thys minstre undo and so brend" (3318-19). His life, like those of Sir Gowther and Robert the Devil, becomes largely one of repentance as he tries to achieve self-knowledge. Initially he berates himself by calling himself worse than Judas and despairing of ever seeing God in eternity, yet wishing for death. However, Geoffrey with Great Tooth is a man much committed to this world; thus when he returns to Guerrande, he immediately sets out for Northumberland to resume his life as a warrior who destroys giants. Grimold, who is Guedon's cousin, is specifically described not only as a proud giant, but also as "a Fend, / A dredful deuill full of cruelte" (4075-76). After an extended exchange of taunts and blows, Grimold is sorely wounded and forswears his pagan gods:

> hys goddys corsed, hys goddys gan renay,
> Enlesse thei wold gif hym Aid or socour,
> Both Margot, polin, Bernagant that houre,
>
> MAhounde, Iupiter, And als other mo;
> hym-selfen bement sorily expresse. (4310-13)

Realizing that he is doomed, the giant flees into a cave, where Geoffrey follows to discover great riches and the tomb of Helmas so that he learns the story of his ancestry. The descent into the mountain's cave is reminiscent of various classical and Celtic underworld visits, but when Geoffrey releases the prisoners (after slaying the giant) a Harrowing of Hell is clearly suggested. The people rejoice and offer praise and thanks to the champion "that thaim deliuerd of this cursed goste" (4809).

Even so impressive a triumph is not long to be indulged, and Geoffrey hastens back to his parents. As father and son talk, Geoffrey reaffirms his guilt (4849 ff.), and also realizes that his mother was the daughter of Helmas. His grief again provokes violence, for he ruthlessly pursues the traitorous uncle who prompted Raymond's betrayal and who in fright accidentally falls and is killed. Once again Geoffrey is forced to recognize his sinfulness and responsibility. His success against Saracen giants has not taught him to control himself and to surrender to God. The lamenting penitent is advised by his father to rebuild the abbey (4971-5000, 5279-87); this is accomplished so that all marvel:

> "Gaffrey is become A monke for all hys lore,
> Neuer trowed man for to se that houre
> A wolfe to become An herdly pastour!" (5115-17)

From violent antagonist and destroyer of the religious community, Geoffrey has become its benefactor, so that he himself is described as a keeper of the flock.

The final stage in Geoffrey's redemption is his pilgrimage to Rome (5209 ff.). Like Raymond, he confesses and is absolved by the Pope with further recommendations for the endowment of the Abbey. Just before his death, Geoffrey is living congenially at Lusignan but is ready to set out to fight another monster when there is need. Thus he remains an active knight in the temporal world but with religious devotion. A fatal illness prevents further knightly accomplishments, and the poet laments that Geoffrey with Great Tooth did not live long enough to capture the Holy Land (6061 ff.). The warrior Christian dies after proper confession and mass: his will appropriately provides for both spiritual and lay matters (6093-98), and he is buried at Maillezais Abbey which he rebuilt after destroying it. There is, then, a continuity to this man's life; he is unfailingly committed to the temporal realm (he cannot like Fromont become a monk or like Raymond become a contemplative hermit), but he grows in grace as he gains tolerance and indeed zeal for the kind of religious life which he himself cannot live.

Thus this son of Raymond and Melusine represents an intermediary stage in religious development, one that is particularly human in its appeal. He arouses his own antipathy, which comes from excessive belief in knightly prowess, and even impresses others; but he does not achieve the inspirational effects of a Lancelot or Guy. The other sons' lives also reflect the interest of the poet of *Partenay* in Christian attitudes. Anthony and Raymond fight Saracens in Bohemia, and their deeds are told in some detail, but there is no complexity in the motives for their actions. Very brief references indicate that Uriens wars against Saracens in Cyprus, and the heirs of Guy in Armenia fight the same dreaded enemy. Thierry maintains a more discreet stability at Partenay. Horrible, the recognized evil son, was, of course, killed at his mother's suggestion (3828 ff.) by suffocation in a cave; naturally he is given noble burial. These sons merit only cursory references, but their inclusion gives comprehensiveness. The family chronicle thus reflects an explicit concern with man's behavior. The poet of *Partenay* dramatically and successfully focuses his attention upon Raymond, Melusine, and their son Geoffrey with the Great Tooth to argue that man's temporal existence is continually disappointing within itself but may be lived creatively through penance so that an eteranl life with God will follow.

This thematic interest is given prominence not only by the greater artistry with which the episodes are handled, but also by the structuring of the poem. Other main parts of the Lusignan story—King Helmas and his betrayal of his promise to his wife Presine (4383 ff.), their daughter

Melior at Sparrow-hawk Castle (5370 ff.), and Palestine's guarding of her father's treasure at Arragon (5704 ff.)—are both brief and subordinate. The Helmas material gives dimension to Geoffrey's story, and the others appear only at the end of the romance to place Melusine in her family context. The crucial place of emphasis at the end of the narrative is divided between praise of the family and meditations upon death and the litany of prayers for "the perdurabilnesse / Off ioy aboue" (6537-38), "the ryght path" (6541), and "the way of sauacion" (6542). The relation between the temporal and the eternal seems, then, to have been the universal theme that gives *Partenay* its real distinction; very appealing are the romance's exploitation of vigorous action and bizarre incident within this ordered frame. A family chronicle is especially adaptable for showing the inevitability of death and arguing that each individual must not only contribute to the continuity of the line but also think of his own salvation. The traditional love of an otherworldly, fairy creature is effectively transformed by Christian belief. Even the magic of a fairy is inferior to the promise of God, and Melusine is mentor to the house of Lusignan so that worldly pursuits are subordinated to spiritual ones. Not all can profit equally from this instruction, for each man lives the Christian experience in his own way: some as knights fight Saracens, others become monks and hermits, another combines the two ways of martial action and prayer, some seem little touched, and yet another is too evil to risk in the world. The poem is thus essentially a very hopeful one in praise of human realization through action and penance, but it is not without skepticism. The physical defects, such as Geoffrey's long tooth, symbolize the blemished quality of man, but each son (except significantly named Horrible) is capable of transcending such limitations as are readers inspired by their story.

There is an impressive variety of deformed or monstrous creatures in these popular Middle English romances. They provide authors and audience with endless opportunities for melodrama, a quality that persists in later fiction. The blinded, maimed Rochester at the end of *Jane Eyre* tells us many things about Charlotte Bronte, not least of which is the continuing need for humans to be reconciled to monstrous appearances and their own limitations. His descendants, for example, Max in Daphne du Maurier's *Rebecca,* are legion. Thrillers often use physical deformity to signal evil. More complex are the uses of monstrosity in William

Faulkner (e.g., Popeye in *Sanctuary*) and in Sherwood Anderson's most brilliant piece *Winesburg, Ohio*. But perhaps the most striking comparison is with the fiction of Flannery O'Connor in which the grotesque is the essential ingredient, and again the framework is relentlessly Christian.

Finally, it is useful to remember that the successful assimilation of the supernatural is a characteristic Shakespearean concern, particularly in the later plays. Just as Edgar imitates the fool's role of Gowther and Robert, so Caliban might well be a son of Partenay and Melusine. The extreme of bestiality in *The Tempest*, Caliban is, if not totally assimilated, at least as carefully controlled on the island as the fiends in a tympanum or well-ordered romance world. Thus even the mature Shakespeare has recourse to the themes and structure of the medieval romance in order to convey the vision of the latest phase of his career. No better illustration of the compatibility of popular art forms with serious moral concerns can be imagined, and in this Shakespeare is true to the tradition of popular Middle English romance. Closely allied to the exploitation of monstrous appearance is that of monstrous actions.

CHAPTER IV

FRIENDSHIP AND BROTHERHOOD

The attractions of the world in medieval romance very frequently
center in fame, as the previous chapters have shown; the king or hero
strives for an excellence and dominance on the field of battle and in
territorial control. Alexander and the Arthur for whom he serves as
prototype care initially for Fortune rather than the soul's salvation.
Practicers of militant Christianity, like Geoffrey with Great Tooth, seem
to give respectability to their campaigns against the Saracens, but in
the process they often do violence to many essential values. Those who
are 'fiendish' in origins, like Gowther and Robert, achieve initial
notoriety for their evil deeds. Certainly there are some splendid examples
of personal relationships in these romances, for example, Arthur's
affection for Gawain or the brotherly concerns of Partenay's sons.
However, another type of popular romance is built more directly upon
individual personal relationships between men, and to these we now
turn our attention.

The values of friendship have been extolled in a variety of cultures,
particularly in classical romances and in Renaissance comparisons
between love and friendship. These ideas also interested many medieval
authors[1] and provided a focus in some of the romances which enjoyed
widespread circulation. The popular theme of sworn brotherhood finds
expression in many different literatures, and often its treatment reveals
much about moral values. Two closely related Middle English romances,
Athelston and *Amis and Amiloun,* use this thematic material[2] and offer
a sharp contrast in their authors' skill in the combination of the popular
Christian view with a more primitive concept of individual loyalty.

Essentially there is a conflict between two worthy claims, adherence to God and to a specific friendship or loyalty. *Athelston* has survived in only one manuscript, and there is no trace of earlier versions. It is the briefer and simpler narrative, being English in origin. Thus it is more direct and serves as a neat introduction to several crucial ideas.

More popular is the story told in the Middle English *Amis and Amiloun,* which survives in four manuscripts, including the Auchinleck. It is, of course, part of a widespread tradition of Latin and French versions with details that have been offered as evidence for its acceptance of the classical virtue of friendship, and others that suggest a hagiographic reading. *Amis and Amiloun* argues movingly for the force and beauty of friendship between men, as well as other intense personal relationships. But its dominant theme asserts the subordinate value of all these to man's love of God, so that even the most satisfying temporal affections are shown to be subsidiary to the eternal, and the miraculous is used to make this vividly clear. This pious tale with its chivalric setting combines a variety of popular elements, so that it is not surprising that it was so often told and perhaps influenced the fourteenth-century author of *Athelston.*

These two Middle English romances, dating from the end of the thirteenth and the second half of the fourteenth century, show effects of sworn brotherhood between four messengers who meet by chance and between two friends who share much in their lives. The sustained popularity of such thematic material is clear from the later success of *Valentine and Orson,* which Henry Watson translated ca. 1502 and which was printed by de Worde and Copland. Here the heroes are twin sons, of noble parentage but through many complications separated and reared by a king and bear, respectively. Angelic visions prompt their reunion, and by magic they learn the identity of their parents. Then follows a series of extraordinary adventures against giants, Saracens, a dragon, false charges of treason, patricide through error, and subsequent penance. This late prose romance, for which the French original has not been found, is one of several narratives that tried to combine as many traditional materials as possible to secure a popular audience. But exotic adventures and some interest in characterization are only part of its appeal. What is most attractive is a high sense of moral purpose that is basic to secure popularity with the English reader, and the brotherly relationship of the heroes holds all together. Watson's extensive use of dialogue that is lively and idiomatic, vivid descriptions, and swift narration attracted not only the popular audience who bought the many printings, but also some of the greatest literary figures— Sidney, Shakespeare, Bunyan, Sterne, Hazlitt, Dickens—who either echo or allude to the romance, as well as the aristocratic audience who saw a pageant on its theme at the coronation of Edward VI in 1542.

The vogue of these romances is in large part due to their treatment of friendship and brotherhood, which provide particularly effective subject matter that characteristically involves testing, a conflict in human associations. Rather than unknown giants or paynims, or grotesqueries in appearance, the strange circumstances in human behavior become the romance's specific focus. But the characteristic element of fantasy is not minimized, for in order to test and clarify the proper nature of friendship and brotherhood the romancers have recourse to the exotic. As in the romances that center on fiendish origins, the terrifying, the miraculous, the melodramatic are freely introduced and made safe. In place of a devilish birth or influence, the patterns of human behavior are shown to involve strange circumstances—being in bed with a friend's wife, attacking an unrecognized brother on the battlefield, the natural man as an outcast of society, murdering one's children deliberately, or one's parent accidentally—which are bizarre and worrying at first glance. Examined in the context of an ordered universe, however, these circumstances, like the gargoyles on cathedrals or the strange creatures who are entwined in floral illuminations, do have their place. This combination of exploitation of weird situations with the careful control of such vagaries results in the perennially popular synthesis: indulgence of the outlandish but reassurance that it is not ultimately destructive.

Athelston

Often *Athelston* is either praised or dispraised according to its critic's delight in the tail-rhyme tradition and shorter romance.[3] In general, it is one of the more highly regarded of these narratives, and certainly there are many memorable particularities—English geography, a lament for a horse's death,[4] swift narration, pungent dialogue. From the point of view of this study, *Athelston* is interesting because of its handling of popular religious ideas. The romancer recognized that there was an opposition in the claims of sworn brotherhood, which characterized both classical and earlier Germanic and French stories of great loyalty between individual men, and the more comprehensive charity of Christianity which extends brotherhood to include many human beings and also a final relationship to God for which the Church is supposed to mediate.

Although there is interest in the conventional motif of a falsely accused queen that we saw in *Emaré*,[5] the basic action is the treasonous betrayal of Earl Wymound which corrupts even King Athelston. Such falsity, however, is not only resisted but vigorously opposed by Alryke, a bishop of the Church, who is also one of the four sworn brethren. The bare outline of the argument is thus a clear victory for the Church over the State, and scholars have long been interested to suggest historical identifications, such as Becket and Henry II, Stephen Langdon and King John, Bishop William Bateman, or more convincingly a composite figure to represent the significance of the Church.[6] There can be no doubt, then, of the religious, homiletic nature of the romance, but *Athelston* lacks the poised grasp of essential Christianity which we find, for example, in *Amis and Amiloun*. As has often been noted, there is little subtlety or discrimination in the presentation of the Church's victory. It comes not through a careful and fully understood Christian ethic, but from an aggressive, militant play of power by the bishop who commands more than the king. Like Turpin in the *Sege of Melayne,* which is another possible source for this romance,[7] Alryke is a startling figure whose efficiency in 'doing God's will' is not debatable, but those methods, like those employed in many other more aggressively 'religious' romances, are hardly in keeping with the fundamental Christianity which he professes to champion. Thus there is a dogmatic rather than an empirical demonstration of Christian value, a not unpopular mode in the Middle Ages, but one less subtle than that of many romances.

Athelston is completely permeated by religious details and allusions. There are numerous references to churches, crosses, Christ, evensong, blessings, the power of God, and the efficacy of prayer; and there is the central confrontation between church and state. The meeting of Alryke and Athelston is perhaps the most vivid illustration. Somewhat belatedly, after an instantaneous seeking of revenge for supposed treason, the King, accompanied by many knowledgeable priests and clerks, goes to church to pray for divine guidance about the fate of his prisoners. When he lifts his eyes, he sees the archbishop in the choir and is immediately ordered not to shed the blood of the innocent. The dramatic dialogue quickly establishes the toughness of these sworn brothers who immediately indulge in violent threats. Little indication of motivation or reasoning is made; Athelston simply surrenders to the power of the Church. Although he himself originally appointed Alryke to the see of Canterbury, the Archbishop's threat to stop the workings of Christianity (masses, baptisms, confessions) is too severe to risk and the people's loyalty goes first to the Church.

Apparently Alryke is motivated by a stern wish for justice, and a ruthless determination that the Church will triumph in temporal affairs. The knight who voices the decision in favor of ecclesiastical authority is very explicit:

> þe kny3t sayde: "Bysschop, turne agayn;
> Off þy body we are ful fayn;
> þy broþir 3it schole we borwe.
> And, but he graunte vs oure bone,
> Hys presoun schal be broken soone,
> Hymselff to mekyl sorwe.
> We schole drawe doun boþe halle and boures;
> Boþe hys castelles and hys toures,
> þey schole lygge lowe and holewe.
> þou3 he be kyng and were þe corown,
> We scholen hym sette in a deep dunioun:
> Oure crystyndom we wole folewe." (519-30)

Thus religious authority triumphs over civil power, but Alryke's pursuit of justice is as relentless as Athelston's. He carefully tries the accused in the repeated ordeal scenes, which build suspense and exploit ideas of justice. Finding Egeland and his family innocent, Alryke immediately demands the name of the traitor. Again there is a conflict between sworn brotherhood and the Church, and again the Church triumphs. But Alryke's immediate violation of the secrecy of confession is yet another failure in his professed Christianity.

In effect, Bishop Alryke succeeds in saving the innocent and punishing the guilty, but there is no sense of mercy or humility in his actions, which are as ruthless as those of the King. It is arguable that this portrayal of inadequacies in the establishment reflects popular reactions, like those that culminated in the uprisings of 1381. Alryke's compassion is suggested by his shedding of tears (367-68) upon initially hearing of the imprisonment, but there are no hints of such feeling in the later narrative. The repetition of the ordeals for Egeland's wife and children makes this abundantly clear by reiterating that human beings are continually tried and judged for their actions with a relentlessness more characteristic of the Old Testament than the New when Christ's mercy mitigates. Indeed the most striking expression of compassion is that of Athelston's queen, who pleads tearfully with her husband when he first imprisons Earl Egeland and his family. The effect of her action is to induce violence in the King who kicks his pregnant wife and kills the heir, thus effectively punishing himself even as he sins (273-96).

The constant judicial attitude of the author of *Athelston* is indicated by his balancing this act with the birth of St. Edmund, who is immediately named heir. Egeland's pregnant wife prays to Christ and then merrily goes through the ordeal untouched. Immediately she has labor pains, and

> Sche knelyd down vpon þe ground,
> And þere was born seynt Edemound:
> I blessyd be þat foode! (648-50)

This event provides both an artistic balance and a religious hope for the future, so that there is a wholeness of argument, however inadequately it is prepared for and developed.

Similarly, the conclusion of the poem leaves no doubt that its author's intention is more moral than political.[8] The explanation for the cause of the events of the narrative action is simple and to the point. Just before he is executed, Wymound is asked why he lied, and he confesses.

> "Certayn, I can non oþer red,
> Now I wot I am but ded;
> I telle ȝow noþyng gladde -
> Certayn, þer was non oþer wyte:
> He louyd hym to mekyl and me to lyte;
> þerfore enuye I hadde." (795-800)

The final emphasis, then, is not so much upon treason or falsehood as upon envy, one of the more insidious of the seven deadly sins, as popular religious tracts constantly argued, and famous knights like Kay, Modred, Ganelon, and countless stewards make clear in other romances. Envy is also the cause, as we shall see, of many actions in *Valentine and Orson*. In the context of "weddyn breþeryn for euermare, / In trewely dede hem bynde" (23-24), "falsnesse" (8), avowed subject of

Athelston, is perhaps the most blatant failure. The romancer, however, as we have seen, concerns himself principally with the idea of the power and righteousness of the Church which mercilessly exacts justice. Thus the focus of the poem is upon a vivid and cruel world. Only the conventional opening lines indicate an awareness of something more:

> Lord, þat is off my₃tys most,
> Fadyr and sone and holy gost,
> Bryng vs out off synne.
> And lene vs grace so for to wyrke,
> To loue boþe God and holy kyrke,
> þat we may heuene wynne. (1-6)

Even the conclusion of the poem does not resume this basic thematic material, which is crucial in so many of the most distinguished Middle English romances, ensuring their popularity by offering a hopeful prospect free of the harshness of immediate reality.

Athelston is, then, an interesting elementary study of a very popular idea. It vividly demonstrates the great limitations and liabilities of the primitive concept of sworn brotherhood and also the inadequacy of a militant church which is motivated by a devotion to justice above mercy. Rooted almost entirely in the sense of this world's action (only the hint of the future in the birth of St. Edmund is enlarging), *Athelston* lacks the complexity and subtlety which we will see in *Amis and Amiloun,* where there is a full exploration of the theme of brotherhood as both good and evil and the larger sense of man's relationship to God in eternity. Here we see merely a negative exposition, for the avowed friendship has no long-lasting impact upon action. The worth of *Athelston* lies in its clarity and directness of presentation of the key issues, and its defect stems from a lack of detailed and convincing thematic exposition which satisfies both intellectually and aesthetically because of more comprehensive resolution of the problems.

Amis and Amiloun

Unlike many of the romances which recount diverse adventures and still retain epic qualities from the *chanson de geste, Amis and Amiloun* is a brief and precisely focused narrative which reveals its author's literary skill and clarity of purpose. The Middle English version is not explicitly associated with Charlemagne, and many of its exact details and certainly its pervasive tone and values reflect the sensibility of a later age. There are fewer characters and incidents, and these are much more fully presented, reflecting an awareness which is both exact and discriminating.

Critical evaluations of *Amis and Amiloun* tend to be somewhat negative, though not always for the same reasons. John Edwin Wells classifies it as a "Legendary Romance of Didactic Intent," one of four narratives "written evidently largely for teaching. All depend upon supernatural intervention in behalf of a pious hero."[9] The poem has attracted several critical reassessments in the last dozen years, and all maintain the ambivalent attitude that is clear in Wells's judgment that the medieval writer's sympathy "lead to loss of moral distinctions."[10] Like *Athelston, Amis and Amiloun* is both praised and blamed for the stylistic quality of its tail-rhyme stanzas. And the introduction of the miraculous is both censured for being melodramatic and celebrated as the essence of wish-fulfillment, that escape from the binding realities of the world which is crucial to romance.[11]

When esteemed, *Amis and Amiloun* has generally been praised for its secular values. Although Laura Hibbard (Loomis) includes it among "Romances of Trial and Faith," she rejects Bédier's theory that the pietistic theme, "Omnem filium quem Deus recepit, corripit, flagellat et castigat," was emphasized in developing the legend.[12] She summarizes: "The most graciously romantic quality in the story comes from its emphasis on friendship as an ideal human relationship, and it is for this quality that the tale is remembered longest as a 'chançoun d'amur, de leauté, et de grant couçur.' "[13]

This reading is most fully presented by MacEdward Leach in a long study of the sources of the romance when he argues against its being an expression of Christian values: "The theme, in general, in the Anglo-Norman version and in the English is the testing of friendship, not an exposition of Christian character or Christian virtue."[14] Although the medieval Christian environment is recognized, he argues that the Middle English poem is essentially non-Christian and non-hagiographic, that it is basically an exposition of friendship, a bond that is stronger than all others.[15] There is a troublesome contradiction here, so that another reading seems in order. This is particularly indicated by Hornstein's continuing the stress on the ideal of friendship as the central theme of the poem that "blurs moral distinctions" and the continued critical arguments in favor of this reading by Kratins and Hume.[16]

In refuting the Christian significance of *Amis and Amiloun,* Leach reveals a sense of Christian value which misses, I think, its essential nature. He writes, for example: "Furthermore (to consider the story in its larger aspects), what has Amiloun done that God should so honour him by marking him out for special chastisement? He has converted no heathen; he has not even killed any. He has made no pilgrimage or crusade. He has given no money to the Church. On the other hand, he has killed a man unjustly, tricked an ordeal, and falsified the holy sacrament of marriage. And he is no different after being healed of the leprosy."[17] The argument here is crucial. As the parable of the vineyard makes clear, and this is the core of the argument about equal rewards learned by the dreamer in *Pearl,* man is foolish indeed to think that the quality of his performance warrants God's attention and generosity. However well man behaves, he still falls far short of perfection, even excellence, so that quibbles about what he deserves from God are ridiculous. The essential point in Christianity is that God *gives* to man; grace is not something merited or earned, but a gift of God. Thus it is the most hopeful of religions, for it truly recognizes and accepts fully the quality of human nature. Man repeatedly makes mistakes, but this is not catastrophic for God's forgiveness is always available. This understanding is vital, for it allows man to survive meaningfully. He need not succumb to the despair which his own inadequacy and failings impel him toward, and he is less likely to exalt his own achievements in the arrogant blindness of pride. Always sustained by a knowledge of God's infinite charity, he can live meaningfully and prudently in this world with assured confidence in the next.

This view of Christianity reflects medieval philosophy uncorrupted by the excesses of classical and modern stress on man's importance, his receiving a life that is defined only by his own efforts and merits. The acceptance of man's limitation under God's control vastly expands human possibilities; ideals that can never be realized absolutely are enjoined because they inspire human performance in its striving for perfection, whether earthly or mystical. The appeal of such a view lies in its simultaneous acceptance of failure and confidence in another opportunity. Such a philosophy embraces the most bizarre and extreme vagaries of human performance because they are contained in an ordered structure. The marvelous is comfortably accommodated, for although human performance is not insignificant, it remains only part of the whole.

Recognition of these essential Christian values leads to understanding of *Amis and Amiloun,*[18] for it is the underlying principle of the thematic material which gives real distinction to the romance's thought and aesthetic. Friendship is certainly a primary concern of the author; however, as will be suggested, it is only one of several vital issues.[19] Although much esteemed in classical thought and literature, friendship is not uniquely non-Christian. As is characteristic in intellectual growth, one system of thought evolves from and develops those which precede it. Similarities between classical friendship and Christian charity are thus notable, but there are also differences.[20] For while the story of *Amis and Amiloun* describes the strong personal attachment of two particular knights, it also is a comment on man's relation to his fellow man within the structure of a God-governed universe. Of great significance in the romance are the thorough expositions of the relationships between husbands and wives, between parents and children/heirs, and between authority and members of the community. These fill a large portion of the narrative; they contribute to the author's purpose of expressing true Christian values, and they provide ample opportunity for the exploitation of his literary finesse and contribute to the story's popularity.

Seen only as an exposition of the theme of friendship, *Amis and Amiloun* is a restricted piece of work in its conception, and because of its mass of apprarently irrelevant detail it becomes a rather incompetent piece in its execution. Seen as an expression of the theme of Christian charity and the vital necessity for humbly choosing this value, the romance is a harmonious whole which richly explores the complexities of human relationships. The concern is not with a single relationship, but with the multiple and often fiercely contradictory involvements of the human being: man with friend, husband with wife, parent with child, lord with servant, man with good and evil, and above all man with God.

An abundance of brief references, such as "god me spede" and "for godes loue," the simple devout oaths and thanksgivings, might be regarded as automatic turns of phrase which give respectability or authenticity to *Amis and Amiloun.* But in addition to these commonplaces there are also carefully developed details and vivid expositions of the significance of God in the lives of the people of the romance world. Some versions of the story, clearly and obviously emphasizing the hagiographic elements, have more references to God, but they are throughout less subtle and discreet than in our romance version. The toughness of the poet's intellect, his freedom from mere lip service, a 'monkish hand,' is clear in the anticlerical qualities of Belisaunt's speech when she taunts Amis for his refusal of her generously offered charms:

> "Sir kni3t, þou hast no croun;
> For god þat bou3t þe dere,
> Wheþer artow prest oþer persoun,
> Oþer þou art monk oþer canoun,
> þat prechest me þus here?
> þou no schust haue ben no kni3t,
> To gon among maidens bri3t,
> þou schust haue ben a frere!
> He þat lerd þe þus to preche,
> þe deuel of helle ichim biteche,
> Mi broþer þei he were! (614-24)

This vibrant young woman[21] is boldly explicit in her indignation. She zestfully makes clear her view of the limitations of clerical types and significantly notes the irrelevance and inappropriateness of their attitudes in certain contexts. Obvious didactic preaching is, then, eschewed. The effect of this passage is to forestall impressions of slavish thinking and writing by suggesting the author's careful awareness.

The opening line, "For goddes loue in trinyte," is the conventional poetic formula to gain the audience's attention; then a quick summary of Amis and Amiloun's ancestry follows. The first main scene takes place when they are twelve years old and the duke of the country holds a feast, "Al for Ihesu Cristes sake / þat is oure sauyoure" (68-69). This is an occasion of great generosity, climaxed by the duke's request that the children be left in his care. The parents agree to this service: "þai 3aue her childer her blisceing / & bisou3t Ihesu, heuen king, / He schuld scheld hem fro care" (127-29). A Christian context, thus established very early in the narrative, is sustained throughout, and at several climactic moments becomes the focus of attention, so that the most consistent feature of *Amis and Amiloun* is such expressions of popular concerns.

There are, for example, supernatural voices. Amiloun is warned when he poses as Amis to undergo the trial by combat: "Com a voice fram heuen adoun, / þat noman herd bot he" (1250-51). Twice the voice identifies itself as sent from Christ (1253, 1261), and Amiloun is warned that if he carries out his deception he will become a leper and lose his worldly position. Not only does Amiloun choose to abide by his sworn friendship, he also proclaims his indifference to the dire consequences of his action: "Lete god don alle his wille" (1284).[22] Here the narrative is explicitly Christian in contrast to the earlier passage which describes Amiloun's dream of a bear attacking Amis (1009-27). Significantly the voice speaks directly; the dialogue gives an immediacy and dramatic quality which are lacking in the first sequence. This artistic distinction indicates a scheme of values; the individual choice and the consequences of Amiloun's actions are much more important than his awareness of his friend's danger.

The appearance of an angel in dreams to both Amis and Amiloun is yet another demonstration of supernatural power, as well as structural balance. Immediate repetition enhances the potency of the message that Amiloun may be cured by being washed in the blood of Amis' children. Again the writer's use of specific Christian matter is clear from the injunction that this deed must be accomplished on Christmas morning (2203 ff., 2325 ff.), an addition of the Middle English author. The associations of generosity and the Slaughter of the Innocents are implicit in this season. A further analogy is suggested between the sacrifice of the children to save a man and the sacrifice of Jesus to save all mankind (2251 ff., 2287 ff.). And the parent's sacrifice of a child repeats the situation of Abraham and Isaac, so popular in medieval visual arts and eloquently expressed in the Brome play and cycles. Thus the theme of the poem is extended beyond the essential idea of friendship or even the conflict of interests which beset the man who is both father and friend. This is made explicit by Amis' words when he finally makes his decision:

> "Mi broþer was so kinde & gode,
> Wiþ grimly wounde he schad his blod
> For mi loue opon a day;
> Whi schuld y þan mi childer spare,
> To bring mi broþer out of care?
> O, certes," he seyd, "nay!
> To help mi broþer now at þis nede,
> God graunt me þer-to wele to spede,
> & Mari, þat best may!" (2296-2304)

The imagery recalls the Crucifixion and serves to enlarge the thematic matter. Certainly Amis sacrifices for his brother (Amiloun), but in doing so he is following a specific injunction from heaven. This devout context is further indicated by his many prayers after the deed (2357 ff.); it is significant that we are instantly told that Christ hears this request and answers his prayer. Thus the scene in which Amis tells his wife what he has done contains no suspense about the fate of the children; we know they are to be restored. What interests us is the reaction of Belisaunt, whose love for her husband and faith in God are put to the ultimate test, since in our version she has no surety of their safety. Significantly she echoes her husband's sentiments precisely: "God may sende ous childer mo" (2393). Thus she, like the two men, shows a substantial evolution of character. The domineering and demanding young thing of the wooing scene, who has been compared to Potiphar's wife, has been replaced by an understanding wife who puts her trust in God. If the dutiful wife seems to exist at the cost of the loving mother, we must remember the analogy of Emaré and Chaucer's Griselda or Constance. We are dealing with characters who, though they suggest a certain realism on one level, are essentially idealistic, not wholly consistent persons, but also vehicles for suggesting a system of value, with specific virtues like obedience.

After the dreams Amiloun had said simply: "Broþer, ich abide her godes wille, / For y may do na mare" (2231-32). This is true Christian wisdom, and it is the value acquired in the course of the story. Each of the four principals had tended to regard himself as the controller of his destiny; indeed the manipulation of the trial by combat is not simply presumptuous but a kind of blasphemy. There is no lack of understanding of the issues involved. Amis is fully cognizant of his lies (904 ff.), and he asks Christ's help. Even Belisaunt's reassurances do not dispel his knowledge of his false position:

> "Ich haue þat wrong & he þe riȝt,
> þerfore icham aferd to fiȝt,
> Al so god me spede,
> For y mot swere, wiþ-outen faile,
> Al so god me spede in bataile,
> His speche is falshede,
> & ȝif y swere, icham forsworn,
> þan liif & soule icham forlorn;
> Certes, y can no rede!" (940-48)

And to Amiloun he says:

"& forsworn man schal neuer spede;
Certes, þer-fore y can no rede,
'Alas' may be mi song!" (1102-3)

Our sympathies are thus elicited. Amis has an attractive honesty about himself, which had been earlier shown in his humble and modest refusals of Belisaunt. Further, he has certainly been the victim of the envy and treachery of the false steward, the archetypal viilain of the romance world, as the poet repeatedly stresses. Amis is, then, an appealing character. Trapped by dreadful circumstances, he tries to save himself, but he does not pretend to be righteous. Somewhat weak, this less than ideal man is the more credible. His fault in loving Belisaunt is a sexual failing (and not a result of his own initiative), clearly less heinous than failures in fundamental charity or honesty. An apt comparison is the thematic material of Shakespeare's *Measure for Measure*. The romance even offers a kind of exoneration of this detail, for Amis carefully places his sword between himself and Amiloun's wife when he (as Amiloun) goes to bed, and indeed he offers a gracious explanation for his abstinence. Thus melodrama is used creatively, not simply indulged. In short, he is hardly a promiscuous man, though he has feeling. Of the two friends Amis is, therefore, the more humanly fallible and less assuming, though not passive. Thus his extraordinary expressions of charity at the end of the romance are predictable and convincing. A man who recognizes and admits his weaknesses is less likely to be pretentious and makes an appealing hero.

One carefull detail makes exquisitely clear the character of Amis, and it is illustrative of the author's literary finesse, since it is not to be found in the Anglo-Norman source. When the friends parted, Amiloun had two exactly matched golden cups made and gave one to Amis. The cups are the means of recognition when Amiloun later appears as a begging leper. What is notable is that Amis does not know the identity of the leper. As a worthy lord he offers wine to the foul leper and his handsome attendant page, and he sends his gift in the precious cup of friendship. Amis, then, does not regard the cup as a private or personal possession. It is not reserved to a single friendship with Amiloun (who has fought for him in trial by combat); it is a means of conveying charity to less fortunate fellow men.

Further, Amis has been much moved by the knight's tale of the generous young man who charitably attends his suffering companion and rejects offers of a rich and easy temporality. The narrative is very explicit here in presenting alternate systems of value, for the author of the romance describes exactly how Amoraunt, Amiloun's faithful nephew Owaines here symbolically named, responds to the suggestion that he think of his own convenience and well-being:

> & he answerd wiþ mild mode
> & swore bi him þat dyed on rode
> Whiles he miȝt walk & wake,
> For to winne al þis warldes gode,
> His hende lord, þat bi him stode,
> Schuld he neuer forsake.
>
> þe gode man wende he hadde ben rage,
> Or he hadde ben a fole-sage
> þat hadde his witt forlorn. (1939-47)

Or as the knight so cryptically concludes his account to Amis: "He nold neuer gon him fro: / þer-fore ich hold him wode" (1991-92). Such summary judgment is most frequently that of the world; the knight is an ordinary man whose concerns and values are basic, so that he does not easily perceive the truth of loving (Amoraunt). Amis, however, possesses understanding and sympathy. Although he gives lip service to the worldly judment (1982-93), he instantly behaves generously. He does not try to single out the young man whose truth and integrity he recognizes and respects. The cup is, then, sent to the leper and his page, and in the name of Saint Martin, who divided his cloak with a beggar and had a vision of Christ making known to His angels this act of charity to Himself. By such actions Amis offers his followers a worthy but unpretentious example. The author of the romance adds depth to the characterization of Amis by the reaction of the squire who has seen Amiloun's matching cup.

> "Certes, sir," he gan to sain,
> "Mani gode dede þou hast lorn,
> & so þou hast lorn þis dede now;
> He is a richer man þan þou,
> Bi þe time þat god was born." (2036-40)

A man of Amis' temperament is, then, regarded as a bit of a fool by the uncharitable world in which he lives and is taken advantage of, but this does not deter him from following his good instincts, even though he preserves outward formalities of ducal pomp to mitigate the obvious discrepancy.

Amis' basic charity does not exclude a precious love for his friend Amiloun. He is, therefore, furious and violently seeks revenge when he thinks that his friend has been killed. His attack on the leper is one of the most vividly described fights in the romance. Here Amoraunt intervenes, graciously and gently stopping the attack, revealing to a stunned Amis the leper's true identity and reminding him of his indebtedness. The well-meaning Amis is desolated by his momentary misunderstanding; he upbraids himself for his failure to recognize Amiloun and is grieved to see him so ill. Amis has, however, neither repulsion from nor anxiety about the leprosy; he lovingly embraces his friend, who is clearly not to be defined by his physical appearance. His only concern is to ask forgiveness:

> "O broþer," he seyd, "par charite,
> þis rewely dede forȝif þou me,
> þat ichaue smiten þe so!" (2143-45)

The concepts of brotherhood and charity are here fused in the first speech which the two exchange after preliminary lamentation and swooning. Clearly the thematic matter of the romance is again seen as both personal and general, and the bizarre circumstance of embracing a leper is fully exploited.

Belisaunt's charity lacks the universal strength of Amis', so that her initial reaction to her husband's bringing a leper into their hall is to think him mad. But she is deeply grieved when she knows Amiloun's identity, and she does not hesitate to embrace the identified friend and indeed personally to administer to his bodily needs, treating him as an honored guest. This care continues unabated for a full year, when "A ful fair grace fel hem þo" (2195). There is thus a full year for the exercise of their charity, so that Belisaunt's immediate acceptance of the slaying of the children is given adequate preparation. Her active exercise of love is carried out with characteristic dynamic energy. Amis' conflict of interests is exploited, not his wife's; her more personal and tardy attainment of love is complete. And all can rejoice in the miracles of Amiloun's cleansing and the restoration of the children.

The wife of Amiloun enjoys no such understanding and happiness. Her character is deliberately contrasted to that of Belisaunt, for her failings and indeed wickedness increase as the story develops. Initially

she mutely accepts Amiloun's attitudes and actions, but only in prosperity is she loyal and true. Once Amiloun's fortunes falter, her love
and gradually even a minimal charity disappear. Even before the first
signs of leprosy, she upbraids her husband for having undergone his
friend's trial by combat: "Wiþ wrong & michel vnri3t / þou slou3 þer a
gentil kni3t; / Ywis it was iuel ydo!" (1492-94). Such severity in judgment is startling, especially since even casual bystanders desire Amis'
victory (1300 ff.). Triumphantly she hails Amiloun's leprosy:

> "þou wreche chaitif,
> Wiþ wrong þe steward les his liif,
> & þat is on þe sene;
> þer-fore, bi Seyn Denis of Fraunce,
> þe is bitid þis hard chaunce,
> Daþet who þe bimene!" (1564-69)

Here we have an archetypal shrew (a familiar figure in fabliaux, drama,
and visual arts), a female who relishes her husband's misfortune because
it enables her to tell him he is bad and to intensify his suffering. Her
singular lack of charity—and to the person for whom she should have
most compassion—is diametrically opposed to the generous love of
others in *Amis and Amiloun.* Her treatment grows steadily more abusive:
she forces Amiloun from their chamber and the high table in hall, and
then she forbids him the castle. Quietly Amiloun accepts his penance
and agrees to obscurity: "of no more ichil þe praye, / Bot of a meles mete
ich day, / For seynt charite" (1606-8). Of his worldly goods, he takes
only his gold cup, and the narrative tells us: "to god of heuen he made
his mon / & þonked him of al his sond" (1619-20). Here the author
explicitly indicates the penitent quality of Amiloun's development, and
this is sharply contrasted not only to his earlier behavior but also to his
wife's present attitude. As he grows in Christian humility, she grows in
pride. A similar contrast to the evil wife's lack of charity is provided by
Amoraunt's unselfish generosity and loyalty. This technique is carried
still further after Amiloun and Amoraunt are banished, for even
strangers in the market town give them food and drink until the famine,
an all too familiar experience in medieval Europe, comes and none
aid them.

> "Wo was hem o liue;
> & his leuedi, for soþe to say,
> Woned þer in þat cuntray

Nouȝt þennes miles fiue,
& liued in ioie boþe niȝt & day,
Whiles he in sorwe & care lay,
Wel iuel mot sche þriue!" (1746-53)

The author of the romance has thus deliberately given us in Amiloun's wife a person of evil character, though she is less obviously defined than the evil steward of the opening sequence. She refuses charity, both in thought and action, to all—and especially to her husband. Only with the promise of Amiloun's permanent absence does she relent; she gives to her husband "so michel of al his gode / As an asse to riden opon" (1771-72). Not surprisingly the narrative relates with exquisite irony how Amiloun, healed of his leprosy, returns to his country:

To speke with his wyf þat tyde;
And for she halp him so at nede,
Wel he þouȝt to guyte hur mede,
No lenger wold he abyde (2433-36).

And the irony is intensified, for the self-righteous wife is herself discovered in a fault; she is about to wed again. A battle ensues, and Amiloun reoccupies his rightful heritage. Significantly, he does not order his wife's death, but provides for her a life of penance. A little hut and a diet of bread and water, the traditional estate of those who seek spiritual renewal (and Amiloun's recent lot), are to be hers.[23] Lest there be any doubt about Amiloun's motives in so treating his wife, the narration cautions and reminds us: "Who þerof rouȝt, he was a queede, / As ȝe haue herd echoon" (2483-84).

Very carefully, then, the author of *Amis and Amiloun* makes clear his view of Christian values (chiefly charity and humility) that abound in popular preaching. It is important to note that Amiloun, not Amis, suffers a long period of penance. Throughout the early part of the narrative Amiloun is the dominant and confident friend. He warns Amis against the steward, he has the cups made, he offers to undertake the combat trial—and he willfully decides to preserve his troth whatever cares God may send as a consequence. There is also the curious detail of his having Amis go to bed with his wife; this, too, is perhaps an arrogant act, an assumption of godlike testing and judgment. At every point he regards himself as righteous, a virtuous man who keeps his word to his friend—even if this means daring God and briefly deceiving his wife as well as exposing her to serious moral danger. Amis, in contrast, was deeply apprehensive, cognizant and repentant of his faults, fully accepting that he could not win the combat if forsworn, yet not anxious to die (like Gawain in his encounter with the Green Knight) because of the steward's treachery.

Amiloun formally adheres to his ideal of knighthood; for example, he generously dismounts in the trial by combat (which he is, in a sense, falsifying by his impersonation), so that he will not have undue advantage over an unhorsed opponent. The literary skill of the romance is again shown in a precise and symbolic detail which describes the knight's resolution to conclude the combat quickly: "þan was sir Amiloun wroþ & wode, / Whan al his armour ran o blode, / þat ere was white so swan" (1357-58). The gleaming white knight must not have his armor besmirched. Finally the formulaic phrase "As prince proude in pride" (1381, 1458) is twice used to suggest Amiloun's manner of going: after the victory and when he returns home. This is echoed when his wife gives the requested ass; she "proude in pride / Schameliche gan to sain" (1793-94). Thus the connotation of the phrase is pejorative, and we re-examine surface values.[24]

As is not infrequent in the best medieval romances, here we find a firm suggestion of the limitations (and indeed destructive quality) of a conventional, surface, and formal adherence to a stringent and exacting code of knighthood with all its excessive demands for 'honor.' Amiloun is certainly not an unworthy figure. Many of his actions lead to virtuous and noble results, and Amiloun always means well. His fault lies in a failure to recognize that he may not be always right, that he is a fallible human being who inevitably will make mistakes and thus should eschew overweening confidence. Most importantly he must come to that crucial wisdom for which the Christian strives: to accept and await God's will, not always to try to force events to conform to the pattern one wishes for oneself.

Amis and Amiloun are, then, not simply identical friends; the romance is much more than an "exposition of the theme of friendship." They share certain characteristics; their time of birth and appearance, for example, are identical, and their early training and experience for knighthood are the same. In their essential natures, their distinctive personalities, however, they are certainly not alike. Thus the course of their lives is not the same, even though the ultimate end (Heaven) is not differentiated because it is eternal transcendence. Each man must follow his own way to salvation; however deep and abiding his friendship, he remains a human being apart. As they were both born at the same time, Amis and Amiloun die on the same day and are laid in one grave. The significant detail is in the romance's last lines:

> And for her trewþ and her godhede
> þe blisse of heuyn þey haue to mede,
> þat lasteþ euer moo. (2506-8)

The juxtaposition of "trewþ" and "godhede" is notable, for it makes clear the author's belief that *Amis and Amiloun* is both a story of friendship and of man's relation to God. The personal friendship presented in the romance is only part of the larger theme of charity, the fundamental and distinctive Christian value. Through precise development of many characters and scenes, which carefully contrast and develop the basic idea, the romance comprehensively reveals the author's understanding and conviction. We are pleased and fascinated by the literary skill in many scenes with pungent dialogue and effective narrative description, and we are moved by the confrontations of basic human feelings, but always we note the sustaining sense of value which gives shape to the whole of the romance and is the basis of its popularity. Within this more comprehensive scheme, the ideal of friendship, sworn brotherhood, is sustained as it could not be in *Athelston,* where conflicting interests led to repeated accusations and ordeals which, while resolving judicial issues, never realized a poise between the diverse individual claims placed on every man. Perhaps the combination of theological interest and individual conscience was what appealed to those who used *Amis and Amiloun* material for a dramatic disguising at the court of Henry VIII.[25] The most intense treatment of the idea of brotherhood comes when the heroes are not only sworn to mutual loyalty but in fact are twin brothers.

Valentine and Orson

The sustained enthusiasm for romances where brotherhood is a main theme is clear from the success of *Valentine and Orson,*[26] one of several late narratives that are "Composites of Courtly Romances."[27] Like *Generydes, Partonope of Blois*, and *Ipomedon,* it is frequently condemned with *Guy of Warwick* as a popular example of the genre.

The diversity of subject matter included in such long narratives makes simple classification difficult. Although *Valentine and Orson* includes folk motifs like the falsely accused and exiled queen and credulous king, and offers a rich compendium of tournaments and battles against giants and Saracens,[28] it is particularly distinguished by its presentation of twin brothers. The many adventures are unified through their constant adherence to "a chivalric ideal of character. Its heroes are bold, unselfish, constant in love, courteous, and devout; models of every knightly virtue."[29]

Stories of twin brothers, and the frequent corollary of Combat of Relations, are commonplaces in many literatures. A short list includes Romulus and Remus, Cain and Abel, Jacob and Esau, Sohrab and Rustem, the Eustace legend, and medieval romances such as *Octavian, Maugis d'Aigremont, Generydes,* and *Tristan de Nanteuil* that exploit the materials of Contrasted Brothers.[30] That this is a dominant idea is indicated by the 1649 printer's note of 'art and nature' in the two sons, but it is perhaps most clearly illustrated by Charles Dickens' reference in *Christmas Carol:* "And Valentine," said Scrooge, "and his wild brother, Orson; there they go!"[31] Here is a striking illustration of continuity in the material of popular fiction through the centuries. Specifically, the interest is in contrast between nature and civilization, and the ways in which parentage and nurture influence character and action. This thematic material is expressed not only in Valentine and Orson, but also in Pepin's illegitimate sons Haufray and Henry, who are envious of both Valentine's favor with his uncle and the future of the rightful heir Charles. Even the giant Ferragus is contrasted with a brother, the Green Knight, since their responses to Valentine, their sister Clerimond, and Christianity are diametrically opposed.

Complicated familial relationships, most often those involving loyalty and honor (usually of brothers, but also between sister and brother or parent and child) dominate much of the action, but the argument is most vivid in the characters of Valentine and Orson. Although their mother, Bellysaunt, is the sister of King Pepin of France and the wife of Emperor Alexander of Constantinople, the twins are not born in a royal situation. Like many hapless ladies in the romance world, Bellysaunt has not been able to escape male prejudices. Both her credulous husband and her sexually biased brother refused to believe her innocent of the false charges made by the Archbishop, whose "loue

clotheD,and this seuen yere thou shalt li vnder the stat
res of thy palays with out speche if god giue the life so
longe,and thou shalt neyther eate nor drinke but of ȳ
relefe of the table,and yf thou do this penaūce thy sin
nes are pardoned the,and not eles. Syr sayde Ualen
tyne all thys shall I do wyth good heart. Then ȳ pope
gaue hym absolucyon,and made hym dyne wyth him.
After diner he departed out of ȳ cite with out speking
vnto his seruaunte,

℣How valentyne in great doloz of his body perfour∘
med his penaunce foz the sleing of his father. Ca.Crii

Ualentine entred in to a wode after ȳ he hade
shozne his hear,and was there eatinge rotes
so longe that none coude knowe him,after he
wente towarde constantynoble,where as was made
much sozowe foz hym,foz whan Orson had red the let∘
tre that valentine gaue Clerimonde he wepte bitterli
Bzother

Valentine and Orson   Copland, 1565

A pilgrim setting forth.

This is a popular 'factotum' cut that could be used to illustrate
many stories; it also appears in Copland's *Four Sons of Aymon* and
Knight of the Swan.

dysordynate" (p. 14) led him first to seek a liaison and then, having been refused, to charge the lady with infidelity because of his own envy and fear. Bellysaunt is banished with only a faithful squire, Blandymayn, to escort her. He is off seeking a midwife so that "all alone without any company, saue God and the blessed virgyn mary, that did helpe her, and succoured her in such manner that she was deliuered of twoo fayre sonnes in the forest" (p. 33). Immediately one son is carried away by a bear and hence known as Orson. Then while the frantic mother crawls in pursuit and collapses, the second infant is discovered by Pepin, who adopts the foundling and rears him in Orleans with the name Valentine. Each grows up in a predictable manner according to his circumstances.

Just as God and the Virgin aid Bellysaunt in her distress caused by an evil religious, so Orson is protected; "God that neuer forgeteth his frendes shewed an euydent myracle" (p. 38). The bear's little cubs accept and play with the baby who is then nurtured by the bear and grows as a wild beast. He is fearless and master over animals and men who enter the forest, killing what he likes and eating raw flesh. Fifteen years old, he roams about naked and cannot speak. Valentine, in contrast, is nurtured by the squire whose name he bears, and then accepted (at the appropriate age of twelve) in Pepin's court, where he gains knightly prowess and attracts the love of the king's daughter Eglantine and the envy of Haufray and Henry. As the French proceed toward Rome, they pass through the forest where Pepin is attacked by the wild Orson, whose exploits are awesome to the French. Returned from a Roman victory, Valentine is urged by the envious Haufray to seek out the wild man; and the youthful knight, making a classic response, accepts the challenge because of his sense of unworthiness at being a foundling. Thus the twins are sharply differentiated in the opening scenes, and their fierce encounter begins a close association that lasts through the long romance.

Not knowing their identities, the brothers ardently want to kill each other, and each displays remarkable strength and stamina. The outcome is decided by God, to Whom Valentine prays as "mine only hope and trust, mine onely refuge and comforte" (p. 69). Significantly, victory comes when, in the midst of combat, Valentine offers his brother Christianity. This is, of course, the favorite episode chosen by English romancers for emphasis in the Charlemagne stories with heroes like Firumbras and Otuel.[32] Valentine argues eloquently:

Alas wylde man, wherfore doest thou not yelde the vnto me thou lyuest here in this woode lyke a beaste, and hathe no knowledge of God, nor of his blyssed mother saynt/ Mary, nor of his holy fayth, for the whiche thy soule is in great daunger. Come on thy way with me & then shalt thou do wysely. I shall make the be baptized, and shall teache the, the holy fayth. And shall geue the flesh and fysshe, bread and wyne ynough for to eate, and clothes and all maner of thinges that appertayneth vnto a mannes body, and shalt vse thy lyfe honestly as every naturall body should doo. (pp. 69-70)

Such an offer of charity, the possibility of becoming man and not beast, cannot be refused. Although Orson knows no words, he instantly understands the essence of the Christian argument that provides for both spiritual and physical well-being. Thus he signifies wholehearted acceptance by docile surrender and avowal of utter loyalty to his brother.

This popular religious argument is maintained throughout *Valentine and Orson,* which abounds in statements about the power of God, prayers for His help, practice of the sacraments of established religion, and which reaches its climax in the final episodes with their emphasis upon penance. So firm a moral statement is characteristic of much popular fiction, and the basis of this story's success. The romance provides an inexhaustible variety of thrills; but as this episode makes clear, there is never any doubt that good will triumph, and it is that kind of reassurance which attracts many readers.

In the first encounter of the twins we have both the fascination of bestial man and of unkown identity (obviously for the antagonists, but also in Valentine's search for knowledge of his parentage). What is most gratifying, however, is the resolution of conflict through clear moral superiority and the promise of a future that comes with the right choice. Valentine is a worthy young man, disadvantaged by circumstances and unfairly the victim of envy, yet nevertheless triumphant, not simply because of his considerable knightly expertise, but through his belief in Christianity. Orson is intriguing because through his beastliness shows a sensibility that promises chivalric nobility; this is to come, of course, with the training of the unsophisticated youth—a motif popular for heroes as diverse as Achilles, Beowulf, Perceval, David Copperfield, and the young men in Horatio Alger, Jr. Valentine is also a fledgling knight who must discover his identity, but predictably the lives of the twins show both similarities and differences.

Orson's early life as a wild man is gradually altered. There are delightfully funny episodes such as his first experience of drinking wine and wanting to give it to the horse because its flavor is so superior to that of water, or Pepin's amused laughter at Orson's eating and drinking habits, but there are also somber scenes in which frightened people like the cook try to hurt primitive Orson. Significantly, Orson's untutored strength does not cause deaths and destruction as in earlier versions. Thus Pepin's first response shows the direction of the action: "And how wel that he is roughe, yf he were clothed as we be, he wold seme / a right fayre knyght" (pp. 73-74). Valentine simply instructs Orson in the decorum of the palace, so that never again does he instigate evil. He does exploit his fearsome manner, for example, in besting Grygar, who has treasonously captured his beloved Valentine when, in envy Haufray and Henry again sought the death of Pepin's favorite. Further, Orson inspires the love of Fezonne, "by the pleasure of God & of the virgin Mary" (p. 103), "for god had put hym on the earth for to be her husband" (p. 106). However, their wedding has to be delayed until he can speak and his brother's lady is also won. In the fight against the paynim Green Knight, Orson's primitive strength is crucial, since only a king's son not suckled by a woman can triumph. But this is muted by Valentine's knightly arguing for mercy that results in the Green Knight's conversion to Christianity. Through the Green Knight the brothers discover their parentage, for he sends them to his sister Clerimond, who lets them speak to the brass head (p. 140). Not only does Orson learn his identity, an acknowledgment of the brotherly bond which already exists with Valentine, but also he gains new skill. Once Valentine, following instructions of the brass head, has cut and taken away the thread under Orson's tongue, "he began for to speke veray ryght and pleasauntly, and that same houre recounted vnto them all his lyfe that he hadde ledde in the forest" (p. 144). This is a final mark of transformation from the wild man to the chivalric knight, and the narrative interest shifts to his brother.

The youthful Valentine's life is marked by his urgent need to know his parentage, a desideratum in the chivalric world. Indeed the envy of Haufray and Henry is engendered by his being a foundling, and they use this to argue an abuse of their sister and thus precipitate Valentine's fighting the wild man. Even while he is tutoring Orson, Valentine is constantly seeking knowledge of his parentage. Thus he denies Pepin's urgings to return to court after the death of Grygar:

Syr sayde valentyne, for goddes sake pardon me, for I shall neuer retourne vnto the tyme that I knowe what I am, and of what place extraught. (p. 95)

In the early episodes success comes to the brothers through a combination of Orson's extraordinary primitive strength with Valentine's recognition of his own physical limitations and trust in God's strength. Almost immediately after the brothers' parentage is revealed, the narrative development is largely through magic, specifically the pagan dwarf Pacolet and his marvelous wooden horse which, with the simple turning of a pin in its head, goes "throughe the ayre more faster than ony byrde coude flee" (p. 142).

Here is the crux of the critical problem in *Valentine and Orson.* Dickson has noted that "there is but one serious flaw in the story, and that is the large part played in the latter half of it by Pacolet's magic and trickery, by which Valentine and his friends profit without sharing the odium. The translator recognized the flaw, and did his best to minimize Valentine's dependence upon magic."[33] Specifically, Henry Watson softens or omits unpleasant features, such as gratuitous speeches of delight about executing pagans and references to magic.[34] This reflects the usual attitude of an English translator to his material, for it is a sure way of heightening the moral tone. Since the Pacolet material is a late addition and magic was a particular focus for the attacks of Renaissance humanists,[35] it provides opportunity for insight into the popularity of romance. The persistence of "Pacolet's horse" as a proverbial equivalent for extraordinary speed and the use of the figures as late as the nineteenth century in puppet shows in Liège, give evidence of continental delight in the material that parallels the many English versions. Similarly Dickson makes a good case for Cervantes' derivation of both a brazen head and a flying wooden horse.[36]

There seems little doubt that these magical elements caused no problem for medieval readers and later ones who delight in the popular elements of romance. The reason is simple; although Valentine profits from magic, it is handled by pagans and ultimately denounced by the Christian hero. Dickson writes of Pacolet in *Valentin et Orson:* "Since he remains a pagan, there is nothing improper in his use of magic and treachery to further Valentine's interests; while the proprieties are saved by the fact that Valentine, though he condones and profits by Pacolet's doings, takes no active part in them, and after Pacolet's death expresses remorse and does penance for this and other sins. The situation is a degenerate development from the beneficent magic of Maugis and Auberon, and, as far as regards the use of magic, it is paralleled in other late romances."[37] Instead of "degenerate" we might simply describe the magic as "different" perhaps as we contrast the two towers of Chartres. Valentine's various encounters with, captures by, and escapes from pagans are certainly less personally distinctive than the combats in which Orson figures. However, the delight of magic charms and flight persists, and its frequency makes the kind of elaborate interlacing that Vinaver so eloquently describes, but that is less accessible to modern readers.[38] There is a pleasure in observing the complexity of episodes and the exotic details of the East, especially the unique account of the shrine of St. Thomas,[39] but there is also an emerging sense that Valentine is not really gaining an identity through the episodes as a worthy knight should.

Watson's translation makes this clear in many ways. In one episode Pacolet, after casting a spell over the hundred guards posted by Lucar, appears as Mahoun to the King of Inde (p. 263). Then he enchants Brandyffer and brings him into the King of Inde's power. Pacolet laughs at Lucar's punishment of the sentries who are drawn at horses' tails and hanged. Watson does not have Valentine laugh, but instead he immediately urges the necessity of releasing his father whom Brandyffer holds in prison. The effect is to indicate that Pacolet's magic, though incidentally helpful and amusing, can be a distraction from what is more important. A reminder of still higher value comes in the next chapter (p. 264) which describes Pepin's thrice repeated vision of the three nails and spear that pierced Christ's body and of a priest saying mass at the Holy Sepulchre. Pepin understands instantly and goes on a pilgrimage to Jerusalem. And he goes incognito as a pilgrim, which is distinctly different from Charlemagne's pilgrimage.[40] This existential approach is what Valentine has yet to embrace; as long as he uses Pacolet's sophisticated magic, he is never relying on his human resources.

Even the death of Pacolet does not force Valentine's self-knowledge, for he takes the dwarf's tablets and continues to use the flying wooden horse. The demands of militant Christianity produce endless battles against pagans, all in Jesus' name, and with betrayals and ruses exonerated. Thus, disguised as a paynim, the Emperor attacks Valentine, who bears Saracen armor; and the much sought father is murdered by his son. Recognition comes from Orson, and the scene is one of the finest dramatic moments in Middle English romance (pp. 308-30).[41] Just as Valentine won Orson the wild man, so Orson comforts his grief-crazed brother with perfect Christian consolation: avoid despair, know that God is powerful enough to pardon even a greater sin than this, comfort will come in penance, and death must be accepted by all.

Such encounters in battle are a commonplace in romance, but the outcome is distinctive in *Valentine and Orson*.[42] The fatal slaying is the catalyst for Valentine's discovery of his essential nature. Previous episodes in his life have dealt with establishing Orson's and his own identity in the world, and Valentine constantly relied upon pagan magic. The brazen oracular head which first told his identity is, of course, the kind of object that appears frequently in classical and medieval literature and in stories about Grosseteste and Roger Bacon at Oxford and others at Orleans.[43] *Valentine and Orson* shows the influence of its use in saints legends because Clerimond is converted, but this is the source of brotherly animosity between the Green Knight and Ferragus, so that there are echoes of diabolic effects. Pacolet's magic had flourished without Valentine's questioning its appropriateness. The shock of murdering his father finally jolts the young man, and thus he renounces such deceptive arts:

Frend sayd valentyne all weping, neuer please it God that I plaie more with suche arte, for it is dampnable. And he that tought it me dyed vnhappely at the laste, and I beleue that for this sinne I haue slain my father. (pp. 310-11)

Admittance of human failing is fundamental, and Valentine's story now enters a final stage with the accomplishment of his penance and gaining salvation, the real achievement of identity.

After so heinous a sin as patricide Valentine's penance must be treated fully to allow readers opportunity to be convinced and to learn a moral lesson. The final portion of *Valentine and Orson* includes the material that we saw essentially in *Sir Gowther* and more fully developed in the very popular *Robert the Devil*, which is undoubtedly a main source.[44] Admittedly the concluding phase of Valentine's life occupies only a small portion of this long composite courtly romance, but it is in the crucial terminal position and thus provides a judgment on all that has transpired. Negative criticism of popular fiction frequently faults the genre for having the indulgence of immoral actions neatly offset by a quick pious conclusion. Such arguments stem from uncertainty about the possibility of conversion; and medieval literature, of course, continually refutes them. The evidence is strong in the popular Corpus Christi plays, or the moralities, as well as the exhortations of homilies and explanations of catechisms. Thus it is not surprising to find the same attitude in the romances. The more obviously exemplary works are neatly categorized, but the critical debate about the conclusion of Chaucer's universally esteemed *Troilus and Criseyde* gives ample testimony of the difficulty with more complex narratives. Sophisticated psychological analyses demand slowly evolving attitudes, but this obscures the clarity of medieval views of good and evil. Valentine has murdered his father, so that his only possible conclusion is that there is something dreadfully wrong about his way of life. As his brother Orson argues, the Christian does not give way to Despair—the sin against the Holy Spirit, made vivid in sculptures like those of Autun or Vezelay —he amends his life by forswearing the knightly endeavors and magical assistance that have been the core of his life. Merely to repent and ask mercy is sufficient theologically, but artistically and practically (since man, although he repents, has a tendency to sin again) the romancer convinces by a full exposition of Valentine's penance, which most closely resembles that of Robert the Devil but is also like that of Guy or Lancelot.

The ultimate aloneness of man before God is thus made clear as it is in visual and dramatic representations of the Last Judgment. Valentine must give up his knightly ways of life and become the penitent who appears a fool to the world. He first goes to Rome and is shriven by the Pope, who

behelde hys gre[a]t repentaunce, & had pyte on hym saynge. My childe discomforte you not, for god is puyssaunt ynoughe for to pardon a more greter thynge. (p. 313)

This exact repetition of the words of Orson when Valentine's murder was recognized (p. 309) provides the fundamental consolation that is so appealing to a popular reader. With the reassuring good news of salvation and the Pope's absolution, Valentine enters his period of penance. He first goes into a wood, after cutting his hair, and lives on roots. This is an interesting variation of Orson's life as a hairy wild man. The brothers share isolation from the world, but there is no ferocity in Valentine's life. Merely to withdraw is, however, not adequate penance, and Valentine returns to Constantinople, the world in which he tried for so long to identify himself. So altered is his appearance that he is not recognized and thus beaten by servants. However, Orson orders the poor mute man left alone, a charity given because of his brother Valentine. Here is the extension of brotherhood to all men, even the unknown poor, and the necessity for the corporal works of mercy is fulfilled. Orson tells the insensitive that they must "suffre and endure of hym" (p. 314), for he recognizes the possibility of the wretched appearance cloaking a man vowed to God, since he has the experience of his own transformation from wild man. Valentine is mocked for his refusal of the best alms that are given him; and, echoing the Crucifixion, he prays, "Veray God pardon all theym that mocke me, for they know not the miserable faut wherbi it behoueth me to liue thus" (p. 315). Here is the classic discrepancy in attitudes between the penitent and those still wholeheartedly committed to the world.

The sympathetic relationship between brothers is consistent throughout the romance; when Valentine left for his penance, "Great sorow made the lady [his wife], and mor greater Orson" (p. 314). But Orson's understanding of the necessity for Valentine's penance is particularly striking. Orson, natural man, began his life as a wild beast and then was converted to a Christian life; Valentine, civilized man, was an active participant in the militant Christianity which characterizes the world of the Charlemagne romances. Thus his seven years of penance, when he is a mute beggar largely thought a fool by the world which had exalted him as a knight, are necessary to offset the effects of a way of life which involves him in serving various Saracens and culminates in his murdering his father. Valentine's adoption of *de contemptu mundi* is not absolute, for he intervenes to prevent Clerimond's being forced to wed again. He asks God's help; and before he has finished his prayer, an angel appears to instruct him in how to serve her without revealing his own identity. To explain that Valentine still lives, he assumes another role; he wears a pilgrim's habit, a reinforcement of the idea of the "pilgrimage of life." Having thus given needed human aid, Valentine continues alone and dies in the best circumstances. His prayer is one which reasserts belief in Redemption:

Veray redemptour of all the worlde consyder not my folyshe youthe the which I haue passed folyshly in pleasures mondaynes, and condampne me not but by thy holy mercy receyue my poore soule into thy blessed handes, and defende me from the deuyll. (p. 324)

Just as an angel had first directed Valentine to discover his parentage at Ferragus' castle and then directed him to help Clerimond, so at the end of his life an angel appears to tell him he will die within four days. Thus he is able to write a letter of explanation to those left in the world and to receive the sacraments before he dies.

Valentine, then, keeps his penance faithfully. Only after his death does anyone know of it. The letter serves to lead others to follow his example, for Clerimond recognizes her failure to perform the corporal works of mercy:

"Alas I haue sene you often in pouertye, colde, and trauayle wythout geuying you any comforte."
(p. 326)

She becomes a nun and then abbess of an abbey founded in honor of St. Valentine, for miracles have happened immediately at his grave. Thus the romance, like *Guy of Warwick,* continues its popular argument for high moral purpose. Valentine, a distinguished knight, has recognized, because of the disaster brought on by his use of magic and deception, that worldly attachments are not what is most important. His wife learns this through his example, as did followers of Lancelot in the stanzaic *Le Morte Arthur,* and the audience for which the romance was written should reach the same conclusion.

The theme has a final reiteration in the character of Orson. While Valentine flew from one adventure to another, from one Saracen force to another, Orson's knightly pursuits were less spectacular. He does take his mother Bellysaunt to Constantinople for reunion with her husband, and he is the victim of envy from Henry and Haufray as Valentine was. The latter involves a plot to kill Pepin and lay the blame on Orson, and the vivid detail of the knife left in the bed by a frightened Garnier (pp. 207-10) probably was used by Shakespeare in the scene of Duncan's murder in *Macbeth.* [45] The evil brothers do succeed in betraying Pepin, whom Orson has accompanied to Jerusalem, so that they are imprisoned until Valentine releases them. Thus Orson remains with his father in Garnyson's strong castle and subsequently becomes involved with the Saracen maiden Galazye, This is the romance's one exception to the heroes' constancy in love, though there are numerous opportunities, especially when Valentine finds himself the object of the passionate Saracen queen Rozemonde. Dickson regards Orson's disloyalty to Fezonne as an illustration of the author's "temptation to include one more story," [46] but it is included for several other reasons. The episode is not exploited; there is a conventional description of her physical beauty (p. 371), and she instantly accuses Haufray of treason against his father Pepin and the twelve peers and puts him in prison. The relationship of Galazye and Orson is as tersely presented as possible. One line in the midst of accounts of prison and wars notes: "That night Orson lays with Galazye, and engendred a sonne that was called Morant the whiche helde the realme of Angorye" (p. 323). Two additional lines (p. 314) explain that Fezonne (conveniently) died of anger when she learned of this event and that within the year Orson wed Galayze. The only dialogue between the two lovers is Orson's acknowledgment that he is the father of the child Galazye is carrying and offer to provide for them. The lady asks instead to go to Constantinople and "put me in to som relgion for to serve God for you and me" (p. 311.) This hardly rates as sizzling, decadent passion. The sexual fault does serve to recall Orson's function as natural man, to iterate that even his full embracing of Christianity does not preclude the possibility of sin (significantly the most human and commonplace), and to reassure the popular audience that such failings can be sorted out. Finally, there is the very practical necessity of having an heir.

When Valentine becomes a penitent, the ruling of the empire of Greece is wholly Orson's responsibility, and he discharges his duty, continuing for seven years after Valentine's death and providing children for the future. With Galazye's death, Orson sorrows and goes into a wood, where like Valentine he eats no meat. One night he has a vision of Judgment, and this makes firm his estimate of temporality and eternity:

hym semed that he sawe all the gates of heuen open, and sawe the Ioyes of the saued, the syeges of the sayntes crowned in glorye, and the aungelles that songe melodyously before the sauyour of the world. After he sawe betwene two hyghe roches in the botom of an obscure valeye the gulfre of helle, where as was the dampned. Some in a brennynge fyre the other in boylynge caudrons, the other hanged by theyr tongues, the other assaylled and enuyronned wyth serpentes, and generally he sawe all the paynes of helle, whiche is horrible and ferefull for to recounte. After the whyche vysyon he wakened all afrayed and ameruaylled of the thynges that he had sene. And in wepyng pyteously came vnto the grene knyght and sayd to hym. Frende I know that the worlde is of lyttel valoure, and of shorte durynge, and that all is but vayne glorye of the pompes of this worlde, displeasaunt vnto god and to the salute of the soule lytle profytable. . . . And knowe that the remnaunte of my lyfe I wyll lede solytaryly and habandone the worlde. And at this same houre I renounce all worldly honoure and take my leue yf you. (pp. 326-27)

The most vividly described vision in *Valentine and Orson,* this passage calls to mind the frequent sculptural representations of the subject, as on the tympanum at Conques or Bourges, and paintings like the contemporary one of Roger van der Weyden at Beaune, or the dominating illustrations of the Hereford Mappa Mundi as well as the very moving final episodes of the Corpus Christi plays. Each in its distinctive artistry compels the beholder to pause and think on his own end, and clearly this is the intention of the romance which is concluded with a bare statement that Orson ended his life as a hermit and that miracles and canonization followed his death. Like *Amis and Amiloun,* then, *Valentine and Orson* concludes with transcendence. The author's final words, simplified from the French original, exhort all to follow their example:

they finisshed their dayes gloriouslye and wente vnto the blysse that neuer shall haue ende, to the which he bryng vs all that suffered deathe for vs on the crosse Amen. (p. 327)

The twins have been sharply differentiated and their ways to God have not been the same, but their ends are alike because they share admittance of human limitations, penance for their sins, belief in God's mercy, and utter devotion.

This reassuring theme has been carefully developed throughout the romance and is the basis of its popularity. Good and evil are clearly distinguished; and the heroes, though they are by no means perfect, consistently do the right thing in the end. This makes the brothers, nature and art, very reassuring, and universalizing of the idea of brotherhood is not difficult. Simplicity and directness, as well as the extensive use of dialogue, give them an immediacy that is not always evident in medieval romances. Similarly, frequent use of proverbs to make moral points explicit provides guidelines for the popular reader. These range over all subjects, as a few examples indicate:

For maryage done agaynst the wyll cometh not lyghtly vnto perfeccyon. (pp. 163-64)

. . . for your shyrte is more nerer your body than your gowne, yo[u] oughte not for to defende the countree of another, and lette your owne be destroyed. (p. 79)

. . . to sone cometh he that bryngeth euil tydynges. (p. 194)

. . . who that god wyl helpe none can hurte them. (p. 244)

For with his treason he founde hym selfe betrayed as it was reason, for a thynge euyll begon can not haue a good ende. (p. 270)

Throughout this romance, then, are many indications of an artist with a strong moral intention and very much aware of what will appeal. The long popularity of *Valentine and Orson* shows how successful the narrative is. Undeniably it is a compendium of favorite materials, particularly magic, exotic details of the east, varied pagan enemies, lush descriptions of interiors, and of fairs and dragons impressive enough to inspire Bunyan's *Pilgrim's Progress.*[47] There is also a topical appeal; Constantinople had been the focus of late crusades at the end of the fifteenth century. Similarly, a broad public is attracted by homely features like the proverbs, reiterating respect and devotion to parents as we will see in *Paris and Vienne,* and having a merchant serve as Bellysaunt's champion (a detail that reflects changing class interests as chivalric tradition alters).[48] Yet, the narrative's strength is its use of the idea of brotherhood through two sharply contrasted protagonists whose exciting worldly adventures entertain but serve a high moral purpose in bringing them ultimately to humility, penance, and trust in God. Inspiring its popular audience is the demonstration that the most basic of man's relationships is one that transcends the temporal; even the strongest ties, like human brotherhood, are insignificant when viewed from the standpoint of eternity.

In romances like *Athelston, Amis and Amiloun,* and *Valentine and Orson* exploration of the ideals of friendship and brotherhood appealed to a popular audience concerned with the claims of close familial ties and sworn oaths of loyalty, matters of urgency in the Middle Ages because of the feudal structure of society. But the sustained popularity of these treatments came not only from such concerns but also from the romancers' exploitation of the exotic in presenting situations where the nature of friendship and brotherhood was tested and clarified. Thus social outcasts, like the leper Amiloun and 'natural' man Orson, must be accepted and integrated in a harmonious society; and melodramatic episodes like a husband's kicking his pregnant wife or being in bed with his friend's wife (at the friend's request), the would-be slaying of a brother or actual killing of a father in combat, and the murder by a father of his innocent children are controlled or made safe through their heightening of the participants' moral awareness.

CHAPTER V

THE DELIGHTS OF LOVE

In the whole range of personal feeling none is more completely associated with the romance than the love of man and woman. Indeed the name itself is used to describe stories of passionate attachment in modern fiction where giants and dragons no longer appear. There is a tendency to consider most fully and often illicit delights, and this may be traceable to enthusiasm for lovers like Tristan and Iseult or Lancelot and Guinevere.[1] But this somewhat obscures part of the main argument about the popularity of Middle English romances as a whole, for certainly it falsifies the English tradition which clearly did little to perpetrate these ideals of illicit love, as comparison with French and German artists makes clear.[2] Many English abridgements of continental models are in love passages; there is no English translation of Andreas Capellanus, nor are there English 'courts of love.' There is no memorable treatment of Tristan, and little attention to Lancelot (except for the stanzaic *Le Morte Arthur*) in separate narratives. In the larger English treatments of Arthurian material (especially Malory) we find a similarly unenthusiastic response to adultery and its almost inevitable chaotic consequences. Avoidance of extremes and exploitation of emotion in French romances is the consistent English response, which clarifies and heightens moral awareness. Middle English romances are often put down not simply because of their lack of stylistic elegance but also because of their lack of Gallic sophistication and the high sentiments of Germans like Wolfram, Gottfried, or Hartmann. But increasingly *amour courtois,* like the extremes of chivalry, is being recognized as a French (both artistic and scholarly) phenomenon that does not apply with great accuracy to Middle English romances which date from a later time and mirror a different ethos.[3] Perhaps the point is most obviously clear in Chaucer's attitude in *Troilus and Criseyde,* upon which so much critical theorizing has centered, but many romances less widely read by modern audiences reflect the same concerns about sexual love.

Ywain and Gawain, both because it is the most accomplished romance of the twelfth century and the only one of Chrétien de Troyes that has a Middle English version, as well as the German of Hartmann von Aue, and because the knight and lady are married, provides a good focus of the argument. The worldly pleasures of knightly fame and camaraderie are weighted against a rather blissful marital situation, so that this romance is another articulation of the most desired popular experiences; the possibilities of sexual relationships are explored. Yet *Ywain and Gawain* has a richer range of understanding of the totality of man's being, for the full import of the narrative is to show that for all their attractiveness neither fame nor love, which is preferred as long as Ywain is not shamed by masculine scorn, can be exalted above God. Thus an orthodox framework is provided for the love of Ywain and Alundyne and for Ywain's knightly ambitions through marriage. This union gives to both a freedom and possibility for self-realization that neither had previously experienced in a personal way, and it also serves as a focus which leads them to the greater understanding that comes with the transcending of self. Marriage, then, makes compatible both sexual passion and knightly ambition. In God's sacrament a reconciliation of divergent human desires is accommodated.

Ywain's satisfaction in his personal relationship with his wife suggests an increasing regard for heterosexual relations that were rather irrelevant to men motivated by a desire for fortune and military prowess. Lancelot's emergence as a hero in later romances reflects this interest. Since it centers upon Lancelot's love for both the Maid of Astolot and Queen Guinevere, the stanzaic *Le Morte Arthur* eloquently argues how attractive a man's love for a woman can be. The presence of the two possible loves, one with youthful innocence and propriety and the other with mature experience and costly betrayal, reduces the English emphasis upon the theme of courtly love/adultery that is typical of many French treatments of the subject. This romance presents a wider range of the possible kinds of satisfaction in sexual relationships that are available to man during his lifetime. But again a clear indication is given of the destructiveness of any love relationship which distracts the individual from his essential moral balance.

As in a romance like *Sir Gawain and the Green Knight* or *Troilus and Criseyde,* a clear case is made for earthly delights. Like fame and beneficent rule, or friendship, love and marriage are worthy states. Indeed the attractions of an individual relationship in contrast to a more generalized one, the possibility for personal rather than public fulfillment, offer additional ranges for investigation. These distinctive qualities provide another popular kind of Middle English romance with thematic possibilities that become increasingly favored in later fiction, deteriorating ultimately into the 'lady's romantic fiction' that has provoked the contempt of a critic like Q. D. Leavis and the witty censure of James Hart.

The lovers of Arthurian romances certainly offered early audiences varied erotic adventures, but these were always part of a larger vision of man's (specifically the seeking knight's) experience. The widespread appeal of this subject matter can be variously illustrated in non-Arthurian narratives. Evolving attitudes are well indicated in the prose *Paris and Vienne,* a mid-fifteenth-century romance which Caxton translated from French in 1485, that both he and rivals frequently printed, that appeared in dramatic form in the mid-sixteenth century, and is to be found in printed texts in eight other languages. The popularity of this narrative stems partially from its including more realistic and local details—as was more typical in later romances—than did tales of Tristan, Lancelot, and Guy. But the lovers, who undergo the usual trials of separation (unwanted suitors and numerous chivalric combats, encounters with exotic foreign places and personages) provide its basic charm. Their steadfast dedication and loyalty, always preserving honesty in expectation of worthy marriage, offer the moral example and inspiration that are crucial for success in popular fiction.

Ywain and Gawain

Considerations of the relation between Middle English romances and the work of Chrétien de Troyes[4] make very clear the English regard for moral value. Significantly "of all Chrétien's surviving romances, only *Yvain,* the most moral and the most eventful, was adopted by the English."[5] Further, the author of *Ywain and Gawain,* who obviously worked directly from a manuscript of *Yvain,* shows throughout a "sterner temperament and more strenuous preoccupations" in his "abridged free translation."[6] At least two scholars have argued that Chrétien used the adventures of his romance as "a carefully contrived set of opportunities for Ywain to redeem himself from the sin of Pride."[7] And a careful analysis of *Ywain and Gawain* reveals that the English author not only follows this essential attitude of Chrétien,[8] but also heightens the theme by carefully eliminating much of the detail and elaborate stylistic effects of the French original and its extreme concern with the niceties of courtly love and chivalric behavior. The result is a briefer narrative, more sharply focused on the protagonist Ywain and his individual struggles. The Middle English poet shows throughout a directness about his devotion to fundamental Christian values. His essential 'English' character, based on firmer moral principles, shows a kinship with the authors of popular romances about Guy and Havelok as does his colloquial quality.

Thus it is again arguable that the traditional minstrel's prayers with which the Middle English romance begins and ends are not only the standard, conventional formulae of minstrel procedure but also a precise expression of the basic point of view that informs the poem.

> Almyghti God þat made mankyn,
> He schilde his servandes out of syn
> And mayntene þam with might and mayne. (1-3)

> Bot Jhesu Criste for his grete grace
> In hevyn-blis grante us a place
> To bide in, if his wills be.
> Amen, amen, par charite. (4029-32)

This addition to Chrétien's text is a concise expression of the order for which every Christian yearns. While alive man prays to God for help to stay free of sin, so that when inevitably death comes he may have eternal happiness in heaven. These two themes are succinctly fused in the final lines of the poem which explain how the principals of the romance "In joy and blis þai led þaire live . . . Until þat ded haves dreven þam down" (4024, 4026). Clearly, then, Ywain's earthly striving and repentance have resulted in his redemption. The enormous efforts of his early life give way to that poised calm which follows the individual's recognition of his fault, his earnest efforts at amendment, his true contrition. And the motto "par charite" epitomizes the idea.

Thus when Ywain and his wife Alundyne are reconciled, he humbly admits his guilt and accepts the mercy of God:

> "Madame," he said, "I have miswroght,
> And þat I have ful dere boght.
> Grete foly I did, þe soth to say,
> When þat I past my terme-day;
> And, sertes, wha so had so bityd,
> þai sold have done right als I dyd.
> Bot I sal never thorgh Goddes grace
> At mi might do more trispase;
> And what man so wil mercy crave,
> By Goddes law he sal it have." (3995-4004)

This recognition of his own failing, significantly a breaking of a vow to return to his wife after one year's seeking of knightly adventures, is crucial to Ywain's character. The contrast between his present humility and earlier pride is vividly made. The values of a man's participation in a world of daring are clearly acknowledged, but as we saw in *Valentine and Orson*, excessive pursuit of this ideal can be disastrous, and this Ywain's way of life has fully illustrated by a maze of crises. Ywain's sincerity in promising not to repeat this 'trespass' is unquestionable, and we see how much he has learned from his suffering in the world. His faith is expressed in the belief that God will have mercy upon him. He also knows that mercy is granted a man not because he is 'good,' but because God forgives those who seek Him. The author of *Ywain and Gawain* has, of course, emphasized in his narrative the means by which an individual achieves self-knowledge in the world.

The exact changes of the Middle English adapter in this passage illustrate how the moral tone is intensified and clarified. He begins the speech with Ywain's admission of responsibility ("I have miswroght"), not the request for a lady's pity on a sinner. Similarly, the idea of Ywain's penitence is combined with stress upon "Goddes grace" and "mercy," which are not contingent upon man's performance. The forgiveness of the lady and the lover's temerity in seeking it are not retained, nor is Laudine's speech of acquiescence. This bolder presentation concentrates upon essential understanding of man's dual nature, for just as the spiritual awareness is heightened, so the possibilities of an earthly love are shown more clearly and directly by the last lines which describe a more intense reconciliation:

> þan sho asented saghteling to mak;
> And sone in armes he gan hir tak
> And kissed hir ful oft sith;
> Was he never are so blith. (4005-9)

Initially Ywain, like so many heroes in popular narratives, is an arrogant young man who is eager to gain reputation through his physical prowess. He is, of course, provoked by the extraordinary pride of Sir Kay, who has boastfully taunted Ywain's cousin Sir Colgrevance, who tells an exciting tale of adventure. However, Ywain does call Colgrevance a "fole" (461) for not having previously told his marvelous story so that Ywain could revenge him. We cannot fail to recall Biblical injunction against calling anyone a "fool," so that Ywain's pride—which is typical of many young knights—is clearly established. The Queen's rebuke of Sir Kay—"What þe devyl es þe withyn" (485)—indicates the dishonor of a chiding, vicious tongue; and her allusion to the Crucifixion (another English addition) emphasizes how great is the discrepancy between two values—the pride of knights and Christian charity. Nevertheless, Ywain still thinks vaingloriously of his own virtuosity, so that he resents the decision of Arthur and other knights to share the quest; indeed he hastily sets out alone to "tak þe grace þat God wald send" (548). And the poet's imagery is suggestively symbolic, for the narrow way is set with thorns and briars.

Appropriately Ywain's first fight is not wholly successful. Riding hard, he relentlessly follows his mortally wounded opponent and is trapped inside the castle gates in an extraordinarily spectacular way:

> At aiþer entre was, iwys,
> Straytly wroght a portculis
> Shod wele with yren and stele
> And also grunden wonder wele.
> Under þat þan was a swyke,
> þat made Syr Ywain to myslike.
> His hors fote toched þareon,
> þan fel þe portculis onone
> Bytwyx him and his hinder arsown,
> Thorgh sadel and stede it smate al down;
> His spores of his heles it schare;
> þan had Ywaine murnyng mare. (673-84)

Such an exciting episode is comparable to the required car chase that is formulaic in modern thrillers, and the consistency of popular taste is supported by the choice of this most dramatic moment for carving

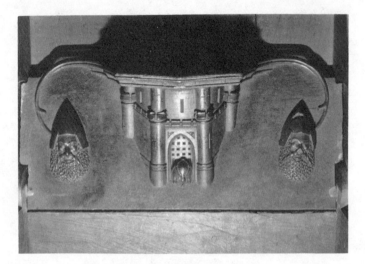

Courtesy of Lincoln Cathedral

Misericords: Ywain's escape through the portcullis. (see p. 124)

Courtesy of Enville Parish Church

on misericords at Lincoln, Chester, Oxford (New College), Boston, and Enville (Staffs.). All show the castle's portcullis crushing the horse's hindquarters, and at Enville the knight's spurs—which were shorn off by the edge of the gate—are prominent. Here, too, the men-at-arms who are to seize Ywain are represented on the supporters as full figures, in contrast to the heads at Lincoln and Chester. *Ywain and Gawain* was translated in the fourteenth century and is included in the Thornton MS of Lincoln, so that it is tempting to speculate about the influence of the literary form. The widespread appearance of the scene in Britain in such arresting misericords suggests the compelling interest of near disaster averted at the last possible moment, and the English preference for high excitement in knightly exploits. The poet tells us that Ywain is unscathed because "A faire grace ʒit fel him swa" (687), but the young man remains oblivious. Even his capture does not mute his pride, for he refuses to believe that he can be hurt. Because of his previous good deed to Lunet, the maiden saves him and indeed feasts him inside the castle. She even woos her lady for Ywain, who falls in love when he observes Alundyne lamenting her slain husband. Thus when Arthur and the knights arrive they find Ywain established as lord of the castle. In disguise Ywain defeats proud Kay, and all are delighted. Ironically we have pride overcoming pride; the poet thus boldly repeats his theme. An interlude of feasting cannot be long protracted, for Ywain must yet come to self-knowledge and humility before he gains the happiness which precedes salvation.

Thus Gawain argues against Ywain's sacrifice of his knightly activities for the enjoyment of his lady. The English poet has very much shortened this section of the poem (1455 ff.), for Gawain simply states the importance of a knight's achievement among his peers. There is no exploitation of a conflict between love and duty, the claims of both are recognized, and we recognize the sanity of the English author. Indeed Alundyne shows herself again a very pragmatic woman. Just as she acquiesced to the argument that she could not remain a widow and that the conquering Ywain was her best choice for a husband, so now she graciously and modestly accedes to her husband's request. She is not, however, a mere pawn in a man's world, for she imposes a limitation of one year's absence. In short, man must participate in the active world, but he must not endlessly exploit his possible success, and he must recognize the complex demands of existence. Further, Alundyne gives

Ywain a ring to assure his safety and victory in the proscribed time, but he is required to use discretion.

Once again Ywain's pride has fatal consequences, for he forgets the time and thus forfeits his wife's love and ring. Finally he confronts the full implications of his behavior, and understanding leads to lamentation for his fault:

> "Allas, I am myne owin bane;
> Allas," he sayd, "þat I was born,
> Have I my leman þus forlorn,
> And al es for myne owen foly.
> Allas, þis dole wil make me dy."
> An evyl toke him als he stode;
> For wa he wex al wilde and wode. (1644-50)

For several years, then, Ywain finds refuge in the solitude of a forest, where a hermit befriends him and they exchange kindnesses. "For if a man be never so wode, / He wil kum whare man dose him gode" (1689-90). Thus the proud and esteemed knight passes a period of purgation, a time in which he is reduced to his essential nature, emphasized by his appearance as "a naked man" (1674, 1713) and the rudimentary nature of his food. Ywain, much as Gowther or Robert or Valentine when they do penance as fools, learns both to receive and give charity.

The next stage in Ywain's redemption is his return to a consciousness of the world. He is seen by three ladies, who "Thorogh Goddes help" (1749) restore his wit by means of an ointment from Morgan the Wise. Ywain's first exclamation, "Lady Saynt Mary" (1792), conveys a sense of traditional Christianity. Still not fully understanding his experience, Ywain is nevertheless gentler and more courteous in manner. He gains quick victories over a knight and a dragon, and wins the offer of a lady's favors. Thus a lion, which symbolizes power and courage but also expresses humble gratitude, and is perhaps allegorically Christ,[9] not only does Ywain no injury, but becomes his follower and great admirer, recognizing the princely quality of the hero and giving the romance's audience the satisfaction of inspiration and indulgence of the unusual.

Returning once again to the chapel in the forest, Ywain injures himself when he swoons and falls on his sword. The aggrieved lion is ready to kill himself, and Ywain again shows humility and self-knowledge which are inspired by the lion's compassion and grief. To the imprisoned Lunet he declares his sorrow, accepting full responsibility for his condition:

> "Nay," he said, "by Saynt Martyne,
> þare es na sorrow mete to myne,
> Ne no wight so wil of wane.
> I was a man, now am I nane;
> Whilom I was a nobil knyght
> And a man of mekyl myght;
> I had knyghtes of my menȝe
> And of reches grete plente;
> I had a ful fayre seignory,
> And al I lost for my foly.
> Mi maste sorow als sal þou here:
> I lost a lady þat was me dere." (2113-24)

In keeping with Ywain's new condition of spiritual awareness, the championing of Lunet (against a false steward's charge of treason) is undertaken with prayers to God, an acceptance of God's will (2201), and a reliance upon God: "Thorgh grace of God in trenyte, / I sal þe wreke of þam al thre" (2205-6).

This attitude is sustained throughout the rest of *Ywain and Gawain*. The giant he next fights is "a devil of mekil pryde" (2250). Those he serves observe, "God has us gude socure sent, / þis knight þat of his grace wil grant / Forto fyght with þe geant" (2318-20). Ywain modestly turns aside their obsequious gratitude. His first act on the morning of battle is to hear mass at the church, and he refuses the generous offer of gifts from those he aids. The narrative then describes a series of adventures in which Ywain and his loyal lion are successful in aiding the unfortunate. Prayers are numerous; Ywain is confident of himself as a true Christian knight: "For with me es bath God and right, / And þai sal help me forto fight, / And my lyon sal help me" (2519-21).

Like Guy of Warwick, Ywain continues his active life as a knight champion, but the attitude and tone of his life are no longer proud and selfish. Indications of the hero's knowledge of his relation to God and his fellow man are more numerous than in the earlier part of the narrative. Thus Ywain still admits that a knight gains renown through fighting, but now his emphasis is upon helping those who are in need:

> "Gladly with þe wil I gane,
> Wheder so þou wil me lede,
> And hertly help þe in þi nede.

> Sen þou haves me so wide soght,
> Sertes, fail þe sal I noght." (2926-30)

Appropriately Ywain's sphere of activity is temporal; he is a knight who evolves from pride to humility, but he does not achieve transcendence in the romance. His opponents are consistently described as devils (3018, 3070, 3155, 3189), prayers are numerous (3352 ff., 3377, 3502 ff., etc.), and he acknowledges his role as the instrument of God (3301 f.). Also his distinctive quality is recognized by other people.

> If God had cumen fra hevyn on hight
> And on þis mold omang þam light,
> þai had noght made mare joy, sertain,
> þan þai made to Syr Ywayne.
> Folk of þe toun com him biforn
> And blissed þe time þat he was born;
> Of his prowes war þai wele payd:
> "In þis werld es none slike," þai said.
> þai cunvayd him out of þe toun
> With ful faire processiowne. (3339-48)

Thus the narrative provides a description of almost ritualistic honor, intensified by the English romancer's use of "processiowne," paid to the popular champion of right values against evil forces in the world.

The theme of pride is repeated in *Ywain and Gawain* with the episode of the older and younger sisters who quarrel about inheritance rights. As defending champions Ywain and Gawain are reconciled. Once their identities have been revealed after fierce battle, each vies with the other to disclaim victory, and we see the virtue of humility in the context of the Round Table. Appropriately Arthur arbitrates the dispute in a way which stops further proud claims.

The final resolution of the complex narrative threads comes with the identification of Ywain as the knight with the lion. This worthy beast is overjoyed and effusive in his welcome (3820 ff.). Thus the poet reinforces our sense of Ywain's purgation. Then the romance is quickly concluded with his being reconciled to his wife. Ywain's last explicit statement of self-knowledge is a formal summary of the significance of the many episodes of the narrative. His admission of guilt, plea for forgiveness, firm promise of amendment, and recognition of God's mercy are the ideal toward which a Christian strives, and medieval narratives which emphasize these ideas sustain their popularity for centuries. In this world man strives judiciously, not excessively or proudly, to achieve an awareness of his role as God's creature; and the securing of this self-knowledge brings great happiness and peace. The poet's ending does not give us a transcendent conclusion, but rather Ywain's prospect for a meaningful and worthy life. Thus his prayer voices the hope of every Christian. What Frappier has described in Chrétien's poem as "a peculiar quality of plenitude and harmony," is certainly not lost in the simplicity and directness of the Middle English narrative. Ywain's potential delights in worldly individual relationships are widely diversified—friendship, knightly camaraderie, love for wife. He does not, however, simply move in the fantasy world which the poem's spell creates in the enactment of the highest ideals of knighthood.[10] Rather his experiences are a cumulative learning to bring him to God, that increasing spiritual maturity which subordinates individual delights to ultimate values for which popular literature traditionally pleads.

Le Morte Arthur

Characteristically regarded as inferior to the alliterative *Morte Arthure*, the stanzaic *Le Morte Arthur* has been noted especially for its choice of subject matter, the tale of the 'Lily Maid of Astolat' and of the Round Table, and praised for its naïveté.[11] More recently it has been discussed as a source for Malory.[12] The poem has, however, yet another distinctive quality which is more significant. This is its diversified exposition of popular Christian values, most particularly its bold presentation of the remorseless conflict between the claims of the temporal and the eternal, here specifically expressed in the appeals of sexual love and ultimately resolved through a knowledge of the nature and value of penitence and dedication to God.

There are fewer formal references to Christianity in *Le Morte Arthur* than in many other medieval romances, but as in *Amis and Amiloun* the author's attitude toward his material is clearly defined by a belief in it with concomitant sympathy for his hero. The poem significantly does not begin with the traditional minstrel's appeal for salvation, and indeed the early sections contain few precise references to Christian belief. What we find, in fact, is a bold exposition of the world of Arthur's court, a world in which the values of a code of knighthood are triumphant.

Within a few hundred lines we know that Lancelot feigns illness to stay behind with the Queen, and that Agraveyne remains to spy upon them. Further, Lancelot's ambition for knightly excellence prompts him to hide his true identity in a disguise which is, however, quickly penetrated by Arthur. Lancelot's distinct character, his apartness from the other knights, is established. Thus the futility of denying one's essential nature is early suggested, and this theme is developed as the poem evolves. Specifically, *Le Morte Arthur* expresses the fundamental idea that man's reason for being is not contained within the possibilities of the ideal Arthurian world.[13] Though this society is based on high principles, regretfully these cannot be sustained by even the noblest of men because of human limitations. Thus from the outset there is a sense of the necessity for an alternative to the chivalric ideal, which combines knightly prowess and love. Knightly endeavors contribute to the poem's appeal, but it is helpful to concentrate upon the presentation of the delights of love since the sexual relations provoke the martial experience and occupy much of the romancer's interest.

No human experience more completely and richly attracts man to the world than love for woman, as Lancelot's story illustrates. The rich possibilities of such a relationship are made abundantly clear. While the Maid of Astolot offers youthful innocence and absolute devotion, Guinevere provides mature experience and the challenges of independence. The two women, though their circumstances are sharply contrasted, are essentially very much alike. Both are fiercely demanding, claiming from Lancelot greater devotion than is compatible with his sustaining his own personal integrity, the achievement of his identity in union with God. The elaborate expectations of Guinevere are legion, but the Maid of Astolot is no less arrogant and absolute. In offering herself to the knight she is sexually forward (197-200), and pride is clear in her letter (1048-95), when she indites Lancelot for refusing her unsolicited love. Adherents of the arbitrary code of knighthood respond to her picturesque appeal, and thus clearly show the limitations of its ideal values.

The poet is, then, showing that catastrophe results not only from adulterous love, but also from a romantic passion which is so excessive that it seeks to consume the individual and fails to recognize the true nature of being. Yet *Le Morte Arthur* is not merely negative in its analysis of sexual desire, for, in fact, Guinevere's love possesses a value which far exceeds the scope of the Maid's. Through her love for Lancelot

Playing chess.
Ivories showing popular romance subjects.
Victoria and Albert Museum. Crown Copyright.

and the catastrophes which result from their personal exploitation of passion, the Queen gains wisdom and maturity. She achieves that crucial self-knowledge which leads her to devotion to God in the fullest sense. Her recognition of personal failing, acceptance of responsibility and choice of a penitent life, show great maturity and strength of character. Sexual failing is certainly not trivial, but it is less annihilating than spiritual pride. The Maid of Astolot, in contrast to Guinevere, is self-destructive. She "dies for love," having learned nothing of her essential human nature and still indulging the naive egoism which expects and demands personal satisfaction above all. The funeral barge and letter are a melodramatic indulgence of egoism. The Maid, like Romeo and Juliet or Tristan and Iseult, has, of course, attracted much sentimental sympathy from later readers of her story. But this is hardly the intention in *Le Morte Arthur.* Thus these two women are part of the central thematic matter of the poem, and the author's attitude to them is clear. Their lives, like that of the hero Lancelot, are expressions of the poet's awareness of the necessity for self-knowledge, discipline, and a choice of values which places God at the center of being. In short, the central themes are those found in much popular medieval literature where *contemptus mundi* is the ultimate resolution. The attraction of the romance lies in its exploitation of the delights of love (and war) before the reassuring resolution is achieved.

The tone of *Le Morte Arthur* is a far cry from the Victorian sentimentality of Tennyson's *Idyll,* for it is an expression of the clear and firm medieval sense of the relations between this world and the next. The author uses literary skills to express his moral purpose and control; thus careful development of memorable characters and a harmonious ordering of material to unify various episodes to illustrate his theme are crucial. As in *Guy of Warwick, Troilus and Criseyde, Amis and Amiloun,* and countless other medieval romances, the mode of fiction admirably serves to convey a serious belief. The attractiveness of temporal and human relationships is given full and eloquent expression, but unfailingly the wise human being (characteristically a fallible but cognizant knight) chooses to dedicate himself to God and strive for eternal happiness. Although this often involves a renunciation of appealing and very valuable and edifying relationships and experiences, the romances make clear that the questing knight properly seeks and achieves a way of eternal life for which we should strive. Thus the Bishop's appeal to

Lancelot that he return Guinevere is not superficial antifeminism, but an attempt to suggest the complexity of human experience.

> "Syr, thynke that ye haue venquysshid many A bataille
>   Throwgh grace that god hathe for you wrought;
> ye shalle do now by my counsayle:
>   Thynke on hym that you dere bought;
> Wemen Ar frele of hyr entayle;
>   Syr, lettes not ynglande go to noght." (2296-2301)

Love and patriotic loyalty have their claims upon individual commitment; however, as is clear here, and as the romance further shows, there are yet higher claims: God's grace is crucial. In *Ywain and Gawain* an earthly reconciliation came through marriage, but illicit and/or unrequited passion is not so accommodated.

Not surprisingly *Le Morte Arthur* concludes with a triumphant and transcendent vision, the achievement of Lancelot's self-knowledge and dedication to God. Significantly the romance is terminated with this knight's death. Like Guy of Warwick he has the fullest understanding, that gained through diverse experiences and complex decisions based on thorough self-knowledge. The death of Arthur receives only brief treatment and the details—a hand from the water to grasp the sword and a rich ship of ladies who bear their "brother" away—are those of Celtic mythology, not Christianity. There is, of course, the stanza of Christian prayer (3408-15) made by Arthur's knights, but the author deliberately subordinates this material. Clearly he is concerned to use instead the explicit penitence and death of Lancelot for a bold exposition of the Christian meaning that is the core of the poem. The analogous experiences of Guinevere and various knights reiterate this crucial thematic material, and this strong emphasis gives artistic harmony to the various story lines as well as intellectual strength.

As is so frequently the case in romance narrative, the king is less fully and humanly realized than his principal knights, and the deceived husband is not easily compatible with the hero-king. Arthur certainly is loyal and appreciative of the prowess and services of members of his court, as his laments for the dead eloquently show. His reputation for excellence is widespread (227 ff., 1048 ff., 2546 f.), and his exploits against Modred remarkable (3082 ff.). However, his absolute adherence to the code of knightly conduct reveals a fatal lack of flexibility, and his judgment of character is lamentably unsophisticated. He is too static and simple to serve as the romance's real protagonist.

When Guinevere is accused (falsely) of poisoning the Scotch knight, Arthur's initial concern is with form, the "right" (912 ff.). Though he does plead for a champion for his wife, he cannot inspire his knights' loyalty and Guinevere must look after herself. Later, when he leaves his country, in order to avenge himself against Lancelot, he follows unwise counsel in choosing Modred as steward (2516 ff.). Motivated by a primitive wish for self-vindication in physical brutality, Arthur thus deserts his kingdom and follows bad advisers. Ironically, Modred desires the Queen, even tries to force a marriage, so that he poses a threat greater than Lancelot's. Arthur's grief for Gawayne, a knight who is capable of courtesy but also of lying to the Queen (1105 ff.), is disturbingly strong, even if he is the beloved nephew. Moreover, Gawayne's relentless seeking of revenge for Gaheriet's death does, after all, bring about the collapse of Arthur's Round Table. This proud man (note, e.g., 2829 ff.) so values his own self-esteem and assertions of righteousness that no repentance and attempts at reconciliation are acceptable to him (2652 ff.). He (Lancelot) who has sinned must be destroyed absolutely. There is no possibility for mercy or evolving sensibility in Gawayne's value system. His primitive ideal of vengeance (2010-13) is like that in several militant romances, and it is typical of many of Arthur's knights, who usually are ireful when opposed (e.g., 1350 ff.). Thus he fails completely to grasp the fundamental Christian qualities of humility and forgiveness. Gawayne's knightly courtesy makes him refuse to witness the Queen's execution, but this is not charity. Arthur's devotion to such an individual cuts deeply against our esteem for him. In short, Arthur, Gawayne, and Modred lack the emerging Christian belief of Lancelot—and his companions who learn from his example. Their shift from 'Arthurian' to Christian values is sparked by Guinevere's self-knowledge and repentance, but the entire narrative carefully evolves to the last triumphant scene.

It is, then, with the erring but learning sinners that the poet's—and our—sympathy and interest lie, for the romance has the popular appeal of accommodated difficulties. The anxieties of critics like Kane, Mehl, and Wertime, who find the morality of the poem inconsistent or best ignored, reflect readings that either expect sinners to be differently viewed or delight in human loyalties and tragic powerlessness rather than the resolution of Christian forgivenss. The attraction of the latter is clear in much medieval literature; a very pertinent example is the inclusion in the Corpus Christi cycles of the episode of The Woman Taken in Adultery (John 8:3-11). The excellent Towneley version, so imbued with the qualities of medieval life, begins with a vignette in the tradition of the fabliau and quickly evolves into an exquisite enunciation of the quality of mercy.

Many references make clear the dangers and evils of civil strife in the kingdom, a temporal reflection of the Arthurian spiritual disharmony. Revealing a notable self-interest and a somewhat confused sense of value, Gawayne advises against Agrawayne's revelation of the Queen's liaison:

> "Wele wote we," sayd syr gawayne,
>   "That we ar of the kyngis kynne,
> And launcelot is so mykill of mayne
>   That suche wordys were better blynne.
> Welle wote thou, brothyr agrawayne
>   There-of shulde we bot harmys wynne;
> yit were it better to hele and layne
>   Than werre and wrake thus to be-gynne." (1688-95)

His argument, ironically, is reinforced by a full enumeration of Lancelot's virtues and his own brotherly devotion, though later, of course, his attitude is vindictive and irrevocable. After the initial confrontation, Lancelot is fully aware of what the future will be, and he notes tersely: "We haue be-gonne thys ilke nyght / That shall brynge many A man full colde" (1886-87). When the siege is advanced, he laments further: "Allas and weilawaye! / That euyr beganne this sorewe sare!" (2116-17) and grieves to fight against his king, who echoes his sentiment (2204-5).

Throughout the romance Lancelot's courtesy is exemplary (2200-1), and he strives to secure peace (2406 ff., 2182 ff., 2318 ff., 2420 ff., 2781 ff., etc.). Significantly Lancelot is persuaded to return Guinevere to Arthur by the Bishop's appeal (2296-2301) when he argues God's primacy. Later Christian gentleness, not simply grief for the many slaughtered, lies at the core of his wish for a truce:

> "Wete ye welle it were grete synne
>   Crysten folke to sle thus more;
> Withe myldenesse we shall be-gynne
>   And god shall wische vs wele to fare." (2600-3)

Frequently in the narrative, then, we find a Lancelot whose sentiments and actions are directed by Christian attitudes. Such episodes occur before the last meeting with the Queen when her example of penance provides the final inspiration and catalyst.

Arthur, and even Gawayne, recognize something of Lancelot's quality, but they do not share it. Interestingly Lancelot's generosity and courtesy—crucial virtues in the Arthurian knightly code—exceed those of his peers who lack his basic Christian charity. Lancelot's strength lies in his humility and self-knowledge. Unlike the others he recognizes his human failings, and this results in his own tolerance and indeed beneficence. Though he deceives Arthur and initially conceals his guilt, he shows neither pleasure nor satisfaction in what he is doing. Instead he continually compensates with forbearance and kindness. Never is he self-righteous like the others who repeatedly indulge in attempts to make explicit and to punish human failings. The balance between true and false accusations suggests the futility of such judgments as do the poet's explicit comments.[14]

The people's acceptance of Modred (3050 ff.) indicates that non-Christian values prevail in this romance world. It is worth noting that Modred ingratiates himself by appealing to cupidity, that frequently besetting sin of the medieval world. He wins support by making feasts and giving gifts (2962 ff., 3044 ff.). He also prefaces his refusal of a truce with a distinctly uon-Christian oath; "And sware by Iudas that Ihesus sold" (3250). And there is perhaps a symbolic reference to the Fall in the use of an adder as the catalyst of the last fatal battle. Similarly Modred vanquishes the Archbishop of Canterbury who rebukes him, in Christ's name, for trying to marry his father's wife (3002 ff.). The dead are robbed on the battlefield (3416 ff.). Even as Arthur is dying, loyal Sir Bedwere twice deceives him. Prompted by his cupidity (a reluctance to lose Excalibur), yet another of Arthur's knights reveals how he is governed by earthly values. How different is Lancelot's increasing disinterest in material gains and physical victories.

The disguised Lancelot of the opening tournament scenes reveals traits of character which subsequently evolve. To offset somewhat his high reputation, Lancelot conceals his identity, thus showing a desire to function as himself. He also chooses to fight with those who have most need. The knight's physical vulnerability appears when he is wounded by Ector; his withdrawal to a forest suggests human fallibility and apartness. Essentially, however, his values in the early part of the narrative are 'Arthurian.' Though severely wounded, he wants to risk his life rather than fail to strive for knightly repute in the forthcoming tournament. Lancelot soon shows, however, a resilience and capacity for self-denigration which are lacking in men like Gawayne and Modred. Chagrin at having been wounded and a desire for self-vindication are quickly replaced by hearty good humor, love, and admiration for a brother's skill. Indeed "launcelot loughe with herte fre" (496); this remarkable detachment indicates his integrity and independence.

Lancelot's firm and direct manner is also clearly shown when he refuses the Maid of Astolot and says that he will not return. Falsely accused by Guinevere, he denies (in Christ's name) that he has been deceitful and rides alone to the forest (764 ff.). Certainly this knight is no futile lover who collapses when his lady frowns. He is not happy with the situation but, as his withdrawal to the solitude of the forest shows, he seeks actively to come to terms with his experience. In short, he is not a slave of passion or of the code of knighthood, but a man seeking to know himself. Further, the Queen's misunderstanding and harsh judgment do not prevent his willingness to be her champion when she is falsely accused. Arthur's other knights are begged by King and Queen for aid, and they refuse; Lancelot gives freely of himself to one who needs help, even though his aid is not requested. The scene of mutual forgiveness between victorious Lancelot and Sir Mador is a worthy illustration of tolerance, and the virtue is quickly (if briefly) shared by other knights.

Such generosity and tolerance are also evident in Lancelot's repeated attempts to avoid bloodshed and fighting Arthur. Although his men chide him, Lancelot shows no anger or impatience. On the battlefield itself he is consistently generous, never exploiting the full resources of his knightly prowess. He insists upon defending the Queen's honor, but he also makes every effort to withdraw, to remove himself so as to avoid offense. Significantly his offer is to go to live in the Holy Land (2664), an appropriate and meaningful attempt at penitence, and a detail not found in the source. Even though Lancelot's good will and intention are contemptuously rebuked, his charity is not only sustained but also increased. His responses to Gawayne's repeated insolence and abuse are an impressive demonstration of self-control, good will, and a sincere humility.

The author of *Le Morte Arthur* has given us, then, in Lancelot an

Lovers riding in the forest.

Jousting

Ivories representing characteristic chivalric activities were essential items in courts, castles, and bourgeois households. This scene is a particularly vigorous representation of the kinds of combat described in nearly every romance.

Courtesy of Virginia Museum

These two woodcuts—Valentine leading Orson bound (above) and Trompart and Clerimond on the wooden horse (below) could only illustrate one story. They are from *Valentine and Orson*. Copland, 1550. Permission of The Huntington Library, San Marino, California.

extraordinarily complex individual. Lancelot is certainly not an ideal man, but he is a very worthy human being who, though he fails in details, strives for and achieves a life in which meaningful values (which are not typical of his society) are operative. In Arthur's visions of the wheel of fortune and impending defeat, a wiser Gawayne, flanked by angels, warns that the King must have a truce to wait for Lancelot's assistance. Thus even this recalcitrant knight (like Troilus, from the vantage point of eternity) sees Lancelot's worth and loyalty. And "Throw the grace of God of hevyn" (3588) Lancelot speeds to Arthur's aid.

Told of Arthur's death and the Queen's flight, Lancelot again seeks solitude when he orders his men not to follow him.

> There had he nouther Roo ne Reste,
>   But forthe he went with drery mode,
> And iij dayes he went euyn weste,
>   As man that cowde nother yvell nor good; (3614-17)

Clearly the narrative suggests a period of indecision, that time in which the seeking individual strives to come to terms with himself and his world after losing so much of what had been central to his existence. In the most intense despair—"All-moste for wepying he was mad" (3623)—Lancelot finds Guinevere. Thus a kind of spiritual progress is suggested, for now Lancelot receives very exact instruction in the way to salvation.

Guinevere publicly accepts her responsibility in the disasters that have befallen Arthur's kingdom.

> "Abbes, to you I knowlache here
>   That throw thys ylke man And me,
> For we to-gedyr han loved vs dere,
>   All thys sorowfull werre hathe be; (3638-41)

The violence of bloodshed and horrors of many deaths have shattered the Queen's former complacency, and her consolation lies in a belief in God's mercy. Thus she acknowledges:

> "Oure wylle hathe be to sore bought sold;
> But god, that All myghtis maye,
>   Now hathe me sette where I wyll hold;
>
> I-sette I am In suche A place,
>   my sowle hele I wyll A-byde,
> Telle god send me som grace,

Throw mercy of hys woundys wyde
That I may do so in thys place
    my synnys to A-mende thys ilke tyde,
After to haue A syght of hys face
    At domys day on hys Ryght syde." (3651-61)

Her wise sense of man's relationship with God is admirable. Unlike so many of the Arthurian knights, she recognizes that the assertion of one's will leads to catastrophe and that no individual can afford the high cost of absolute self-satisfaction. Further, she knows that salvation comes not because of her more virtuous attitude but through God's power. Thus she certainly dedicates herself to amending her sins and following a way of life conducive to salvation, but the operative ideas are "grace" and "mercy," and her hope lies in the eternal not the temporal. In short, Guinevere has a true sense of the meaning of Christianity.

This awareness is most vividly manifested in the Queen's new attitude toward Lancelot. From a chiding and demanding virago she has evolved into a humble and compassionate human being.[15] She is able not only to relinquish Lancelot, but also to wish him well and even to suggest that he marry and to pray for his happiness. This is a far cry from her angry indignation about his supposed feelings for the Maid of Astolot. She has thus not only reached a significant decision about the course of her own life; she also accepts the fundamental apartness of the human being. Thus she does not try to impose her own values upon others. Recognizing that each person's most basic obligation is to achieve his own salvation, she works toward this end but without trying to force anyone to her decision.

Admiration and an inspiration to emulate so pure a vision are almost inevitable, and Lancelot's response is instantaneous. He wishes to share the kind of life that Guinevere will live:

"Vnto god I yiffe a heste to holde,
    The same desteny that yow is dyghte
I will Resseyve in som house bolde,
    To plese here-After god All-myght" (3686-89)

As happily as he lived before, Lancelot now argues, "All blyve to penance I wyll me take" (3706), and he seeks a hermitage. The last parting of the lovers is a sorrowful one, but new joy awaits them. The Queen's final words, a concise statement of the theme *de contemptu mundi*, make clear how the author intends us to evaluate their decision.

> "lett vs thynk on hym that vs hathe bought
> And we shall please god ther-fore;
> Thynke on thys world how there is noght
> But warre And stryffe And batayle sore." (3718-21)

The emotional distress of the lovers makes clear how costly is their decision, the only possible one since illicit love is not otherwise reconcilable. They resolve upon a life of penance and total separation because they now regard the salvation of their souls as more important than earthly satisfactions. Here is no easy resolve of old age or waning passion, but a strenuous decision of mature and vigorous individuals who know exactly what they are doing and why.

Once again Lancelot ventures alone into the forest, that solitary place in which he always achieves self-knowledge. His way is not easy, as his lament makes clear:

> "Ryghtwosse god! what is my Rede?
> Allas! for-bare, why was I borne?" (3740-41)

A night of near madness and despair ends with daylight, and Lancelot sees a chapel and hears a bell summoning to Mass. As we might expect in the romance world, this is the chapel where Arthur is buried and the Archbishop of Canterbury and Sir Bedwere are in attendance. Lancelot explains that he wishes to serve God, "That myght-full kynge of mercy free." Requesting the sacraments, he is shriven by the Archbishop:

> That holy bisshope nold not blynne,
> But blythe was to do hys boone;
> He resseyuyd hym with wele and wynne
> And thankyd Ihesu trew in trone,
> And shroffe hym ther of hys synne,
> As clene as he had neuyr done none;
> And sythe he kyste hym cheke and chynne
> And an Abbyte there dyd hym vpon. (3786-93)

Within a short time Lancelot is joined by Bors and seven of his other knights who follow the life of penance and prayer, so that their former appearance and manner of knighthood are no longer evident.

One of the most striking evidences of Lancelot's sanctity, as with Valentine and Guy of Warwick, is a fore-knowledge of the time of his death. Very straightforwardly he acknowledges his mortality in language with liturgical echoes:

> he sayd: "bretherne, I may no lenger A-byde,
>   my baleffull blode of lyffe is bare;
> What bote is it to hele And hyde?
>   my fowle flesshe will to erthe fare." (3838-41)

His wish is that his body be taken to Joyous Gard on the morrow for burial. Lancelot's spiritual progress is contrasted with that of his companions who attempt to deny his statements by arguing that he is but indisposed and will soon recover. However, Lancelot carries out calmly his preparations for a Christian death; he calls the Archbishop,

> And shrove hym of hys synnes clene,
> Off All hys synnes loude and stylle,
>   And of hys synnes myche dyd he mene;
> There he Resseyved with good wylle
>   God, mary-is sonne, mayden clene. (3859-63)

The repetition of "synnes" here is significant, for it makes emphatic Lancelot's nature as a fallible human being who by his own self-knowledge and repentance, as well as his careful use of the sacraments of the Church, has achieved spiritual poise.

The distinctive quality of Lancelot's condition is revealed to the Archbishop, himself a faithful penitent for many years, in a dream. Like Troilus from the eighth sphere, the Archbishop laughs when he has a proper vision of transcendence:

> "here was launcelot bryght of blee
>   With Angellis xxx thousand and sevyn;
> hym they bare vp on hye;
>   A-gaynste hym openyd the gatys of hevyn;
> Suche A syght Ryght now I see,
>   Is none in erthe that myght it nevyn." (3876-81)

A glimpse of heavenly joy brings great happiness and awareness. Those so privileged do indeed laugh, both with bliss and amusement at the triviality of temporal awareness. Again Lancelot's knightly companions lack such grace, for even when told of the vision, they insist that Lancelot is alive, thus revealing their essentially worldly values. When there is no longer any doubt about the death, appropriately the Archbishop makes a first lament for the dead (3890-95) which is followed by services and a trip to Joyous Gard. The appearance of Lancelot's brother Ector leads to a reiteration of intensely personal grief. A continuance of the effects of Lancelot's self-knowledge and dedication to God is then assured when Ector emulates his way of life. Further, the loyal followers pray to Christ and the Virgin for their lord's soul's place in Heaven, so that their sense of God is heightened.

Finally, we are told that Guinevere is buried with Arthur at the chapel, which is called Glastonbury. The brevity of treatment of this detail in the narrative again indicates that Lancelot is the hero, the character whose experiences are to command our attention. To him alone is granted a distinct and memorable Christian death. Guinevere has been a major part of his life, first as his love and then as his guide to a life of penance. Lancelot's self-realization, his willing of himself to God, and his blessing of knowing the time of his death so that he is humbly and fully prepared to meet God, are very individual and independent acts. As is true of Guy of Warwick, however, this sanctification of the knight, though a distinctly individual experience, is not selfish and isolated. His grace is not merely personal; it also touches and inspires others, so that they too are drawn to knowledge of and dedication to Christian values.

Thus the stanzaic *Le Morte Arthur,* like so many of the best medieval romances, has a broadly based appeal; it contains memorable details and episodes that excite the imagination and please aesthetic sensibility. Its author best shows his literary sense and skills, however, in fusing these excellent particularities into a whole which gains its harmonious unity from a pervasive theme—a fundamental awareness of and commitment to a sense of values which is truly Christian. Not knightly prowess, generosity, and courtesy, but elemental charity, humility, and self-knowledge are the traits which distinguish the knight whose story here informs and inspires us. We are led to recognize the limitations of a value system in which personal pleasure and knightly excellence are the only goals. Lancelot fights ably, but without the easy satisfactions of an earlier, simpler knighthood. The attractions of sexual relationships are very clearly articulated in the two possible loves, but neither can provide a satisfactory commitment. The Maid of Astolot offers a love which Lancelot does not share, and the intense mutual passion of Lancelot and Guinevere cannot be accommodated because it exists outside marriage and violates other personal loyalties. The significance of such relationships is made clear both through their being stressed in *Le Morte Arthur* and by the romancer's obvious sympathy for Lancelot, the worthy man who is yet tragically impelled to erring behavior and betrayal through personal desires. Thus the dilemma is resolved, not through the married happiness that Ywain finds ultimately with Alundyne but with the renunciation of false ideals and the option for high moral value that is available when earthly attachments are transcended.

The economy of episodes in *Le Morte Arthur,* which concentrates on the two incompatible loves that provoke martial action and the limiting values of the Arthurian world that these reveal, gives an urgency and directness to the romance that has long been admired. Without digressions the story moves inexorably to the collapse of the Arthurian society. Thus rather than disapproving of Lancelot, the poet treats him with compassion as the most excellent product of a code of behavior that is doomed because its values are faulty in their extreme expectations of human performance. And this sympathy is not misplaced because Lancelot is a man who knows himself, admits his failings, amends his life, and inspires others to do the same. Again the popularity of the romance lies in its dual presentation: the excitement of the desires that so often fatally attract the human being are balanced by the comfort of a resolution that shows man and woman able to overcome their immediate limitations. The cost is the foregoing of sexual satisfactions. The emotional appeals of love sacrificed for the sake of the beloved and concomitant inspiration toward high moral purpose are sustained and exploited in popular fiction as diverse as Dickens' *A Tale of Two Cities* and Waugh's *Brideshead Revisited.* But a happier resolution in this life, with the subsequent prospect of heavenly bliss as well, was favored by readers of Middle English romance, where optimism is preferred.

Paris and Vienne

The contributions of William Caxton, both as translator and printer, to the popularity of Middle English romances are the commonplaces of literary history,[16] for they are the most varied and far-reaching. His unfailing capacity to recognize and foster the tastes of his audience can be singled out as the earliest illustration of modern exploitation of the market for fiction. An enthusiasm for religious/didactic works and romances best describes this taste, which is satisfied and perpetuated throughout the history of fiction. *Paris and Vienne* well illustrates the general characteristics of Caxton's career; as a work of his maturity the romance is one of his most aesthetically satisfying, being both brief and in very readable prose; and the young lovers are among the most attractive and virtuous in fiction.

As is not often the case, *Paris and Vienne* can be dated exactly; the French manuscripts are precise in giving evidence for 1432, and Caxton tells us that he finished his translation 31 August 1485 and printed it in December of the same year.[17] The names of the lovers indicate the precise locale of the romance, which contains details about the south of France. Pierre de la Çypede (probably Squire of Marseilles) says that he translated from Provencal, and there are arguments for a Catalan original. There is general agreement that Caxton's rendering is a fine illustration of good fifteenth-century prose, using an enriched style and presenting few syntactical confusions.[18]

The popularity of *Paris and Vienne* is, however, not a result of these stylistic excellences and use of local color, but of the crucial combination of love and adventure with moral tone which offers the excitement and uplifting that readers of popular fiction characteristically seek. The unusual success of the romance, like that of *Valentine and Orson,* has been attributed to its presentation of so many favorite episodes. MacEdward Leach argues: "it is the stock motifs that carry the story," and he lists stock situations: "the knight fighting incognito in the tournament, the religious as intermediary between the lovers, the elopement, the ring token, the exile and return theme, the rescue of the prisoner by getting the jailor drunk, the disguise of the hero, the ruse by which the heroine avoids an unwanted marriage."[19] But such riches are not unfamiliar, so that Caxton's alterations—though not vast—are notable. His distinctive additions always point to moral orthodoxy—the avoidance of negative and the increasing of positive religious references, the heightening of allusions to chivalry (especially its ceremonials), glorification of England, and praise of the aristocracy.[20] In short, the traditional, basic values are heightened to make *Paris and Vienne* even more popularly appealing as a story of worthy love.

In contrast to Lancelot and Guinevere (or the Maid of Astolot), Paris and Vienne share a legitimate and mutual love that ultimately is sanctified in marriage. Parental opposition, stemming from their fathers' arbitrary valuing of worthiness based on birth, leads to years of separation and suffering. But this time is devoted to the extraordinary maturation of the young man, repeated demonstrations of the young woman's courage and loyalty, and the gradual increasing awareness of the fathers. Thus the marriage is a harmonious celebration, a union sought both by the lovers and their parents; in short, personal feeling and social demands are satisfied, and the happy ending is achieved through charity and humility, those basic Christian virtues that are necessary for right living, as well as through religious intermediaries who advance the plot.

Like Guy of Warwick, Paris is a worthy young man who loves a girl that is his social superior. The daughter of the dauphin of Vienne, an only child conceived after seven years of continued prayer, should be given to someone of higher estate than the son of one of his nobles. Like Tristan, Paris has first appealed to his lady with music. Inevitably Paris must prove himself through tournaments; his victories are remarkable, and thus he wins the lady Vienne's love, which is freely and directly given. There is, then, none of the classic futility of unknown and un-requited passion. Parental consent is not so easily acquired: James, Paris' father, hesitates before he timidly and apologetically asks for the marriage, and the dauphin is so enraged that he banishes Paris. As are many romantic lovers, the young man is so despairing that he thinks of suicide, from which Vienne quickly dissuades him (pp. 38-39).[21] Even exiled in Genoa he is sustained by her encouragement, financial and spiritual, and he admits responsibility for her plight. Thus he is rid of self-pity and is able to go on a pilgrimage to the Holy Land, where his religious practices and beliefs are strengthened. In the process he develops resilience, so that he can live humbly when his finances near exhaustion in Egypt. Quite fortuitously he gains favor with the Sultan by his skill with a falcon, and he is in a favored position that enables him to help others and himself.

The effect of these years of experience is clearly shown by Paris' response to news of the imprisonment in Alexandria of Vienne's father, who has been sent by the King of France on Pope Innocent's crusade. Still in his luxurious disguise as a Moor and speaking this language, he exploits his advantages to aid the man who banished him, for he effects the dauphin's escape. With holy vows Godfrey promises great riches to his rescuer; he wants only freedom and a mere living for himself

(p. 68). This proud man, who has consistently played the heavy father—by refusing Vienne's choice and urging other 'nobler' suitors and by forcing his daughter to fast and remain in prison—now promises Paris, whose identity he does not know but whom he recognizes as a savior, whatever he may demand when they reach France. Paris is decorous in behavior, avoiding ostentation and continuing religious observances. He refuses the kingdom, but he does accept the offer of the lady Vienne as wife. And so clearly has he proved his personal worth that Godfrey is "meruayllously glad and Ioyous" (p. 76) to honor his promise and sanction the marriage he had so violently opposed—even when Paris' real identity is revealed. The abashed young suitor has matured into an assured knight who ultimately becomes dauphin himself. His quickness in going to his own father and mother and to his friend Edward is further evidence of the fineness of his sentiments.

Respect for their elders is characteristic of the young people in this romance, a further illustration of the admiration and gratitude that Caxton often expressed. However tyrannical the fathers, children are deferential. Vienne and Paris refuse to give up their mutual love, but they are solicitous, genuinely grieved by the pain thus caused. Paris, then, writes to his father for forgiveness before he sets out for the Holy Land, asks that his friend Edward supplant him as heir, and offers prayers (p. 45). His openness in telling his love and asking his father's intercession indicates concern to behave correctly. The favored choice is, then, away from histrionic extremes, and the attempted elopement is a last resort. Paris is also courteous to his mother when he finds his treasured things taken from the chamber where she was to keep them safe. Vienne's first request of the dauphin after they are reconciled is that Paris' father Jacques be released from prison. Edward brings his friend's letter to the worried father. In short, youth respects age in a most reassuring way. The lovers insist that true marriage can exist only with mutual love (p. 30), but this individual emotion cannot flourish in a vacuum. It is but part of the large complex of human experience which must be viewed as part of God's provenance in a defined social structure.

Vienne's relationship with her father is a strenuous one, but the same view of obligations prevails. She is adamant in her refusal to marry anyone but Paris, and she suffers many hardships for this love. She does not complain, but accepts the consequences of her choice, and short of giving in to pressures to marry, she is deferential to Godfrey.

A good example of this filial loyalty occurs in the very moving scene when she returns after her failed elopement. The dauphin

made toward hyr heuy and euyll chere / But not wythstondyng Vyenne kneled doun on bothe hyr knees to the erthe sayeng and in wepyng / Redoubted fader I see wel and knowe in my selfe that I haue mesprysed and faylled toward you / wherof I haue grete desplaysyr / Neuertheles folysshe loue hath enforced me to loue hym / whyche is wel worthy to be byloued of the moost grettest lady of the Royame of fraunce allewaye seen the noblenes that is in hym / For I wene that in alle the world is none to hym lyke ne pareylle /

And also I thynke that I am not the first that haue trespaced by semblable reasons / wherfore redoubted fader I am in your mercy / and take of me vengeaunce / suche as shal playse you / and to me chastysement / and example to other Neuertheles I wyl wel that ye knowe and that I swere by my soule / that I am as pure and clene of my body as I was that I departed fro hens / (p. 41)

Vienne's extraordinary honesty and directness here are characteristic. She is a young woman who knows her own mind and has a very sure sense of the possibilities open to her.

The flight of the lovers was thwarted because of a flooding river, which stopped Paris and Vienne long enough for the dauphin's men to catch up. Paris' response had been despair and an attempt at suicide, but Vienne stopped this disaster with arguments against destruction of the soul and precipitation of her own death, exhortations to manliness under stress, and the simple observation: "thys is noo newe thynge that the persones that lyuen in thys world haue trybulacyons" (p. 39). Then she urges Paris to flee, since she knows that her father—however angry and punitive—will not kill her, while Paris was certain to be captured, which would mean the death of both of them. She bravely reassures him of her undying love, expresses hope in ultimate happiness, and offers a diamond gold ring as token of her love. Here she is both practical and disciplined, so that the only viable solution is realized, however emotionally distressing it is. Left alone, she allows herself a good cry as preparation for returning to her father's mercy. This indicates the tensions she feels, making her vulnerability apparent, but also emphasizing her determination and strength of character.

Faced with the dual claims of a lover and a father, Vienne (like any mature woman) prefers the husband-to-be, but this choice does not destroy other claims, and it cannot be made without inevitable pain. Although the dauphin is not convinced by her sincerity and will not admit the rightness of her decision, she treats him with a care and sanity that anticipate Desdemona and from which Cordelia could learn a great deal. The reassurance about her chastity indicates that no violence has been done to the family of the dauphin of Vienne. The young woman is very conscious of her virtue; the first promise asked of Paris before they fled was "that ye touche not my body vnto the tyme that we be lawfully maryed" (p. 34), and the sleeping arrangements at the chapel insure this crucial virtue in popular fiction.

Such emphasis upon legitimate love is the more striking because the narrative so frequently makes clear that Vienne is a very passionate young woman, though one totally without sexual wiles. She is interested by the 'wooing' musicians, she speculates about admirers at the jousts, she is impatient to know her lover's identity and suffers maladies of a lover. Once Paris is identified, she is vigorous in rejecting objections to his lower station and quickly expedites their declaration of mutual love. Before each threat she is unwavering in her loyalty to Paris as her worthiest and only love. And when finally they are reunited, she delights in embraces and kisses (p. 75). Her friend Ysabel voices the anxieties about Vienne's choice, but these are quickly dispelled. Whether disguising herself as a man to elope or placing bits of rotten hen under her arms to create a stench that repels all suitors, Vienne is splendidly unpretentious and inexhaustively inventive. She has neither the egotism, the inaccessibility and strenuous demands of one kind of heroine that is typified by Guinevere and Felice, nor the agressiveness of a forth-putting damsel like Rozemond or Floripas. In short, she is unerringly attractive because she is warmly human. Capable of great love—sexual, filial, friendly— she perseveres, in spite of trials and sufferings that would lead many to despair, with common sense and unswerving belief in human and divine love. She is the triumphant heroine who is to become central in Lodge's *Rosalynde* and the dazzling virtuoso of Shakespeare's *As You Like It*. Vienne even reassures us by the obvious correctness of her choice of lover. The competent and charming feminine creature is one whose popularity is assured, and Vienne is a refreshing and pleasing contrast to women who do not possess both beauty and intelligence, or who are so worrying in their choice of weak or incompetent men.

The action of *Paris and Vienne* covers a long span of time. She is but fifteen at the beginning of the story, and twenty-five years old about halfway through the narrative. The ten-year interval is a time of learning, penance, and pilgrimage for Paris and Vienne, who trust always in God and pray for the happy fulfillment which is finally theirs. As is so often true in romances and modern popular fiction, the lovers must suffer a long separation to prove their loves and to convince the world in which they live of the rightness of their union. Had they merely eloped, there would be no comforting moral of self-sacrifice rewarded by great happiness and repeated opportunities for dedication to God and preserving social order. As lovers Paris and Vienne are very much less self-centered than most, and their love does not infringe on the rights of others or lead to a neglect of duty, but they still undergo a testing and penance. Thus strengthened, their love serves others as well as themselves; it becomes fruitful. The proper perspective is made explicit in the last summary paragraph that notes their forty years together: "and ledde a good and holy lyf / in so moche that after thentendement of somme men they be sayntes in heuen" (p. 77). Their lives are, then, inspirational in showing how happiness and goodness can be realized by strict adherence to a high moral standard.

Because *Paris and Vienne* describes both personal satisfaction and public propriety it offers a pleasing morality to the popular audience who delight in the possibility of happiness and goodness. Like Ywain, Paris has many important personal relationships—friendship, filial devotion, service to his lord—but his love of Vienne is most crucial. This, however, can be achieved only after a pilgrimage and penance, which heighten his awareness, and within a marriage that is based on mutual love and the approval of the society in which the lovers must function. The illicit pleasures of Lancelot or Tristan are a far remove from this substantial morality. Even more significant is the personality of Vienne, a young woman free of conventional role-playing which prohibited direct expression of love (except by Saracen maidens). Caxton can certainly be described as more medieval than humanistic,[22] for his belief is in Christian values with an emphasis upon the necessity for penance and muted earthly delights since man's proper goal is eternity with God. Nevertheless, the romance has more details about the realities of sexual passion and the institution of marriage that are interesting to an audience at the end of the fifteenth century. These ideas are to become prime thematic interests in writers like Shakespeare and Spenser, whose interest in the romances and enthusiasm for the sanctity of love in marriage are notable. And generations of readers of popular fiction continue to find such love affairs reassuring and uplifting, for though the very specific religious framework fades, the ideals of chastity and constancy inspire for centuries.

CHAPTER VI

THE MOST POPULAR HERO: *GUY OF WARWICK*

The romance of *Guy of Warwick* was among the most popular during the Middle Ages, as is attested in several ways: by its survival in several French and English versions (as well as separate favorite portions), by its inclusion in the Auchinleck Manuscript, and of course by Chaucer's using many of its familiar details for his travesty, the tale of *Sir Thopas*. This popularity is further indicated by its constant inclusion in the listing of romances made by Renaissance humanists; it was continually printed into the seventeenth century, and it remained in vogue until the nineteenth century.[1] Indeed there was even a new nineteenth-century prose translation of Regnault's French edition of 7 March 1525. This "long-secluded devotional" was made by Caroline Clive in 1821, kept by the daughters of the Meysey family for generations, and has only recently been published.[2]

Such sustained evidence of interest in Guy's story and popular enthusiasm for the romance has inevitably resulted in varied comments concerning its success. A. Ewert, writing about the Anglo-Norman version, advances two reasons for the six centuries of its popularity: enthusiasm for a national hero and the combination of many adventures.[3] The first is the most rudimentary of explanations and the argument for composite quality is certainly strong since this became a favored type of romance in the fifteenth century, as was noted earlier in the discussion of *Valentine and Orson*.[4] Each point is valid, but certainly additional reasons can be advanced. M. D. Legge expands Ewert's brief hint in her theory of the "Ancestral Romance" in Anglo-Norman literature. She argues that such works filled the need for an "exemplum" of loyalty in the period of the Third Crusade, and she offers William Marshall as a historical model. Nevertheless, her evaluation is essentially negative, for she finds the widespread popularity of the heroes Guy and Bevis surprising. Fame for Roland or Tristan is understandable, but enthusiasm for a champion like Guy or Bevis is "just a matter of taste, the hardest thing in the world to understand."[5]

The types of figures compared immediately suggest elements in "taste." The favored Roland deliberately forces his defeat and the death of thousands of Franks; Tristan is an adulterer whose disloyalty to his uncle occasions not only Mark's personal anguish but also strife within the king's rule. Not surprisingly such heroes are unpopular with English writers. The Middle English treatments of Roland concentrate on his combats and conversions of the Saracens Otuel and Vernagu. This material is obviously much closer in theme to the celebrated exploits of Guy and Bevis. Similarly, Tristan appears only in the brief and undistinguished *Sir Tristrem* and in Malory's comprehensive narrative, where the 'Book of Tristan' is, though crucial for purposes of analogy, recognizably the weakest section.[6] And the history of Lancelot (for whom Tristan is the archetype) in English, as was noted earlier,[7] reflects the same values. The "taste" which contributes to the popularity of Middle English romances is, then, closely tied to the moral concerns of the narratives.

The curious unwillingness to attribute the romance's popularity to anything but the most arbitrary vagaries is evident in subsequent critical comments about the Middle English version of *Guy*. Thus Charles Dunn's summary in *A Manual of the Writings in Middle English* is an epitome of the opposition to the poem's popularity: "The Middle English *Guy of Warwick* does not deserve to have excelled the superior and more original *Bevis of Hampton* in popularity. Its incidents are unduly repetitive and prolix; the Middle English adapters show no inventiveness or critical sense; and the metrical inconsistency of the Advocates version is scarcely effective. Appropriately, Chaucer in the tale of *Sir Thopas* parodies *Guy* more completely than any other romance. The extent of its appeal is presumably dependent more upon the fame of Warwick Castle than upon its literary merit."[8]

Less sweeping but nevertheless grudging, is Dieter Mehl's recent evaluation, which classifies *Guy* as a "Novel" but describes the poem as "a particularly mixed patchwork composition" that lacks a logical linkage of episodes and is not an organic whole. Yet he argues that its popularity stems from "this rather patchwork quality," but perhaps more importantly comes from the romance's presentation of Guy as a champion of God. Thus he concludes: "It is a truly exemplary and homiletic romance. Guy is not only a successful lover and a brave fighter, but he is above all a model of Christian piety and penitence."[9] Here, as in several other portions of this comprehensive study, there is a recognition of moral values, but this is consistently de-emphasized. The exemplary character, especially in the second part of the narrative, had earlier been argued by Hanspeter Schelp, who concludes: "Die antitypischen Spannungen zweischen Ritterromanze und Legende werden in diesem Werk auf dem Feld der unterhaltenden Gattung ausgetragen und für die Zwecke des Exemplarischen nutzbar gemacht."[10]

An earlier positive response to *Guy of Warwick* was briefly expressed by George Kane. He is frankly enthusiastic about the poem, and in contrast to the preoccupation with length that is notable in the criticism of Mehl and Dunn, Kane especially praises the poem's rapidity of movement. He regards this as "a highly developed special skill" which results in quick and easy reading. The poem's meaning for Kane lies in its sustaining principles: "the chivalry by which its personages govern their conduct, the decent loyalty in keeping faith and friendship by which the author clearly set great store."[11]

Thus although the high sense of moral purpose which typifies the most popular English fiction throughout the ages has been noticed in *Guy of Warwick,* there has still not been a full examination of the narrative for its literary merits and thematic values, nor a recognition of the irony in its condemnation by Renaissance humanists as immoral and frivolous and even its citation in the eighteenth century as the cause of a life of crime.[12] The neglect of *Guy* by recent scholars and critics, or its summary dismissal by many who do notice it, should be replaced by more thorough and sympathetic analysis. As the romance with greatest sustained popularity with the reading public throughout the centuries and the object of divergent critical responses—usually brief but disconcertingly absolute—*Guy of Warwick* provides the most comprehensive argument for the popularity of Middle English romance.

Typical in many ways, the narrative relates Guy's numerous adventures in foreign lands and at home, his fighting against other knights in tournaments and in treacherous betrayals and ambushes, and also his overcoming several giants and numberless paynims. Guy is prompted to such redoubtable deeds in the first half of the narrative by his impulsive wish to achieve knightly prowess and reputation so that he may win the fair Felice, who has scorned him because of his less than noble birth. The classic motivations, sexual desire and ambition, govern Guy's youth and hold audience interest. After he has won and wed the fair Felice, the remainder of his adventures stem from his wish to serve God, to behave virtuously for motives which are less selfish then his egoistic all-consuming passions, and very reassuring to those hearing his tale. The romance is, however, neither an endless series of adventures loosely held together by the presence of a single protagonist, nor a collection of feats arbitrarily explained by alternate motivations. It is an artistically realized whole, for it chronicles a man's mature life; it records his growing awareness of who he is and his enunciation of a distinctive scheme of values. In short, it is a *psychomachia*, a record of a man's continual trials and his evolving awareness. It leaves the reader with a paramount sense of the knight's human quality, not his fantastic exploits. The incredible skills and physical strength are but a part of Guy's story. Although these exotic details fascinate and thrill, providing the surface texture as in Homer's *Odyssey* or much modern fiction of adventure, they are not the substance. Far more significant is the enunciation of values, the process by which man learns what is important to his nature. This is presented not only in Guy himself, but also in the persons and episodes which are a part of his story and so frequently clarify his development.

The poet is very explicit about his purpose in the opening lines when he tells us that many adventures occurred in previous times, and he exhorts:

> Therfore schulde man with gladde chere
> Lerne goodnesse, vndirstonde, and here:
> Who myke it hereth and vndirstondeth it
> By resoun he shulde bee wyse of witte;
> And y it holde a fayre mastrye,
> To occupye wisedome and leue folye. (Caius, 15-20)[13]

Pulpit literature provides evidence that this inspirational intention was realized. G. R. Owst observes: "The poem of 'Sir Isumbras' and the 'Romance of Sir Guy of Warwick,' though scorned by the moralist

Nassington as we have seen, here show their influence at work upon the older compilers of pulpit narrations—narrations therefore that are likely to have still coloured more than one English discourse in Nassington's own day." And a footnote adds: "The tale of Guy of Warwick and the Dragon actually appears, e.g., in Felton's Sermons (cf. MS. Harl., 4, fol. 31; etc.)."[14] The fight with Colbrond was particularly popular; it appears separately in the works of a fifteenth-century moralist, John Lydgate, whose interpretation of Guy's life is epitomized in a few lines:

> Forsook the world, onknowne to euery wight,
> Of hih perfeccyoun to leven in penaunce,
> Lefft wyf and kyn, and bekam Goddis knyght (193-95)[15]

Later enthusiasm for the Colbrond episode is provided in Ellis' *Specimens of Early English Metrical Romances,* where it is the longest single quotation included.[16] The appeal of the patriotic champion, who fights an alien giant that represents a threatening nation of invaders, must always be strong; but Guy's hold upon the popular imagination is heightened through his embodiment of moral virtue as well as physical prowess.

Dozens of brief expressions of the importance of God appear in *Guy of Warwick*, many in the earlier part of the narrative when the hero is ostensibly oriented toward self-aggrandizement. Such passages are the commonplaces of most medieval literature and easily are regarded as merely formulaic. But in *Guy of Warwick* they also contribute to the narrative's fundamental purpose, which is to show the complex and bizarre episodes that occur in the life of a powerful and ambitious man who, though always involved in strenuous and potentially disastrous circumstances, succeeds ultimately in transforming these through choices that reflect an increasingly heightened sense of moral value. In the Middle Ages this sense came from a perception of the significance of God in man's life, that awareness which gives a firm and aspiring shape to human experience. Thus the audience has the satisfaction both of participating in outlandish, dangerous, and exotic activities that thrill and of feeling reassured and inspired by a hero who assimilates and controls through his recognition of a moral framework. The entire romance is pervaded by religious awareness, but this quality is intensified as the story evolves through Guy's self-knowledge. The concluding half has not only brief religious references, but also increasingly complex analyses and prayers. Finally the real climax of the narrative comes at the end: the pilgrim Guy is ritualistically led into Winchester as the procession of clergy sing the "Te deum laudamus"; the angel Michael appears to him in his sleep to name the time of his death and foretell his going to heaven; Guy transmits his vision to Felice, and then he dies and his soul is taken to heaven by St. Michael and bright angels; finally, miraculous qualities are immediately associated with Guy.

Significantly Guy does not die in battle, as do so many worthy heroes like Beowulf, Roland, Hector, Gawain, and Arthur. He is dressed and conducts himself as a pilgrim, both actually and symbolically, throughout much of the narrative. He dons knightly armor when he fights—in the latter part of the narrative for the sake of others always, not his own glory—but unfailingly he returns to his essential self, carefully shunning worldly reputation and praise and goods. In short, he is essential man. That he also happens to be an extraordinarily powerful and successful knight adds much delight and suspense to the story, but the limitations of this role are very clear indeed to Guy, as they are to the chastened Gawain after his encounter with the Green Knight, like whom Guy has made his discovery through his own perceptions. No supernatural being, or vision, reveals to Guy what he is; he learns by his experiences and his evaluations of them. Furthermore, the brilliance and clarity of his vision are communicable. Guy's friends, his king, his wife—all accept what he has learned and reveals to them. And because their lives have been touched, clarified and enriched by his understanding, they grow too. They transcend in small measure as he has in the largest sense.

This moral purposefulness of the *Romance of Guy of Warwick*, which is in accord with essential Christian thinking, is the distinguishing characteristic of the romance. Guy follows many precepts of the Sermon on the Mount; he foregoes temporality to gain eternity. His decision comes not when he is an aged or declining knight, but when he is a man at a height of power and happiness. He is known and acclaimed throughout the world and just happily married to Felice; further, there is every propspect that his life will so continue. Thus his choice of vocation is not a reflection of the tardy penitent anxiety of a dying man. Unlike artists who show St. Joseph, for example, as aged, this writer emphasizes Guy's virility. On a fine summer's day, after a successful day's hunting, much refreshed by a good meal, and in merry spirits with his

companions, he yet knows man's fundamental apartness, and he goes
alone up to a turret:

> The Contree he behelde aboute farre,
> And the skye thikke with sterre,
> And the weder that was mery and bright.
> Guy bethoughte him anone right
> That god him had so moche honour doo
> In all londes that he come to,
> That he come neuere in noo fighte
> Bot he was holde the best knyghte,
> And neuer for his creatour,
> That had doon him so grete honour.
> Sore to sighe he beganne,
> And in his mynde bethoughte him anone
> That all his lif he wolde chaunge tho,
> And in goddis seruyse he wolde him do. (Caius, 7395-7408)

Perception of the marvel of the universe, specifically an awareness of the
grandeur and immensity of creation, serves as a catalyst to Guy's awareness. Cast against the firmament his size takes on a new definition. Guy
sees his exploits not as a vindication of his own worth and an exhibition
of his power and strength but as a manifestation of God's generosity,
an honor which is God-given not man-deserved. This is an extraordinary,
almost mystical moment of self-knowledge, and Guy's subsequent
life is determined by his prescient discovery.[17] Moreover, his knowledge
affects the lives of all he meets and indeed informs the lives of those
who hear his story.

   Explaining to Felice that he is grieved because his passion for her
has led him to thoughtless and endless fighting and killing, Guy regrets
his failure to keep a proper perspective. He also recognizes that man
(woman) asks more of man than does God:

> "And if y had doon so well,
> Withoute more the haluen dell
> Hadde for goddes loue wroughte,
> That in so moche honour had me broughte,
> In heuen, for sothe, y were,
> In blisse for euere angellis fere.
> And for him did y neuere nought" (Caius, 7419-25)

The ambitious and incredible striving for excellence in knighthood that
has characterized Guy's life stemmed from false values. Certainly he has
helped many unfortunate people—as well as made a few ghastly

mistakes—through his pursuit of his occupation, and Felice herself proved a very worthy woman, not merely a vainglorious seeker. But in a Christian scheme the mere conscientious and successful adherence to duty and friends is not enough. God is more forgiving and forbearing than demanding humans, but man must deliberately choose to serve Him.

Guy's particular strength is that he reaches this conclusion in spite of all his worldly ease, the fearing respect of his enemies, and the adulation of his associates. His choice is a deliberate one, made in preference to other attractive possibilities and at some high cost. It is, briefly, not a simple or naive decision, but one which has been anticipated by much of the previous narrative and is subsequently confirmed as the narrative evolves to its climactic conclusion.

Further, the narrative is not a dichotomy. Guy leaves his wife behind, but his penance, like that of the young husband in the St. Alexis legend, is for her as well as for himself:

> "And of all the goodnesse that y doo shall,
> I graunte the euere haluendell" (Caius, 7429-30)

There is no doubt of the effectiveness of his decision, as the development of Felice's character shows. By the end of the narrative she has altered as significantly in character as he; her goodness, abounding charity, and humility are legend. Thus she is briefly united with Guy in temporality just before his death, and finally she shares his company in eternity. Guy is her mentor, but the youthful promise of her great learning and accomplishment (Caius, 59-94) is amply realized. The marriage of these two is, then, a transcendent reality, not the effect of mere coquettish and knightly games. The poet is thus not a simple and naive propagandist; his vision comes from wide experience as the sophistication of much of his narrative makes clear. There are many splendid scenes with incisive dialogue and challenging interplay of personalities.

An excellent illustration of this complex awareness comes when Duke Segyn petitions the Emperor of Germany for forgiveness. The preliminary circumstances are involved; Duke Segyn has been besieged because he accidentally slew the Emperor's nephew at a tournament, and Guy, who has helped to release Segyn, also serves as mediator. Bearing an olive branch as peace token, Guy meets the Emperor, who is out hunting, and convinces him that he should go to Arascon, where he and his men are courteously received. The following morning a repentant Segyn tries to make peace with his lord; he asks his hostages to intercede for him, and he presents himself to the Emperor in abject and public humility.

> Than he threwe his mantell of:
> Many man had grete rewthe therof.
> In his sherte he stode allone:
> For him was made mikell mone.
> To the Emperour he gooth soo,
> An Olyue boughwe in his handes twoo,
> That pees shuld beetoken betwene theim.
> All weping his wey forth he doth kenne.
> Thurgh the strete barefote he gooth
> And barehede in his sherte forsoth
> With a roope aboute his swere:
> Many man behelde him there.
> Erles and Dukes of grete valour
> For him they preide to the Emperour:
> On their knees vpon the stoon
> For him they besoughte euerychoon,
> That he wolde haue mercy of Segwyn
> For goddis loue and seynte Martyn.
> With that is Segwyn to the Chirche come,
> On his knees he felle full sone:
> Of the Emperour he besoughte mercy
> For goddis loue and oure Lady. (Caius, 2611-32)

Here the poet vividly and dramatically presents the Christian penitent. Segyn has been ostracized because of a crime against family, one which demands that the bereaved relatives seek revenge in the old primitive Germanic tradition of wergild.[18] The theme of revenge is a commonplace of different literatures; it appears frequently in the medieval romances, and this episode is one of the most striking illustrations in *Guy of Warwick*. With it the author introduces the concept of penance very early in the narrative structure.

Segyn's plea is highly effective and emotional. The slow approach to the Church, where the Emperor has gone to hear Mass, serves to create an atmosphere, to build a climate of opinion. The reactions of bystanders indicate a sympathy for Segyn, so that the poet has already evoked pity before he begins to speak. Urging the futility of his life while he must know the Emperor's wrath, Segyn with a dramatic gesture worthy (and anticipatory perhaps) of Shakespeare's Richard III brings the issue to an immediate and startling crisis when he says:

> "Here my swerde, thou take it,
> And myn hede of thou smyte,
> Or what thy wille is, doo by me
> (Myn owne Lorde, y woll it so bee)" (Caius, 2641-44)

Thus the forceful alternatives, either forgiveness or destruction, are posed; lack of charity for the Christian means annihilation.

Before the Emperor can reply, many nobles who are present advance the argument. The Emperor's son observes that Segyn has treated him kindly as a prisoner, and Duke Reyner argues self-defense as justification of the initial offense. Both, however, reinforce their pleas with a threat of violence if the Emperor is not merciful. Sir Gandimer goes so far as to say that he will start a war in revenge, and the Emperor's steward will desert him. Guy and Tirri avoid such a blatant tension of opposing moralities. Their arguments suggest a more Christian attitude —"Sir, for goddis Loue y bidde the, / On this Duke thou haue mercy and pitee" (Caius, 2687-88)—that is reinforced by the claims of fellowship and their offers of loyalty.

After this elaborate exposition, the Emperor reaches a calm and admirable decision. His judgment emphasizes the most relevant point, that forgiveness for the Christian is crucial. Further, this is the more attractive when humility, not arrogant threats, prevails.

> "All my wrathe y foryiue him
> For loue of the soules of my kynn.
> And for y him so mylde see.
> Vnderstonde nowe and herken to me:
> For he me crieth mercy withoute pride,
> Mercy he shall haue to his mede." (Caius, 2711-16)

Not revenge, but love, fortified by respect for that true sense of worth which inevitably banishes pride, has prevailed. The sophistication of argument is noteworthy, for we have here a conflict between elemental, primitive longing for revenge and the virtue of forgiveness based on charity. In short, the episode is an archetypical presentation of Christianity's salient quality.

Such essential confrontations appear in much medieval literature, which inevitably reflects the antagonisms between older and newer schemes of thought. In the *Chanson de Roland,* for example, no such subtlety occurs; revenge is much more automatically believed in, and the contradiction between basic Christianity and the ferocious behavior of many knights of Christendom is certainly not recognized by the protagonists and only just perceived by the poet.

The astuteness of perception in this scene of *Guy of Warwick* is still further evidenced in a small episode that appears in the Auchinleck Manuscript, which often has modifications that make the romance more readily accessible. Duke Otoun is infuriated by the emperor's decision and fails absolutely to understand what has in fact been decided. He forcefully urges the necessity for revenge, chiding the Emperor for so lightly treating his sister's grief and anger. Hanging, that most ignoble fate for a knight, would have been appropriate for Segyn. Such bold and vigorous "justice" would also have served a didactic purpose of warning traitors like Guy, who while alive is always a threat. Here we have a repetition of the earlier arguments with the gratuitously added insult to Guy, who proferred the most Christian plea for mercy.

The tension of ideologies is instantly clear, for Guy responds with vehemence and violent physical activity.

> Als a wilde bore he lepe him to:
> "Otus!" quaþ Gij, "þou schalt daye,
> When þou of tresoun clepes ous baye,
> Boþe Segyn & eke me:
> þou it schal abie, bi mi leute!"
> Him he smot wiþ his fest
> Amide the teþ, riȝt al in ernest. (Auchinleck, 2738-44)

Confronted with an insult, an aspersion against his knightly integrity, Guy loses control absolutely. Mercy is not meted to those who call him traitor, and he acts instantly and in a fashion that hardly preserves knightly dignity and decorum, let alone Christian forbearance. The animal imagery reinforces this idea. In church, it should be remembered, and fresh from an argument for kind charity, he lapses into a very primitive response and indeed resorts to fisticuffs.

Here we have the youthful Guy, a man who has not yet perceived fully the proper nature of his relation to God, but who clearly has a sense of the values of Christianity which are to become the essentials of his mature life. His enunciation of the concept of mercy is eloquent, but he has not yet fully assimilated this most demanding code of behavior. It is relatively easy to advocate forgiveness; it is not so easy to practice it in one's life. Guy will not tolerate an insult to the personal reputation and dignity which are so much his goals at this stage of his career. On the other hand, he does possess something of the vision which the older Emperor—who is a kind of mentor at this point of the narrative—holds firmly and indeed augments further with the marriage of Duke Segyn to his fair sister Erneborwe.

Outbursts of temper are not uncharacteristic in the youthful Guy. Indeed the poet often uses the hero's lapses into anger to make clear his human limitations and to indicate many essential contradictions between the requirements of the knightly code that is Guy's initial standard and the essential Christian values which increasingly determine his attitudes and behavior. As a striving knight he cannot allow himself to be insulted and must destroy whoever dares to abuse him. The quick jibe and taunt are commonplaces of romance, since verbal utterances characteristically precede and precipitate physical combats. As Guy's reputation increases, his sense of his own dignity forces him increasingly to kill rather than permit a slight to go unanswered. In the latter half of the narrative Guy's identity is seldom known, and frequently his opponents ironically express great longing for the privilege of fighting the "great Guy of Warwick." The pretensions of his early life are then no longer relevant, and often the hero refuses to give his name or reveals his identity only after a promise of secrecy or just as he is leaving the scene. Prior to his exercise of this modest and humble manner, however, Guy often has an opportunity to see himself forced to horrible deeds (often quite ignoble and undignified in themselves) to maintain an unchallengeable facade. The remarkable irony of the episode of Earl Florentin and his son is a good illustration of this, and the narrative here shows extraordinary literary finesse. The poet's handling of dramatic irony is memorable, and the scenes have many vivid details.

In pursuit of a boar on a hunting expedition Guy kills his quarry but only after straying from his companions and wandering into a private forest in Brittany. Recognizing his aloneness, he sounds his horn, and thus his intrusive presence is announced to the Earl Florentin, who sends his son to the hunter. This young man reproaches Guy for poaching and demands his horse. Such insult to knightly dignity is denied by Guy, who, however, offers to accompany Florentin's son and even to give his horn—if it is asked for in a nice way. The impetuous young man is infuriated by this taunt, so that he both seizes the reins of Guy's horse and strikes Sir Guy with a staff. Again we see crude and unknightly behavior stemming from preoccupation with the forms of knightly tradition and prerogative.

Guy's response is instantaneous and unequivocal:

> "Wicke man, þou hast me smite:
> þou schalt it abigge, god it wite!"
> Wiþ his horn he him smot,
> His breyn he schadde fot hot.
> "Now, lording," quaþ Gij, "þe swin þou nim,
> & alle þi wille do wiþ him.
> Na more smite þou no kniȝt:
> þat þou me smot, þou dest vnriȝt." (Auchinleck, 6805-12)

Again the hero's physical prowess is impressive, but his moral stature diminished. The boar is irrelevant, but prestige is crucial. Thus a man's life is quickly taken with self-righteousness, and Guy casually rides away with no thought except a wish for a comfortable castle in which to refresh himself. Such impatient and callous behavior is certainly characteristic of many knights in romances, but the poet of *Guy of Warwick* has created a hero for whom these simple and arbitrary rules of behavior, so rooted in worldly pride, are not adequate.

Very soon Guy meets a countryman who identifies the nearby castle as that of "þe gode erl Florentin. / Better man drank neuer win" (6829-30). Ironically, then, Guy seeks hospitality from the dignified and worthy old man whose son he has just so cavalierly murdered.[19] The courtesy of Guy's speech, which calls for God's blessing and asks refreshment "par charite," is sharply contrasted with his earlier carping and cold comment. Graciously entertained, Guy is interrupted by the sound of tolling bells and lamentation. Subtly then the poet introduces a new tone which modulates into violent grief when the body of Earl Florentin's son is brought into the hall. The irony of the moment is exquisite.

> "Leue sone," he seyd, "who slouȝ þe?
> Now wold god, þat is so fre,
> þat he were here in my beylie!
> Nold ich it lete for al Romanie,
> þat he no were anon y-slawe,
> For-brent, & þat dust to-blowe." (Auchinleck, 6867-72)

When an attendant squire identifies Guy as the slayer, Earl Florentin's response is singular. The code of hospitality is forgotten, and he seizes the nearest weapon, an andiron, to seek immediate revenge. Guy's plea of self-defense is unheeded, and a furious fight ensues in the hall. Armed with an axe, Guy defends himself and is able to kill the steward and many knights. Then he pleads the case for hospitality (6911-30). He argues that the Earl will defame himself if a guest is killed in his hall; then he requests his horse and free passage. Earl Florentin is wretched, and grief for his lost son momentarily consumes him while he laments. His sense of knightly propriety restrains him, however, and he grants Guy's request, lest he and his men be guilty of an unworthy act. Hospitality thus is given a stronger claim than revenge.

Guy is pursued, of course, and he kills two more knights before he is attacked by the elderly earl himself. The scene is, then, bizarre. The combat is hardly inspired, since old Florentin has not fought in fifteen years. Although Guy unhorses him, he spares his life and repays the hospitality of the castle by returning Florentin's horse. But the speech which accompanies this munificence is hardly courteous:

> "Her ich ȝiue þe þi stede,
> For þou ȝeue me þe mete at nede.
> In chaumber þou schust ligge stille,
> Oþer to chirche gon to bid godis wille.
> þi court ichil quite-cleym þe.
> Ded ich wold raþer be,
> Ar ich wold wiþ þe ete
> At souper oþer at oþer mete." (Auchinleck, 6989-96)

The gratuitous taunts about the futility of Florentin's effort, and the suggestion that he go to church since he can no longer survive manfully, are neither gracious nor charitable. And the childish jibe "I'd rather be dead than eat with you" is indeed ridiculous. Guy, then, is hardly an admirable or impressive figure throughout this episode. He is guilty of wholesale slaughter, and his most clearly defined antagonists are an impetuous boy and weak old man. Although Sir Guy is forced to plead hospitality in order to escape the championing knightly company—who are more likely peers—he, nevertheless, kills as many as possible once he is in an advantageous position. His many insults are not only calculated but also revealing, for they show us an incipient perception of how much he has been disadvantaged. The brief narrative account of his continuing to fight—and kill—as he makes his way back to Lorraine and his companions does not mitigate the effect. If he is hardpressed, this seems small inconvenience when contrasted to the desolation he has caused: a broken and solitary Earl Florentin buries his son.

There is quite excellent narrative writing here. There are suspense and excitement in the revealing of what has happened; the dialogue is brisk and pungent, the descriptions and details are vivid, and the basic revelations of characters and attitudes are thought-provoking. The author has given us a sophisticated literary experience. Guy emerges not as a totally faultless hero, but as a human guilty of serious failure. His anger stems from his pride and reveals a fatal lack of discipline; physical deeds of violence are reinforced by vitriolic jibes at those who are hopelessly and obviously weaker than he. Essentially Guy shows an inherent failure to realize himself; he must perpetrate horrors to sustain the dignity of the role he has chosen, and we perceive the basic inadequacy of the code which results in such grotesque contradictions. The contrast between such faltering and the assurance of the later Guy is crucial. Such scenes predispose us to the change; this particular episode is significantly the last before Guy bids farewell to Tirri and returns to England, where he soon weds Felice.

The somber qualities of this last exploit in foreign lands presage what is to follow. Guy's next feat, the slaying of the Irish dragon for King Athelstan, is the last before the achievement of his sole objective— marriage to Felice. Several changes in treatment and attitude are notable. Guy's fervent prayer significantly precedes this combat:

> "God," he seyd, "fader almi3t,
> þat made þe day & ni3t also,
> & for ous sinful þoldest wo,
> & heldest Daniel fram þe lyoun,
> Saue me fram þis foule dragoun." (Auchinleck, 7222-26)

This recognition of God's power is more heartfelt than many of his previous, briefer prayers. It is also noteworthy that God is regarded not merely as Creator and Savior, but also as the protector of fighters like Daniel. The hero's exploits are, in short, not a mark of his excellence, but indicate God's will. Evolution of the narrative is also manifest in the lengthy details of the combat: Guy is compelled to fight much more carefully and calculatingly than in other engagements, and his companions "for him were in moche drede" (Caius, 7300), and "for him bad to god almi3t" (Auchinleck, 7300). No longer, then, is there an absolute expectation of immediate success.

The alteration in hierarchy of value is clearly indicated by the narrative structure and many details of description and characterization. This is shown explicitly in two ways by the Auchinleck manuscript; the verse becomes stanzaic and the poet includes two stanzas of summary and evaluation which indicate the advantages of Guy's career. Both are means to direct popular response to the hero.

> God graunt hem heuen blis to mede
> þat herken to mi romaunce rede
> Al of a gentil kni3t:
> þe best bodi he was at nede
> þat euer mi3t bistriden stede,
>   & freest founde in fi3t.
> þe word of him ful wide it ran,
> Ouer al þis warld þe priis he wan
>   As man most of mi3t
> Balder bern was non in bi:
> His name was hoten sir Gij
>   Of Warwike, wise & wi3t.
>
> ¶Wi3t he was, for soþe to say,
> & holden for priis in eueri play
>   As kni3t of gret bounde.
> Out of þis lond he went his way
> þurch mani diuers cuntray,
>   þat was bi3ond þe see.
> Seþþen he com into Inglond,
> & Aþelston þe king he fond,
>   þat was boþe hende & fre.
> For his loue, ich vnder-stond,
> He slou3 a dragoun in Norþhumberlond,
>   Ful fer in þe norþ cuntre. (Auchinleck, 1-2)

Not infrequently the poet suggests his point of view, but there are few instances in which his judgment is more straightforward.[20] As was previously observed, the clarity of the poet's vision comes most impressively with the conclusion. Interestingly the Caius manuscript, lacking this median indication, has a fuller treatment of this incident than does the Auchinleck, which has a single stanza reiterating the virtues of Guy and explaining that his decision to serve God has led to his everlasting happiness. The statement is a direct and unequivocal affirmation of what we have observed for ourselves in the development of Guy's story.

¶Now haue ȝe herd, lordinges, of Gij,
þat in his time was so hardi,
    & holden hende & fre,
  & euer he loued treuþe & riȝt,
  & serued god wiþ al his miȝt,
        þat sit in trinite,
  & per-fore at his ending day
He went to þe ioie þat lasteþ ay,
        & euer-more schal be.
Now god leue ous to liue so,
þat we may þat ioie com to.
        Amen, par charite. (Auchinleck, 299)

The "par charite" is a nice summary of the essential Christian idea, the crucial combination of love of God and of fellow man. Guy's initial selfish love for Felice was but a brief aberration; Felice and Guy achieve significant union and eternal happiness when their love is sustained by oneness with God. To a modern, and perhaps to a medieval, reader, the harshness of separation and self-sacrifice are difficult to comprehend. But the narrative is, of course, not simply a literal story of alterations of passion and ambitions; it is an enunciation of the necessity for man to be with God. No human love, however intense or noble, is all-encompassing. To believe that it is, is to forfeit reality; and the enormous difficulty of attaining the vision of *Guy of Warwick* lies in the characteristic incapacity of human beings to perceive this truth. When all seems best with Guy, he is actually least well-placed. The worthy knight, slowly attaining the object of his love and incidentally garnering a tremendous skill and reputation as well as the adulation and fear of many, is actually less viable than the poor, unrecognized pilgrim who shuns permanent temporal involvements which will limit his capacity for true self-realization in God's service.

The crucial nature of this paradoxical situation appears not only in the explicit statements and events of the narrative. Again the writer shows his sophistication by choosing a literary technique that is appropriate; his manner mirrors his matter. No device is more frequently and brilliantly exploited in this romance than disguise. There are numerous episodes in which identity is not known or is mistaken, and the writer's command of irony shows a finesse often denied to authors of romance. Disguise here evolves from military strategy to something more profound. Thus the device of unknown identity is used with skill and distinction, so that it is not merely a rather obvious way of advancing the story, but a subtle indication of the confusions in men's minds about alternative values, the seeming impossibility for most of recognizing—let alone choosing—what is essential.

Even between the best and most loyal and devoted of friends such confusions seem to be characteristic. Guy's relationship with Tirri is one of his most significant and fully sustained personal involvements, and episodes centered upon the two men appear throughout the romance. Friendship, as with Amis and Amiloun or Ywain and Gawain, is, then, one of the individual's greatest possibilities. The poet of *Guy* often uses the device of unknown or mistaken identity; such episodes form an excellent basis for discussion. Interestingly, the most obvious example of conventional disguise is part of Guy's early attempt to help Tirri, who has treacherously been taken prisoner by the duke Otoun of Pavia. This unworthy noble plans to wed Tirri's faithful love Oisel, so that the situation is grave, and Guy's intervention is crucial to avoid catastrophe.

Although Guy's old friend Amis of Mounteyn offers him five hundred knights for a direct attack, Guy chooses to rely solely upon his own ingenuity and skill; he accepts only a much-needed horse from his friend:

> ¶Gij him di3t in a-queyntise,
> & com to Paui in squier wise.
> An vnement purchast he
> þat made his visage out of ble:
> His here, þat was 3alu and bri3t,
> Blac it bicome anon ri3t.
> Nas no man in þis world so wise of si3t
> þat afterward him knowe mi3t. (Auchinleck, 6103-10)[21]

Thus Guy's characteristic bright and excellent features are concealed, and he is able to approach the Duke unrecognized. The blackening of his features is perhaps symbolic, since duplicity is the key of Guy's strategy. He first ingratiates himself with the gift of his powerful steed. Then a deliciously ironic dialogue takes place, as the duke explains about his prisoners.

> "Ac on of hem is schaped fro me.
> Now wold god, þat alle may se,
> þat he were now in þis halle:
> Wel iuel him schuld sone bifalle.
> Wel sone he schuld an-honged be
> Wiþ gode ri3t, y telle it te."

"Sir," quaþ Gij, "who [may] þat be?
In gret periil now is he."
"Ichil þe telle," quaþ þe douk þo:
"Gij of Warwike, þat is mi fo.
Siker no be ich neuer mo
þe whiles þat he oliues go.
Ich wold now he stode þe bi."
"Sir," quaþ he, "y knowe wele Gij:
He slou₃ on of mi neye kin;
þer-fore ich am ri₃t wroþ wiþ him,
& wiþ þerl Tirri also:
He is mi dedliche fo.
þurch felonie mi fader he slou₃,
Mi broþer he deserited wiþ wou₃.
God lete me neuer ded be
Er ich him to mi wille se." (Auchinleck, 6145-66)

Guy's daring exploitation of his situation results in his being made jailor, so that he is able quickly to free Tirri. His deliberate pretense of sharing Otoun's animosity reveals not only a clever plan to free his friend but also an almost childish delight in the irony of the situation. The naive question "Sir, who [may] þat be?" (echoed by Chaucer in *The Book of the Duchess* for the narrator's tone?) is coupled with the very accurate observation "In gret perill now is he" to show masterly control. The author is incisive here, and Otoun's remarks prolong the irony when he wishes that Guy stood beside him. This prompts Guy to make flamboyant claims of enmity: his family, as well as he, have been wronged by the notorious Guy. And the last hope—to control Guy—is richly suggestive. Otoun accepts the surface value, Guy is amused by the idea of being controlled by himself, and the reader gains another suggestion about the important theme of self-knowledge and discipline. Not accidentally Guy's wish takes the form of a prayer, which is indeed answered since he dies only when his will has been curbed and he has given himself totally to God.

Here, then, we have exciting suspense, occasioned by the possibility of discovery, and a dashing display of bravado. Neat discovery of the plot by a Lombard who hears the friends talking increases the tension and provides Guy with another opportunity to confront the Duke. That Guy relishes the personal triumph over his enemy becomes even more evident as the episode develops. He sends the released Tirri to his friend Amis, so that he alone faces Otoun at the church. Well armed and mounted, Guy boldly confronts the would-be bridegroom, accuses him of treachery, and bluntly identifies himself:

"Icham Gij þat to þe speke:
3ete today y þenk to ben awreke."
þurch þe bodi he smot him anon. (Auchinleck, 6425-27)

A more economic conclusion it is hard to imagine, and Guy's exit is in the finest swashbuckling tradition, still much beloved by the cinema; he takes Oisel in his arms and gallops away. He is, of course, pursued but only briefly except by a nephew Berard, whom he stops to fight. Later in the narrative Guy encounters again and kills in Tirri's behalf this arch and treacherous enemy.

A more effective and exciting presentation could hardly be accomplished.[22] The narrative reveals its author's literary finesse in a variety of ways. As sheer suspense it is remarkable; economically we are given the situation, and the dialogue subtly underlines the irony which follows inevitably from disguised identity. Tension is heightened when the hero is overheard and thus almost exposed before he is able to carry out his plan. Guy's killing of his would-be exposer and brilliant explanation to the Duke sustain this tone. The bravado of a public and direct confrontation affords much satisfaction; Guy not only saves his friend and his lady, but he also indulges in histrionic accusation and acknowledged revenge. His escape is spectacular, and again the narrator allows a significant pause. Even though he is still rescuing the lady Oisel, confident Guy stops long enough to fight Berard in terms which please him—as a properly attired knight—but not in fisticuffs. Thus the hero triumphs in all possible ways. His physical prowess is reinforced by his verbal facility and ingenuity in planning and in his brilliant improvisation when executing the threatened plan. Especially notable are his supreme self-confidence and his egoistic delight in his own capacities. Finally, the memorable introduction of Berard prepares the reader for subsequent action and provides unity in the narrative action. A close connection between two episodes is realized by the reappearance of characters, and more importantly the thematic matter of the romance gains continuity by the repetition of the literary technique of unknown identity.

Neither Guy nor Tirri recognizes his former boon companion when they meet after long separation later in the narrative. Guy, as a pilgrim, is returning from Constantinople and encounters Tirri, who is also attired as a pilgrim, at Spire in Germany. The contrast between the two men is remarkable. In his most eloquent speeches in the romance Tirri bewails his fate, lamenting his past and lost glory and longing for death. As in *ubi sunt* expressions, Tirri vividly describes his previous well-being and his present distress. Fortitude is clearly not his virtue; he who was formerly companion of Guy of Warwick and enjoyed great wealth is now "a pore caytyfe" that hates his life when he is compelled to beg for food to sustain himself. In this highly emotional context, Guy offers to share his last penny and poses the familiar knightly question, "What is thi name?" Thus the writer gains some variety in Tirri's long monologue with incisive questions. After he has revealed his identity, Tirri continues to explain the particulars of his life, specifically that Berard has become the Emperor's steward and caused Tirri's ruin. Much detail (Caius, 9136-87) establishes the power and knightly skill of this old enemy. Released on condition that he bring Guy as his champion, Tirri has unsuccessfully sought his friend in many lands and believes him dead. Now his period of clemency is over and he expects to be hanged when he appears before the Emperor. Again the situation is urgent, and Guy suggests that they proceed to court. He has still not revealed his own identity; indeed Tirri has not asked the scruffy pilgrim who he is. Thus Guy's outward appearance totally belies his inner self. Even though the kind pilgrim's sympathetic response is so extreme that he swoons, Tirri does not grasp that Guy has an identity. The irony of Guy's explanation that this "evyll" has just come upon him is not perceived by the self-centered Tirri whose sole concern seems to be the recitation of his own griefs. Thus Guy conceals his tears from his old friend as they proceed, and the suspense is sustained.

This involved exposition is necessary, and the emotional context somewhat alleviates its potential tediousness. The author of *Guy of Warwick* is too much an artist, however, to rely upon this alone. He uses a natural plea of fatigue to gain a pause in the action. Tirri rests and sleeps, and a supernatural phenonemon occurs: an ermine creeps from his mouth and runs to a neighboring hill. Waking, Tirri tells of a dream of being with Guy and finding a treasure. From this point on, the pilgrim Guy controls the narrative; he interprets the dream and Tirri follows his instructions. They do indeed discover a magnificent treasure, but Guy is interested in only one item—a marvelous sword—and bids Tirri take all the rest. Perhaps in keeping with the experience of the supernatural, we observe now an astounding change in Tirri's values.

Previously aggrieved by his loss of material wealth, he now declares:

> "Sir, . . . at your wyll.
> Of treasure have I sone my fyll." (Caius, 9423-24)

Thus they proceed quickly to the important task of clearing Tirri's name.

As pilgrim Guy requests charity of the Emperor and is taken to court. The Emperor inquires about the pilgrim's travels and asks specifically what his own reputation is in other lands. An incisive Guy replies that the Emperor is regarded as shameful for his harsh and unjust treatment of Tirri, which stems from his believing the false steward Berard. What the Emperor thought of such blunt evaluation is never told, for an irate Berard "faryd as a wod man" (Caius, 9481) or "As a wilde bore he lepe him to" (Auchinleck, 173:2) and has to be restrained. But for discourtesy to the Emperor, Berard would shake the pilgrim's beard and thus knock out all his teeth! In fact, Guy taxes his adversary with discourtesy as he reiterates the accuracy of his statements. The irony of identity unknown is repeated when Berard wishes the pilgrim were Guy. Quickly the Emperor agrees to a combat, and he offers the pilgrim all necessary equipment and indeed entrusts him to his daughter. Thus, although Guy's identity is not known, his calm manner has been sufficiently distinguished to lead to his being nobly treated.

The importance of physical appearance is demonstrated the next morning when Guy appears for the scheduled combat.

> All they sware be seynt Richere
> That was not the pore palmere
> That toke the bateyle for to fy₃te:
> He semyd well a dow₃ty knyght. (Caius, 9608-11)

The details of the engagement are precisely given, and the effect upon the bystanders of Guy's fighting is even more startling than his appearance:

> They seyd a-mong hem eche man
> That seyen the bateyle than
> That Gye was erthly man none:
> Of hevyn he was an angell one,
> Other ellys a man of fer londe. (Caius, 9664-68)

And after Guy's victory, the watching crowds "Seyd he was a kny₃t of fe[i]r[y]-land" (Caius, 9985). Recognition becomes even more

complicated when Tirri, who has been praying in church for aid, goes to
the battle plain to see his champion:

> "Lord," quod terry at the laste,
> "That ys not the same palmere
> That was yesterday my fere.
> Thys ys a bold man and a wyght:
> Hyt semyth hym to be a gentyll kny$_3$t.
> He was lene and febull of myght,
> An hongry man and euyll I-dyght;
> This man ys wyght and no-thyng wan:
> I wene hit ys none erthly man.
> When I hym se I thynke on Gye:
> He ys full lyke hym, securlye.
> Yf Gye were not ded, I wold seye
> That this were he, be thys daye." (Caius, 9703-15)

Such confusion of identity reflects the incapacity of the human being to
recognize essentials. If Tirri not only fails to recognize his friend and
champion whom he has not seen for years, but also cannot recognize
the man with whom he spent the previous day and to whom he has
entrusted his life, then indeed his vision is unsure. Tirri is always
tantalized by the image of Guy that he keeps in his mind and heart;
actually he is so influenced by this that his capacity to recognize what is
in fact before him is lessened. Thus his return to the church and prayers
to God for succor mark a wise decision—though we are saddened that
he fails to know God's bounty when He has sent the prayed-for
champion Guy.

A final test occurs when Guy returns to the church to bring Tirri
to the Emperor. In spite of the Emperor's wish to clothe him even more
elegantly after his victory, Guy insists that he have only his humble
pilgrim's attire. Tirri's brief confidence after the supernatural sign
has not persisted, for he instantly accuses the pilgrim Guy of betrayal
and lavishly bewails his sad fate, moaning against the complicity of
men. This self-pity is repeated by Tirri when at last he appears before
the Emperor, who restores his former possessions and makes him
steward in Berard's place. Still Tirri has no idea of the pilgrim's identity
and explains that he did not believe in his ability to fight. Yet Tirri asks
the Emperor to reward him appropriately, since he was victorious, and
he also offers his own lands to the still unrecognized Guy when they
return to his estates.

> He yave hyt all to sir Gye,
> But he wold none, securly:
> Of gold and syluer had he no thought,
> But to serue god, that hym bowght.
> And he bad yeve some pore man with hys hond,
> And with that other a-store hys land. (Caius, 10142-47)

Thus Guy perseveres in his chosen anonymity, relinquishing the consolations of material bounty as well as his former reputation and companionship. As a person he has indeed evolved beyond temporal concerns.

Guy is not, however, coldly detached from his fellow man, nor has he lost all touch of humanity. When he takes his leave of Tirri, Guy chides gently:

> "Thys is Gye that thow syeste here:
> Thow owtest me to know in som manere.
> Gye of Warwyke ys my name:
> To tell the hyt ys no shame." (Caius, 10190-94)

The voluble Tirri is at last rendered speechless and swoons. He revives, then, to lament his failure to recognize all the obvious attributes of Guy and to ask forgiveness. The scene overflows with sympathy, culminating in swoons. Even after so many indications of Guy's identity and purpose Tirri still adheres to the old values, for he again offers all his wealth to Guy and alternatively begs to accompany him.

Faced with such obtuseness, Guy has no alternative but to speak forcefully, indeed didactically, in a last effort to make Tirri comprehend that he is not the same Guy of their youth, that his moral vision is quite altered.

> "My frend," quod Gye, "let be thy fare:
> Therof speke thow no mare.
> Wend thow home, as I the seye,
> And trewly serve thy lord to paye.
> Be not prowd in no manere:
> Help thy lord in hys mystere.
> Lyve in pease and not in stryfe:
> Dysheryt no man, be thy lyfe.
> Yf thow do, wyt thow well
> In hevyn shalt thow have no deale." (Caius, 10250-59)

The general principles here are simple and crucial: live in the world of men, observe right obligations, love and be just with all. Guy cites Berard as an antithetical illustration, so that his lesson has immediate relevance. For men of Tirri's ilk, the pattern of life outlined is more viable than that which Guy must follow. Salvation is certainly within Tirri's scope, for all his inadequacies and failings. His way, however, is not that of a man like Guy: "Dwell thow here; for I wyll fare" (Caius, 10268). Guy's role is, then, messianic; he not only has the vision, but also he communicates it to others. Simple recognition of his chosen moral value is not forthcoming, but always there is another opportunity for the human being to make the right choice. The hierarchal scheme is neatly indicated by the narrative writer's last detail; the devoted Oisel upbraids her husband for not having kept Guy with them—by force, if necessary.

This long section of narrative is highly significant for the enunciation of the fundamental theme of the romance, which it makes very explicit. It should again be noted, however, that the author, while furthering his argument, does not fail to keep his narrative lively. There are more long speeches than usual, but these are sharply focused by pointed interruptions of the telling nature of their argument. Further, the episode contains in addition to the supernatural dream a subsidiary part which is both highly amusing and an additional illustration of the basic theme.

After a full day's fighting neither Guy nor Berard has achieved victory, so that the Emperor stops the fighting because of darkness. Guy retires in the Emperor's care and falls into such an exhausted sleep that he does not awaken when four knights—sent by the treacherous Berard—lift his bed and cast it into the sea. Later Guy wakens, sees the stars, and finds himself adrift and far from sight of land. The situation is certainly a startling one, and Guy is nonplused. He immediately utters a remarkable prayer to God, which is a full exposition of his chosen values and his immediate circumstances.

> "God," he seyd, "all weldande,
> That stablyssheth both watre and londe,
> Lord, now thow thynke on mee;
> For I am be-trayed now, I see.
> Lord, who hath do me thys ded?
> And I fyght for no mede,
> Ne for syluer ne for golde,
> But for my brother, my trowth to hold,

> And for to delyuer hym owte of peryle,
> That longe hath bene in excile
> Also power as he may bee.
> When I hym saw I had pyte:
> Some-tyme he was a noble kny₃t.
> I wold dye for sir terry is ryght.
> For he ys now so wrechyd a wyght,
> A-geyne Berrarde I toke the fyght." (Caius, 9776-91)

Guy accepts his present situation with great calmness, although he instantly realizes that he is in grave danger. He wonders who has betrayed him, but he expresses no desire for vengeance. His principal concern is for his friend Tirri, whom he sought to aid because of a sense of justice and pity for his sad plight. Guy would have been very pleased to help successfully his friend, but he simply recognizes, "I am ded, well I wote" (Caius, 9800). Thus he merely prays that the traitorous Berard will receive his just due.

The restraint and unselfishness of Guy's manner are exemplary. He is faintly curious about why he has suffered misfortune, for he has a true sense of his right behavior. He does not, however, either question or resent his fate; he accepts it calmly without apprehensions and personal regrets. His only concern is for others, that Tirri will be cleared of unjust accusations and that a vicious man like Berard will not escape justice. How vibrantly different, then, is Guy from Tirri—and indeed most humans. His sure self-knowledge and commitment to proper values give him great reserves of strength. Even the almost certain prospect of a solitary and bizarre death does not ruffle his sense of identity, his dignity as a sound human being. Similarly, imminent rescue is not cause for undue excitement and emotion. Guy's first words are to reassure the startled fisherman that he is not an evil spirit, and then he plainly describes what manner of man he is:

> "My frend," quod Gye, "have thow no dred;
> I leve in god, so god me spede." (Caius, 9818-19)

Having identified himself, Guy makes a simple and straight-forward request for assistance that again emphasizes his life in God:

> "My dere frend, helpe me nowe.
> For the trouth god yave the,
> Att thys tyme have rewth on me." (Caius, 9839-41)

The fisherman safely takes Guy ashore and restores him to the Emperor so that the combat can continue. Guy was unhesitatingly identified by the fisherman, so that proper treatment was immediately forthcoming. The certainty of Guy's manner and statements left no possibility for another alternative.

Before concluding this discussion of the use of identity and irony in the romance of *Guy of Warwick*, we should notice one final passage in which Guy describes himself somewhat ambiguously. King Triamour is to fight a gigantic black Saracen, but he gains leave to get a substitute. Thus he sends Earl Jonas, under threat of death to himself and his family, to find Guy. The youthful English knight of wide reputation cannot be found, but the matured Guy as an unknown pilgrim agrees to help. So pathetic is his appearance that the King believes he must have served a bad lord. Guy's reply to this remark is a discriminating judgment of his past circumstances and his present values.

> "Sir," he seyd, "well may fall,
> But myn Estate know ye not all.
> For soth, I was in good servyse;
> My lord me lovyd in all wyse.
> For hym I had grete honoure
> Of kyng, prince, and maydens in bowre.
> But for a lytill hastines
> All I loste, both more and lesse.
> Tho went I fro my contree,
> Tyll it myght after better be.,
> Thus will I walke in this estate,
> Tyll his wrath be abate.
> When he and I accordyd be,
> Then will I wende to my contree." (Caius, 8015-28)

Obviously Triamour accepts a surface meaning, that this is a description of the temporal lord of the poorly clad man who was once a knight. Guy is, of course, describing his relationship with God. God gave him many honors, but Guy's casual acceptance of this magnificence led to his loss, for well he knows that he did not properly serve God when all his activities were centered upon his self-advancement. Thus he has changed to an outwardly poor appearance as a kind of penance, and his faith leads him to know that when all is well God will call him to Heaven, for the sureness of his vision is clear. Here, however, Guy's spiritual conviction is still essentially private, so that he limits his explanation to an ambiguous comment. Again the narrative writer demonstrates his literary sophistication by presenting subtle and complex characterization.

Guy's restraint, though it is now inherent in his new vision, perhaps also owes something to the character of Triamour. However, Guy's assertion of his faith increases in boldness as the scene develops. He agrees to undertake the battle "With helpe of God in trinite" (Caius, 8035) or "þurch Godes help & our leuedi" (Auchinleck, 86:5). When Triamour answers with a Saracen prayer— "Mahoun me helpe & turmegaunte" (Caius, 8042)—Guy is blunt and absolute in his rejection of such belief and forcefully asserts his Christian point of view.

> "Nay," quod Gye, "but Mary is sonne,
> That for vs on the rode was done:
> He be myn helpe for his mercye;
> For I the sey well sikerlye
> That Mahoun hath no poweste
> Nother to helpe the ne me." (Caius, 8043-49)

Certainly the king is convinced by Guy's assertions, for he promises as tokens of victory not only that his Christian prisoners will be released, but also that Christians will be well treated in the country and statues raised in God's honor. Actually there is a paucity of precise references to Saracen belief[23] in this romance, so that Guy's effective implementation of Christianity in this scene is the more striking. Part of Guy's motivation in helping Jonas has been his explanation that his sons will be devoted champions of the faith (Caius, 7879-80). Moreover, the narrative contains many subsequent references to make of this combat an explicit meeting of Christian and pagan forces. "But god of hevyn thynke on Gye, / He shall be ded full hastilye" (Caius, 8177-78).

Guy precisely identifies his opponent Amoraunt; "Hit is the devyll, it is no man" (Caius, 8153).[24] Imaginatively, then, the giant is presented as a formidable adversary; in Christian terms he is inhuman, lacking (as a Saracen, denying the Incarnation) that essential awareness which assures eternal salvation. In contrast, Guy's resources are not only Christian but also encompass much of the strength and goodness of antiquity. His helmet was Alexander's, and his sword was Hector's. Thus the discriminating Christian is singularly well armed; having abstracted the finest in earlier pre-Christian knightly tradition, he uses it as a reinforcement of his own strengths. In contrast, Amoraunt's sword once belonged to Hercules (who is traditionally damned) and was "put in water of hell." Certainly Guy has urgent need of every possible resource, for Amoraunt is a terrifyingly effective combatant, whose gods are exactly opposed to Guy's belief. Where the Christian knight prays to God and the Virgin (Caius, 8195 ff., 8236 ff., 8490, 8511, 8525), the pagan giant addresses his requests to Termagant (Caius, 8302; Auchinleck, 126.2). And after the combat the duality of belief is still explicit (Caius, 8580 ff.). Further, Amoraunt cleverly appeals to Guy's Christian charity (he even addresses him as "thow crysten manne," Caius, 8324) to stop the fighting to allow him to have a drink, which gives him renewed strength. Later, when Guy asks the same privilege, his language reflects his essential value:

> "Do me now that ilke deed
> That I dyd to the in thy nede" (Caius, 8408-9)

Refused, he first appeals, "For Iesu crystes love" (Caius, 8417), and then asks Amoraunt as "an hende knyght" to honor their agreement. Thus Guy gives precedence to Christian appeal, not knightly claims.

Such values are, however, irrelevant to Amoraunt; only victory is significant, so that concerns with moral and social codes are of no interest. He says bluntly, "I will to no covenaunte stonde" (Caius, 8431). A dramatic contrast thus exists between these antagonists, and this is the more compelling when Amoraunt explains that his absolute striving for victory stems from his wish to marry the sowdan's daughter. He declares, "I haue her desyred ouer all thyng; / I shall her haue, that mayden yenge" (Caius, 8440-41). So might have spoken a younger and insensitive Guy of Warwick, seeking honor so that he might win fair Felice. In several ways, then, the narrative writer pointedly indicates the essential differences between the two knights, and he unifies the romance through repetition of a motif. Curiosity about the real identity of John (Guy) so piques Amoraunt that he offers to let him drink if he will reveal his true name. Again this crucial question of recognition is highly significant, as will be discussed later. Amoraunt's determination to win increases when he knows that he is actually fighting Guy of Warwick, the man he most fervently longs to kill; thus he heeds not at all the niceties of promises, and the fighting continues at a furious rate.

The combat proceeds in a very interesting manner. With a prayer, "kyng of heven," quod sir Gye, / "But I drynke shortly I dye" (Caius, 8490-91), Guy rushes out into the dangerously deep river.

> But Iesu cryste hym ther did kepe,
> Out of the water shall he not wyn:
> He was nere-hand a-drownyd thereyn.

> Now ys Gye in a stronge case:
> The water ouer hys gyrdyll was.
> Hys hed he smote depe down:
> The water was ouer hys crown.
> Ameraund smote at hym so wele,
> That in the water he made hym knele.
> The water hym closyd all abowte:
> He held hym in, he myght not oute.
> When sir Gye had dronke I-nough
> He thankyd god, and faste he lough.
> Vp he sterte as kny3t full stoute:
> The water ran down hym all abowte.
> He shoke hys hed, & seyd full ryght:
> "I-thankyd be Iesu full of my3te.
> In cold water hast thow bathid me,
> But name had I none for the." (Caius, 8499-8517)

Neatly, then, the narrative description balances the ways in which the two knights drink. Being given no courtesy or ease by the pagan, Guy has to struggle, just as his Christianity is continually tested and must be reasserted through continued survival. Much of the description of Guy's immersion suggests the sacrament of baptism, a counterfoil to Amoraunt's claim of restorative gifts. Thus the supernatural powers of the two ideologies are suggestively juxtaposed. But Guy's recognition of the effect of the water is more dignified and calm (less, however, in Auchinleck than in Caius). His laugh, like that of Troilus from the eighth sphere, expresses an agreeable but modest confidence, and he is quick and careful in his expression of thanksgiving to God and Christ, Who are his sources of strength. Even his charge of treachery in his opponent is somewhat muted and left until later. Finally, the last lines of Guy's speech are ambiguous, though minimally they suggest his apartness and independence and increase our awareness of the richness of the narrative's texture.

The physical details of the conclusion of this fight are vivid and heroic, and in several ways they recall the *Beowulf*. Not only is there the partial fighting in water, which was noted above, but also a kind of dismemberment, which is later repeated in the Colbrond episode; Amoraunt loses first his right hand, then his left arm, and finally his head. Such physical desecration is typical in romance narratives; indeed many details of physical brutality appear consistently in *Guy of Warwick* to reveal skill in writing colorful and vigorous descriptions that reflect the realities of medieval warfare. Here, however, the engagement is unusually prolonged as Amoraunt is reduced to an animal state when at the end he "rode as an hound" and charged against Guy.

Once the victory is his, Guy withdraws quickly and modestly from the scene, Triamour expresses his thanks profusely, frees and rewards Earl Jonas as promised, and offers the champion many gifts, land, and repute. Guy's comments are notable. He answers Triamour's first effusiveness with a prayer:

> "Sir," he seyd, "graunte mercy!
> God yow yeld and seynt marye." (Caius 8584-85)

Guy's terse reply to the offer of a place in his kingdom and the appellation "trew kny3t" is somewhat ambiguous:

> "Sir," quod Gye, "graunte mercye!
> I will hit not, sekerlye." (Caius, 8594-95)

Obviously this may be read as a simple refusal of material rewards and temporal position, but also there is the suggestion of Guy's devotion to God's will, not his own. The Saracen Triamour does not press his case, and Guy withdraws to Jerusalem (again perhaps symbolic) with Earl Jonas.

Throughout this episode Guy's identity has remained unknown except briefly by Amoraunt whose ironic wish to fight this English knight is realized. At his first meeting with Triamour, Guy, it will be recalled, spoke ambiguously both of his past and his present circumstances. He admitted that he was an English knight and commented ironically about his identity. Thus to the King's vigorous abuse of Guy and Herhaud was given a simple reply:

> "Syr," he seyd, "full well know I Gye
> And herrawd also; both two
> I know hem well, so must I goo." (Caius, 8004-6)

But, as has been noted, niceties of courtesy do not concern the pagans whose interests are expediency. Earl Jonas, however, is a more sensitive individual; this is illustrated by his deep concern for his fifteen sons, movingly expressed in a manner reminiscent of Ugolino (Caius, 7873-83). It is thus not surprising that he wants to know the identity of the man who has saved him and his family and also furthered the cause of Christianity.

Unlike some of those whose causes Guy has championed, Jonas has maintained a charitable concern for the pilgrim as well as anxiety about his own cause. When first the pilgrim (Guy) offered to undertake the fight, Jonas had tried to dissuade him for fear that Amoraunt would slay him. Very significantly it was Guy's exposition of his trust in God that convinced the old man of his acceptability:

> "Pylgryme," quod Gye, "dred the nowght.
> God ys myghtfull as I haue thought.
> Many on hath provyd to do me scathe,
> And with hys eyen lokyd wrathe,
> Yet fled I neuer fro hym in bateyle.
> I tryste on god, he wyll not fayle.
> Though thow thinke I feble be,
> He ys of so grete poweste,
> That he may yeve me grace & myght
> To slee that Geaunte in that fyght." (Caius, 7923-32)

Here we have one of the more precise expositions in the romance of essential Christian belief, and the passage is a memorable expression of Guy's awareness. He recognizes fully how hazardous has been his existence, and he acknowledges completely that God is responsible for his successes and his safety. Thus his trust, his faith in God, is absolute; God's power makes all things possible. After this moving and brilliant explanation Earl Jonas offers no further objections. Indeed he simply agrees with Guy's essential argument:

> "Sir," quod the pilgrym, "graunt mercye!
> He that was borne of that mayd marye
> Yelde the or thow be dede." (Caius, 7933-35)

There is, then, complete accord between these two in their understanding of Christianity. Guy's dedication to the service of others is paralleled by Jonas' wish that he and his sons may also further Christian belief; not accidentally both appear in the guise of pilgrims.

The narrative episode ends harmoniously when the two men speak again with mutual understanding. Earl Jonas repeats the conventional formula, but his request to know Guy's identity is phrased in terms of their belief.

> "Sir kny3t," he seid, "what is thi name?
> Tell me, so god shyld the from shame.
> Thow seydyst that thow hy3tyst Iohn:

> Thow hast a nother name, be my crown.
> For that goddis love I byd the
> That sufferd deth vppon a Rood tre,
> And with his preciouse blode vs all dere bow3t,
> Tell me thi name here, and lye me nought."
>
> Then seyd Gye, "thow shalt here,
> For thow me askyst in feyre manere.
> Loke thow discouer me neuer more,
> For grete shame and synne yt wore.
> Gye of Warewyke ys my name:
> Though I be pore thynketh me no shame." (Caius, 8606-19)

Here we have both Guy's acknowledgment of his identity as the renowned knight and his wish to preserve his anonymity. His poor appearance is thus not cause for concern or shame, but part of his chosen way. He does not hesitate, then, to reveal his identity to one who will comprehend his choice of values.

But even Earl Jonas does not possess the detachment from the world that is Guy's gift and understanding. He is awed by the reputation that has attracted so many, with esteem or animosity. Thus he too makes the characteristic offer of his lands and fealty; for "Ther was neuer on erth a trewer kny3t" (Caius, 8629). Modestly Guy offers his thanks and good wishes, but affirms that he must go his own way:

> "Sir, much thanke and graunt mercye!
> To well ye quyte me my servyse
> Yf that ye dyd in such a wise.
> To my land now will I fare:
> Haue good day for euer-mare." (Caius, 8641-43)

The poise of sentiments is exemplary here. Guy can admit his worldly reputation but gently restrain those who seek his excessive glory. Yet he pursues without interruption his chosen vocation, satisfied and strengthened by serving others. In the Triamour-Amoraunt episode the narrative writer explicitly emphasizes the confrontation of Christian with non-Christian through precise references and symbolism. The essential structure and the techniques of unknown identity and irony are repeated to sustain the basic theme of the romance. The episode abounds in exciting and exotic details. Suspense is carefully maintained and increased by subtle irony, and lively and incisive dialogue gives vigor to the narrative. Thus the author of *Guy of Warwick* fully uses the resources of his medium; he combines a skillful exposition of his moral purpose with literary skill.

The last combat in the romance of *Guy of Warwick* reiterates these carefully developed intentions. It repeats many of the techniques used in earlier episodes, but introduces certain new details which make it a transcendent expression of the vision of the romance as well as a summary of its previous excellences. There is a kind of hierarchal structure in the grouping of Guy's most significant exploits. Thus Guy's aid to Tirri against Berard on the continent follows the Amoraunt encounter, which is the most impressive of his battles in the Holy Land, and his last combat is on his native soil when he fights to defend England against the African giant Colbrond, champion of the Danish king who has invaded the country and threatens Athelstan and his land.

The dominant theme of Christianity which has become increasingly potent as the romance narrative developed is here given its most comprehensive exposition.[25] As soon as Guy lands in England he hears that Athelstan has assembled at Winchester all his nobles and clergy for three days and nights of fasting: "That god shuld send a man of my3t / That with the Geaunt durst fy3t" (Caius, 10306-7). He learns further that Herhaud is out seeking the stolen Reinbrun and that Earl Rohaunt is now long dead. Here also Guy is told of the many works of charity performed by his wife Felice, who prays constantly for her husband. Thus immediately the penitential theme is established, and not by Guy alone. The poet suggests a significant dimension of Athelstan's personality, and he also gives very important information about the development of Felice's character, which in some ways parallels Guy's own.

Athelstan's appeal to his lords is moving, but none dares to fight Colbrond. Eloquently we are told:

> They stode all styll, and lokyd down,
> As a man had shavyn ther crown. (Caius, 10394-95)

Thus the king has cogent reasons for regretting the absence of Guy, and he fiercely accuses himself of responsibility. In terms now very familiar to us, Athelstan argues that his failures in generosity and urging have led Guy to leave his native land. Thus again we see the complete incapacity to understand the motives and methods of Guy's chosen way and the near impossibility of human comprehension of total dedication to God. But, unlike Tirri, Athelstan does not indulge in endless self-pity and lamentation. Sensibly he retires at night to bed and:

> All that ny3t he lay wakand,
> And euer to god fast byddand
> That he wold hym send a man
> That durst do the bateyle than.
> And god of hevyn for-yate hym nou3t:
> As he lay in grettest thou3t,
> An angell come to hym full ry3t,
> And spake to hym from hevyn bry3t:
> "Sir kyng," he seyd, "slepyst thow?
> To the me sent my lord Iesu:
> He had the aryse vp full erlye,
> And to the church thow wend in hye.
> A pylgrym shalt thow fynd thare;
> Take hym home with the full yare.
> Byd him for love and charyte,
> And for god, that dyed on tre,
> That he for the take the bateyle,
> And so he wyll, with-owten fayle."
> With that the angell went awaye:
> The kyng gan wake, hyt was nere daye. (Caius, 10434-53)

The king's faith in God is explicit. He has found no succor among his people, but he does not despair. To the man with such trust, God is always helpful. Again we find a variation of the theme of man's apartness and need for self-determination. Athelstan's dream is a vivid enrichment of the romance. Dramatically the narrative is expanded by the angel's dialogue, which also provides additional statement of basic belief. The emphasis here is upon Christ's aid to man, and instructions to the sleeping man are very precise and fully reassuring. England's champion will appear in the guise of a pilgrim and appropriately will be at church. Significantly, aid is to be requested "for love and charyte"—precisely the motivations which have determined the course of the second part of Guy's life and which must be the basis for true Christian living.

Without a moment's hesitation Athelstan accepts the validity of his vision. Fully confident, he goes early to the church to await the promised pilgrim. His manner is gracious and firm; and although pilgrim Guy is at first hesitant, he quickly accedes to the king's request. Athelstan exactly fulfills the injunction of the angel when he asks aid:

> "Pylgrym," he seyd, "for charyte
> And for hys love that dyed on tree,
> Helpe me now in this mystere
> With thy strenght and thi powere." (Caius, 10476-79))

Simply the extremity of England's situation is made clear; the fearsome strength of the adversary and the nation's vulnerability are explained and Guy's assistance is asked, "for charyte" and "for hys love . . . That made both ny3t and daye" (Caius, 10492-93). No embellishment mars the concise simplicity of the request.

After Guy's pleading that he is too weak to undertake the battle, Athelstan and his lords humble themselves before the poor pilgrim. However, their kneeling is not to Guy of Warwick, great knight and champion, but to a pilgrim champion promised by an angel. Thus they ask help "For Goddus love & for hys sake" (Caius, 10505) and "for charyte" (Caius, 10509), repeating the only cogent justifications for seeking aid. Before such argument Guy's hesitancy disappears; his acceptance is made in the same terms as the petitioners' request, "With help of god wyll I not fayle" (Caius, 10513); and Athelstan replies, "He shall hym slee with goddys my3t" (Caius, 10519). In every detail, then, Guy's last temporal challange is defined by his dedication of himself as a servant of God. Love of Him, and thus of fellow man, is the true charity, so that the appeals to pity, human vanity, or justice recede into comparative irrelevance.

A precise description of Guy's armor balances neatly the elaborate details of Colbrond's black appearance (Caius, 10590-623), but scarcely interrupts the narrative before the romancer further elaborates his essential theme. As has been noted in earlier episodes, Guy characteristically makes increasingly more explicit his dedication. Here his prayer before battle expresses his knowledge of God's omnipotence with a plea for both immediate victory and everlasting salvation.

> "Lord," he seyd, "for thy passyoun,
> That savyd danyell fro the lyon,
> Save me from thys fowle fellown,
> And bryng me to savacioun,
> And lend me grace thys ilke daye
> (For well I wot that thow maye)
> To slee thys thefe with myn hond,
> And fro trowage save thys lond."
> He blyssed hym with hys hand ry3t,
> And on hys sted he lepyd full ry3t:
> Styrrop ther towchyd he none;
> Therof spake many one. (Caius, 10560-71)

Again the directness of expression is notable. This is more effective than the obvious elaboration in the Auchinleck Manuscript, which adds

Lazarus and Susannah to examples of those God has helped and modulates into a prayer to the Virgin (252). And the author's detail of Guy's physical resources (his leaping onto his horse, fully armed, without even the use of a stirrup) is that aesthetic enrichment of which we have seen so many illustrations. Such poise and delicacy in physical movement reflect the hero's sane balance, and they contrast boldly with the vigor and violence, the sheer brutality of the actual fighting. Momentarily Guy is disadvantaged when he breaks his sword, and he turns to God for understanding:

> "God," he seyd, "that dyed on Rood,
> Why am I thus evyll dyght?" (Caius, 10691-92)[26]

A taunting Colbrond asks him to surrender, and even offers riches and amnesty, but Guy's faith is unshaken:

> "Nay," quod Gye, "so must I thee,
> Shall I neuer traytoure bee.
> Though my swerd be now a-wey,
> My lord of heven, that well maye,
> May make the lose thy good brond,
> That ys so sykur in thy hand." (Caius, 10712-17)

He boldly asks for one of Colbrond's battle-axes to continue the fight. With a pagan prayer, "So me helpe tormagaunte" (Caius, 10723; Auchinleck 266:7 "Apolin"), Colbrond refuses. Thus Guy uses the oldest of ruses to get an axe: he says that someone is behind Colbrond, and then darts past unscathed while his enemy is momentarily off balance. The battle is then short-lived, for it goes just as Guy had hoped:

> As Iesu cryste ys wyll was
> (Hyt was a full wondre cas),
> The swerd in-to the ground gan dryve
> Thre fote also blyve,
> And, as he after the swerd gan stoupe,
> Gye hym smote with-owte dow3te. (Caius, 10748-52)

So exact a realization leaves little doubt that Guy is indeed God's servant, one whose faith leads to a successful fulfillment of unselfish purpose. Quickly, as with Amoraunt, Guy smites away the giant's right arm and then his head—and thus England is saved from the Danish threat.

In joy and triumph Athelstan and his lords lead Guy to the capital.

> They toke sir Gye hem amonge,
> And led him forth with mery song
> To wynchestre, the good cyte.
> All the clergy of that contree
> Comyn with gret precession,
> And ladden sir Gye into the town.
> And as they gan hym homward bryng,
> "Te deum laudamus" gan they syng.
> Gye on-armyd hym there,
> And askyd hys slavyn and no more. (Caius, 10776-85)

This ritualistic treatment of Guy is in keeping with the purpose of the romance. The "Te deum" is well chosen, for it is one of the most exquisite and best loved of medieval hymns, and its characteristic terminal position at matins (the midnight office), repeated in liturgical plays, appropriately suggests that Guy's story is near conclusion. Such great respect is, it will be recalled, given to the victorious champion promised by the Angel in Athelstan's dream; Guy's identity has remained unknown, and there have been no ironic hints of identification in the narrative.

As is traditional, and understandably human, Athelstan fervently desires to know the name and story of the man who has saved England. Thus he repeats those most compelling reasons for acceding to his request.

> "Mercy, pylgryme," quod the kyng,
> "For hys love that mad all thyng,
> And shed hys blod on the rode
> For mannus sowle and mannus good,
> Tell me now, with-owt blame,
> Where were thou bore, & what ys thy name?" (Caius, 10806-11)

Guy does not hesitate; the servant of God has no inclination to refuse what is asked in His name. But the wary hero, anxious not to become embroiled in a confusion of values, is even more circumspect than is his custom. Perhaps disconcerted by his ceremonial treatment, or wishing to avoid the complications of royal fealty, Guy readily agrees—but on condition that Athelstan alone accompany him to the edge of town. Kings, like lesser nobles, fail to grasp the true significance of Guy's vocation: Athelstan falls upon his knees, implores Guy to stay, and offers half England as an inducement. Like others whom Guy has aided, Athelstan is gently tutored, so that he abides by Guy's wishes, letting him go and keeping his secret.

Nearing the end of his pilgrimage, Guy approaches Warwick and the last test of his unknown identity. He mingles with the poor at the gates of the city and is anxious lest he be recognized. Not even his faithful wife Felice, who ceaselessly and tirelessly performs charitable works while she prays for her husband, sees beneath Guy's outward, wretched appearance. But Felice, who in the beginning of the romance disdained the love of handsome and esteemed youthful Guy because he was not worthy of her, now completely and freely shares with an unknown wretch, offering him comfort and sustenance for as long as he shall live. Like Guy, Felice now lives by a truly Christian scheme of values; she does not judge and demand, but gives freely of all her resources even to the apparently least distinguished of God's creatures. There is perhaps no more dramatic illustration of the influence of Guy of Warwick's dedication to God. Previously imperious, Felice is now mild and gentle, truly compassionate in attitude and manner. Indeed Guy's promise to her that half his penance would be to her benefit seems amply fulfilled.

While the author of the romance is thus clearly advancing this argument, he again shows his delicacy and literary skill. The control and restraint of this scene are admirable, for we have a judicious selection of detail to make clear the character of the new Felice. Several earlier references have prepared us for the change, and the single scene of her daily charity provides evidence of her reputation. Thus the author prepares for their last meeting, when Guy is dying and their love is eloquently expressed. This alone would have been too intense a moment, so that we have a gradual development. Also once Guy has seen her, he need have no further apprehensions and can approach his death with supreme detachment and confidence. Felice's well-being is assured, for she has achieved a way of life and prayer that is the feminine analogue to Guy's masculine knighthood for God. Her mode is less exotic, less violent and varied, but nonetheless meaningful.

One problem of the romance of *Guy of Warwick* in very human terms is the hero's seeming abandonment of his wife, as we saw in *Ywain and Gawain*. This scene, like their last meeting before Guy's death, mitigates the apparent callousness. (Similarly, Guy's request that Athelstan behave kindly to his son Reinbrun allays some misgivings.) The love of the two is not lessened by their long separation; indeed the whole point is that it achieves true realization through their mutual dedication to God. The romance is not concerned with domestic bliss; it is an argument of the essential aloneness of every human being and the necessity for his seeking his salvation by giving himself to God in Whose name he unselfishly serves his fellow man. The cost of choosing the essential Christian values before immediate, personal, temporal satisfactions is inevitably high; and this the romance makes clear by Guy's foregoing an easy and pleasurable life with loving Felice and his admiring friends. Their mutual enjoyment of eternal life—which the narrative dramatically suggests in the last moving scene—is the chosen alternative; in short, it would have profited them nothing to gain the whole world and lose their immortal souls. Inevitably the two levels of meaning—symbolic and personal/literal—do not always coexist with perfect east in this romance. The individual demands of both are often apparently at variance, just as they are in Chaucer's *Man of Law's Tale* or *Emaré.* What is impressive is the literary skill of the author of the romance of *Guy of Warwick* in so minimizing these seeming contradictions that he gives us a narrative which, while never straying from its exposition of the basic theme of Christian value, yet remains an exciting and believable story of the romance world. His sustained control is remarkable, and the gradual intensification of details as well as the more explicit and fuller exposition of thematic material result in a work which is both meaningful and delightful to read.

Clearly, then, the ultimate purpose of the romance is to indicate the significance of Christian values and to suggest, by means of a worthy knightly protagonist, how each human being must strive to free himself of egocentric concerns and submit himself and his will to God. As is so often the case in medieval romance the knight is not to be read merely as an exceptional human, or even as a realizable ideal, but rather as a symbolic absolute that serves as a guide and inspiration. Guy of Warwick's every act and deed are not praiseworthy, for the romance leaves him with convincingly human attributes and limitations that allow him to function as a possible model and also to serve as a protagonist with whom we can empathize as well as respect.

The richness of Guy's experience and the consequence of his difficult but worthy choice of Christianity are made abundantly clear at his death, that time when each man is judged. Throughout much of the narrative Guy has ventured abroad, first to perform valorous deeds for his own reputation and then to serve God by helping his fellow men.

Significantly he returns to Warwick, to his origins, to die; and indeed he spends his last days at a hermitage in a forest. There he has the daily benefits of Confession and Mass, and his solitary contemplation is not interrupted by the discreet service of a single page. Exact knowledge of the time of one's death is indeed rare, but this privilege is given to Guy:

> ¶In slepe as Gij lay ani3t,
> God sent an angel bri3t
> > Fram heuen to him þare.
> "Gij," seyd þe angel, "slepestow?
> Hider me sent þe king Iesu
> > To bid þe make þe 3are;
> For bi þe ei3tenday at morwe
> He schal deliuer þe out of þi sorwe,
> > Out of þis warld to fare.
> To heuen þou schalt com him to,
> & liue wiþ ous euer-mo
> > In ioie wiþouten care." (Auchinleck, 284)[27]

As in several other crucial scenes, the narrator uses the appearance of an angel in a dream to convey important information. Guy is allowed the advantages of knowing exactly when he will die, so that he can be indeed prepared. Significantly the angel contrasts temporal existence (sorrow) with eternity (joy without care). Even in this marvelous episode, the author preserves his hero's balance between human and ideal traits. Guys asks the angel whether he is God. Thus subtly is indicated the almost overwhelming radiance of the angel and Guy's own mortal limitations of perception. Michael's reply precisely explains:

> "God hath me to the now sent:
> Thow haste hym seruyd with good entent.
> I shall come with angellys bryght,
> And bryng thy sowle to hevyn ly3t." (Caius, 10847-50)

Heaven is the reward of the man who serves God "with good entent"; so simple is the design of being. For this gift, a worthy man is indeed grateful:

> Gye thankyd god of hys present.
> He was glad of hys maundement
> That god of hevyn hym had sent. (Caius, 10852-54)

Guy is, exceedingly happy that he will die; it is for such a death then that he has prayed; and although no one ever deserves heaven, Guy has behaved as well as he possibly could and not forgotten the limitations of his own nature.

While he lives Guy retains, however, some temporal concern. His last attention to a worldly matter appropriately involves Felice. He sends his page with news of his death, instructions for his burial, and a promise of their eternal union: "And sey her she shall dye in hye / After me full hastylye" (Caius, 10885-86). Their last meeting is movingly described, and so complete is their understanding that no words are necessary between them.

> She arose & went in Ryȝt drerly:
> Her lordys body she lay ther bye.
> Rewly she cryed ther for the nonys,
> And he lokyd on her onys:
> He kyssed her fayre & curtesly;
> With that he dyed hastylye.
> Ther dyed the noble knyȝt sir Gye:
> Seynt Mighell was ther full redye
> With mercy song of angellys bryȝt,
> And bare hys soule to hevyn lyȝt,
> And presentyd hit to the hevyn kyng;
> Ther shall he be with-owte endyng. (Caius, 10937-48)

It is hard to imagine a more appealing death; there is no physical suffering or spiritual anguish and fear. A serene and loving tone is pervasive. In his last moments Guy of Warwick's two loves, Felice (human and temporal) and God (divine and eternal) are perfectly harmonized. Perhaps the "mery song of angellys bryȝt" best epitomizes the feeling of the scene, and the sure confidence and faith of the narrative reiterate the poet's vision.

There is, of course, lamentation for the death of Guy of Warwick, but this is comparatively restrained in the tradition of expressions of grief.[28] The writer does not linger over the reactions of Felice and the many other mourners. Instead we are again given a single memorable detail:

> God dyd hym there gret honoure:
> Fro hym ther cam a swete sauoure. (Caius, 10959-60)

Such preservation from immediate physical decay is a mark of God's bestowing of honor and indicates the excellence of the deceased. So Hector and Lancelot, to choose diverse examples, are distinguished in other medieval romances. To understand the impact of this singular quality, we need only recall the amusing, but pointed, detail of a medieval painting of the raising of Lazarus: a wary bystander holds his nose. Formal lamentation is appropriately left to Athelstan, King of England, who fully summarizes the career of the 'flower of Christendom' (Caius, 10975-11022). Again the calmness of tone is notable. Guy's exploits are precisely recalled, and his humility and modesty are noted. But there is no excessive bewailing; no violent anxieties about the loss and future of those remaining mar the beauty of the scene. As far as is possible in this world, Guy has set all in order, so that his death is accepted as part of the harmony of existence. The extraordinary quality of Guy is almost immediately evidenced after his death when his body proves impossible to move. Thus Felice explains her husband's choice of a burial place and avows her determination to remain with him until she joins him in death.

Felice's manner of life does not markedly change; she prays constantly for Guy, continues her works of charity, and prays soon to join her husband in death. After forty days the promise is fulfilled; Felice dies quietly and is buried beside Guy:

> To-gedyr be they in company
> In blysse: I hope to oure lady,
> Iesus graunt vs so to do,
> That we may com hym to.
> Lordyngis, now have ye herd
> Of Gye of Warewyke, how he fard,
> And how he led hys long lyfe
> In bateyle and in stryfe,
> But euer he lovyd hevyn kyng
> Moste ouer all thyng,
> And god hath a-quyt hys mede,
> In geste as ye have herd rede. (Caius, 11060-71)

The relevance of the story of Guy of Warwick is, then, very clear. Love and service to God lead to salvation, which every man should seek. This passage, like the opening and concluding lines of the romance, is not a mere formula, a conventional obeisance to God that is required of the medieval writer. It is an explicit and concise statement of the purpose which the author of the romance of *Guy of Warwick* has made consistently and vividly clear through his literary finesse in skillfully presenting Guy and other characters and the episodes in which they figure.

This centrality of intention and purpose gives cogency to the romance, though it does not exclude other details. The narrative is a rich mine of interesting particularities. It abounds in details of knightly customs; for example, the shame attached to hanging, exact descriptions of armor and fighting techniques, the courtesy of providing a visiting knight with rich and elegant clothing, the frequent games of chess, vivid pictures of marriage and other ceremonial feasts, the formal manners of tournaments, and so on. Similarly the writer uses the conventional abrupt shifts in narrative; an unpretentious indication that he is going to shift the story line suffices without apology or explanation.

> Nowe of a straunge case y shall you telle,
> Ye that woll a while duelle. (Caius, 1267-68)

satisfactorily marks a new beginning. At best there is a certain charm to these many beginnings:

> It was vpon a somers daye,
> Guy oute at a wyndowe laye
> As he lay, come ridyng a knyghte. (Caius, 4939-41)

Memorable, quotable poetic expressions are not the strength of this romance, though there are effective descriptions—of a storm or armor, or the exact death blow, for example. The narrative is, moreover, very readable as the many adventures are unfolded with ease and vivacity. Further, the dialogue is characteristically very lively and straightforward, sometimes devastatingly witty, and always pointed and direct.

Reasons for the long and widespread popularity of the romance of *Guy of Warwick* are thus easily advanced. The narrative utilizes many of the same details and archetypes, the love of exotic places and characters, the excitement of suspense, the clash of good and evil, which are to be found throughout many other such narratives. And it also reveals its author as a man who possessed subtle understanding and delicate sensibility as well as considerable technical skill. He knew the effectiveness of dialogue and the possibilities inherent in a conventional technique like unknown identity, and thus he exploited fully such resources. Judged by these criteria *Guy of Warwick* has distinctive excellences, and naturally was a favorite of the genre. However, its claims to our concern go far beyond historical interests, for the romance has a sureness and singleness of purpose which give it a remarkable quality not simply as an aesthetic piece but also as the clear vision of an ordered mind. That the vision is of the essential nature of Christianity, the relation man must recognize between the temporal world and eternity, is its great value and relevance to the medieval reader at least. But the purity of conception and the skill of the writer in executing his design through carefully and gracefully evolving argument also make the romance of *Guy of Warwick* an admirable intellectual and aesthetic achievement, a culminating illustration of the distinctive Middle English romance.

CONCLUSION

The vitality of recent interest in medieval studies is evidenced by the abundance of criticism written in the last twenty-five years, and examination of less familiar texts seems inevitable. The universally admired *Troilus and Criseyde, Sir Gawin and the Green Knight*, and Malory have been the focus of much of this enthusiasm, and each year sees some expansion of interest in romances that had survived only as children's stories or been preserved as antiquarian documents. Yet most of the Middle English romances here presented have received very little critical attention, and they represent only a fraction of the available texts.

The history of critical attitudes toward romance suggests some striking points. First there is their enormous popularity through several centuries with a wide audience indicated by surviving manuscripts and early texts as well as catalogues that list favorite heroes. With the humanists came objections to medieval romance because it transforms classical ideals through the introduction of new ideas, most obviously a view of human nature that is defined by Christian belief. Antipathy toward such medieval distortions of classical material led to academic antagonism that was reinforced by Reformation prejudices against the popish origins of medieval romance. Nevertheless, many of the greatest English writers—Shakespeare, Milton, Bunyan, Dr. Johnson—continued to read the romances, to express enthusiasm for their stories, and to employ romance modes in their own writings, just as Dickens, Tolkien, and T. H. White have in later centuries. And all reach a large audience. The contrast in attitudes is provocative; what is decried as immoral and distracting by one group is esteemed by another as inspiring and refreshing.

From the eighteenth century onwards, the circumstances become ever more complicated. Antiquarians seek out the old texts, which also survive in simplified forms, and writers of both prose and verse exploit the form. The proliferation of novelistic 'romances' down to the present day has inevitably resulted in some narratives that lack distinction—in much the same way that the original medieval romances vary in interest and quality. The extremes of sentiment and sensation often dominate without the firm sense of moral purpose which gave distinction to the romance in the Middle Ages. The mysterious and monstrous are exploited by Romantics in ways which prove quite different from what we encounter in *Kyng Alisaunder, Robert the Deuyll, Amis and Amiloun,* and *Guy of Warwick,* where the threat of the bizarre is contained by a world in which all things are not only possible but readily accommodated without ultimate harm to accepted values. Trials, suffering, misunderstandings, the inexplicable, grotesque distortions— all are controlled in God's universe; and the protagonists of romance proceed through an infinite variety of experiences that culminate in their greater understanding and provide inspiration for all who know their stories. Very rarely is there a lingering, an indulgence in the emotional and peculiar for its own sake. Episodes are designed to further the awareness of the knights and ladies, and their less sentient followers, so that they achieve the crucial knowledge of human limitation which results in necessary humility and dedication to something beyond this world. Thus participation—by both protagonists and audience—in the attractions and delights of earthly life is made safe through its subordination to an awareness of eternity. This combination of indulgence to human frailty with the reassurance of ultimate sanctity is unfailing in its popular appeal, as studies of more recent fiction make clear. But academic readers, like their prototypes among Renaissance humanists, tend to be uncomfortable with this happy harmony of apparently contradictory possibilities.

The recognition and acceptance of this equipoise has characterized recent critical evaluations of the literary gems of romance from Chrétien and Wolfram to *Troilus and Criseyde* and *Sir Gawain and the Green Knight,* where high moral purpose is rendered acceptable when clothed with extraordinary literary finesse. My examination of representative texts from the huge supply of largely unnoticed Middle English romances indicates an unexpected similarity in argument and intention and also, I think, provides evidence of greater literary excellence than has been recognized, though this is an even more controversial assertion. An aesthetic for medieval audiences has not been defined, so that critical evaluations are rather more tenative than with later works. Of course, the aesthetics of modern audiences do not show unanimity, but reflect varying sensibilities as well as the quality of the work being considered. The complexity of responses is clear in judgments by the critics and popular audiences of modern users of Arthurian materials as diverse as Alfred Tennyson, T. S. Eliot, Charles Williams, C. S. Lewis, T. H. White, and Mary Stewart.

Middle English romances are largely unified through their concern with ultimate values and their combination of high moral purpose with frank indulgence in the bizarre and more disturbing possibilities of behavior, and in portrayal of the inexplicable; they are less integrated through particular aspects of formal composition. With the stylistic emphasis that has characterized English literary studies since the impact of New Criticism, it is not surprising that Middle English romances have attracted little enthusiasm. This is especially true of huge works, like *Guy of Warwick* (which has even been labeled as laughable for its excesses) and *Valentine and Orson,* but even the shorter pieces have been faulted for metrical inadequacies. Although some of these negative responses are legitimate, they have been too widespread and constricting.

By focusing on "popularity" a much needed re-evaluation can be made. My approach to the narratives themselves has been to define their fundamental argument, that larger scheme of value into which everything fits. What emerges very clearly is the place of the romance in the English moral tradition. A. B. Taylor's conclusion is worth quoting as an epitome: "Perhaps it was this strong ethical flavor that ensured the popularity of medieval romance until fairly recent times."[1] But he perpetuates the idea that romance is appropriate to modern children who respond to the same qualities that "appealed to the child-like mind of our ancestors." This kind of modern sophistication is both inadequate and inappropriate.

When a modern commentator has less confidence and a lack of firm belief, the romance mode appears to him too simple and unconvincing, an escapist trifle that cannot be talked about as serious literature. This stance is one taken by many modern critics, and the crudities of later popular fiction have contributed a disreputable aura, while demonstrating how essential to popularity some stabilizing ideas remain. The single audience of earlier periods has also been replaced by increasingly polarized groups. Even at the beginning of the nineteenth century William Thoms could preface his collection with confidence about his audience: "the Editor determined upon laying before the public in a form accessible alike to *the man of letters,* and *the general reader,* a collection of the more rare and interesting of these productions."[2] As the work of Leavis and Hart makes very clear, no modern editor could presuppose a comparable identity and harmony of interest and response. Thus even medievalists are apologetic, especially American ones who cannot rely on the residual sympathies of historical interests. But this is not so surprising when we see the old humanist prejudices perpetuated; there are many inexpensive editions of classical authors but a paucity of medieval (and especially Middle English) romances, to be found in the racks of university bookstores. A correction of this imbalance is not likely to occur quickly or easily, but clearly I hope for some shifting of balance in favor of the romances. What is required for an acceptance of this view is an extension of the sympathetic response given to the "literary gems" (such as *Sir Gawain and the Green Knight*) to the less widely recognized examples; the firm moral principles that give intellectual distinction are the same, and the artistry is less discrepant than is usually assumed.

Many contrasts can be shown between the medieval and classical ethos. Nowhere is this more precisely indicated than in the *lai* of *Sir Orfeo*; quite simply the story has a happy ending. A cheerful resolution is insisted upon. Strange things happen, loss of the beloved and of noble position, journey to the otherworld, tests of marriage, friendship, and feudal loyalty—all are experienced, but the poet concludes:

> þus com Sir Orfeo out of his care.
> God graunt ous alle welle to fare. (603-4)[3]

Penetration into and graceful escape from fairyland is achieved, husband and wife are happily united, order in the kingdom is not only maintained, but the rightful ruler is loved and supported by a faithful steward who serves honorably in his lord's absence. Here there is very little (but note lines 387 ff. which give the lie to arguments that the minstrel is unaware) of the sinister fable of Orpheus, for the vision is not rooted in unhappiness and frustration of man's wishes and ambition, but in a quiet harmony that comes from perseverance in adversity and tolerance of human failing and the unexpected and unusual. Further, "the beauty of it loses nothing by the course which it has preferred to take, the happy ending."[4]

It is fashionable, particularly among modern intellectuals, to argue that such hopeful, cheerful attitudes reflect lack of intelligence and moral responsibility, that mere happiness is not allowable. But even a cursory glance at the quality of medieval life reflected in its literature provides ample evidence for awareness of misery, if one requires this recognition. The world of romance provides an alternative, and as Tolkien has argued these narratives satisfy the fundamental desire for the "consolation of the happy ending." *Eucatastrophe* (Tolkien's word for this happy quality) provides "a catch of breath, a beat and lifting of the heart, a piercing of joy and heart's desire."[5] Undeniably there is escapism, but this is not unworthy, an easy avoidance of the unpleasant. Rather its hopefulness makes possible arduous yet sustained endeavor, for the unbearable and inexplicable are accommodated rather than merely decried and indulged. By admitting human and worldly limitations and stressing belief in eternity, Christianity is the most cheerful of religions because of confidence in God's mercy and ultimate generosity. Permeated with these values, Middle English romance both inspires and reassures. Thus it is not surprising that the genre's popularity lasted for centuries; but it is regrettable that high moral purpose, exciting adventures, and comforting reassurance however appealing are no longer rated as serious literature. Yet the persistence of these popular elements even in modern thrillers, which so aptly can be defined in existential terms, attest their primordial quality. Thus any reader who recognizes literature as a significant human record should cultivate a less supercilious attitude to popular literature; this is both appropriate and necessary.

NOTES

CHAPTER I

[1]See J. Burke Severs, ed., *A Manual of the Writings in Middle English 1050-1500,* Fascicule 1 (New Haven: Archon, 1967), which is described as "preempting the field, overshadowing its competitors . . . quite the best bibliography available for any literary field or for any separate genre" by Lillian Herlands Hornstein, in "Middle English Romances," in *Recent Middle English Scholarship and Criticism: Survey and Desiderata,* ed. J. Burke Severs (Pittsburgh, Pa.: Duquesne Univ. Press, 1971), pp. 58-59. Helaine Newstead gives a broad, general definition of the material in *A Manual,* pp. 11-12.

[2]*Principles of Literary Criticism* (New York: Harcourt, Brace & World, 1925), p. 203.

[3]*Medieval Secular Literature* (Berkeley and Los Angeles: Univ. of California Press, 1965), p. 21.

[4]Matthews, p. 6.

[5]Dieter Mehl, *The Middle English Romances of the Thirteenth and Fourteenth Centuries* (London: Routledge and Kegan Paul, 1969), makes this clear in his "Introduction," pp. 1-29. Ojars Kratins, "The Middle English *Amis and Amiloun:* Chivalric Romance or Secular Hagiography?" *PMLA,* 81 (1966), 347-54, considers one part of the problem. Reinold Hoops, *Der Begriff 'Romance' in der mittelenglischen und frühenenglischen Literatur,* Anglistiche Forschungen, 68 (Heidelberg, 1929), provides classified meanings and uses of "romance" and references to these in primary texts from the earliest appearances through the mid-seventeenth century. D. M. Hill, "Romance as Epic," *English Studies,* 44 (1963), 95-107, provides a comprehensive view of the two forms and conflicting judgments. Paul Strohm, *"Storie, Spelle, Geste, Romaunce, Tragedie:* Generic Distinctions in the Middle English Troy Narrative," *Speculum* 46 (1971), 348-59, illustrates the problem. N.E. Griffin, "The Definition of Romance," *PMLA,* 38 (1923), 50-70; Dorothy Everett, "A Characterization of the English Medieval Romances," in *Essays on Middle English Literature,* ed. P. Kean (Oxford: Clarendon Press, 1955), pp. 1-22; Derek Pearsall, "The Development of Middle English Romance," *Medieval Studies,* 27 (1965), 91-116.

[6]Eugene Vinaver, *The Rise of Romance* (Oxford: Oxford Univ.

Press, 1971), p. 138.

[7]Hornstein, *Recent Middle English Scholarship,* p. 69.

[8]*The Tragedy of Arthur* (Berkeley and Los Angeles: Univ. of California Press, 1960), pp. vii-viii.

[9]Charles Moorman, *A Knyght Ther Was* (Lexington: Univ. of Kentucky Press, 1967), is not unusual in his high praise of Chrétien and *Sir Gawain and the Green Knight* and dismissal of other romances, e.g., pp. 7, 76-77. See Mehl, pp. 1 ff., for a brief summary of the key issues and history of criticism. A. B. Taylor, *An Introduction to Medieval Romance* (1930; rpt. New York: Barnes & Noble, 1969), is startling in its relentless and aggressive assertion of French superiority. Note especially pp. 148-53 for unmitigated condescension and pp. 163-64 for niggling praise of the English. M. A. Gist, *Love and War in the Middle English Romances* (Philadelphia: Univ. of Pennsylvania Press, 1949), makes useful comparisons; note particularly pp. 8-9. Adelaide Evans Harris, *The Heroine of the Middle English Romances,* Western Reserve Univ. Bulletin, No. 31 (Cleveland: Western Reserve Univ. Press, 1928), p. 6, argues for the superior morality of English versions. James H. Blessing, "A Comparison of Some Middle English Romances with the Old French Antecedents," Diss. Stanford 1960, specifically compares key examples to demonstrate strengths of the English adaptations. Margaret Schlauch, *English Medieval Literature and Its Social Foundations* (Warsaw: Panstwowe Wydawnictwo Nankowe, 1956), p. 175, points out differences in stress on action and adventure, less overrefinement, and emphasis upon conventional morality. John Speirs, *Medieval English Poetry, The Non-Chaucerian Tradition* (London: Faber & Faber, 1957), pp. 108 ff., argues English excellence in "mythic" awareness. A. C. Baugh, "The Middle English Romance. Some Questions of Creation, Presentation, and Preservation," *Speculum,* 42 (1967), 17, notes the more substantial quality of the English audience. W. P. Ker, *Medieval English Literature* (1912; reissued London: Oxford Univ. Press, 1969), pp. 59 ff., early urged recognition of distinct English virtues. There is incidental support of the English versions in *The Middle Ages,* ed. W. F. Bolton (London: Sphere Books, 1970); see esp. Rosemary Woolf, "Later Poetry: The Popular Tradition," pp. 263-77, and D. J. Williams, "Alliterative Poetry in the Fourteenth and Fifteenth Centuries," pp. 121, 126. Since writing this, I have seen John Stevens, *Medieval Romance* (London: Hutchinson Univ. Library, 1973) which

makes an eloquent plea for the genre as narrative fiction with universal appeal, using similar broad categories of human experience, but stressing French originals and English "literary gems"; Maldwyn Mills, *Six Middle English Romances* (London: Dent, 1973) includes less familiar texts.

[10]See, e.g., W. T. H. Jackson's general survey in *The Literature of the Middle Ages* (New York: Columbia Univ. Press, 1960). Note especially his conclusions, pp. 154-59.

[11]Ronald S. Crane, *The Vogue of Medieval Chivalric Romance during the English Renaissance* (Menasha, Wis.: George Banta Publishing, 1919), and "The Vogue of *Guy of Warwick* from the Close of the Middle Ages to the Romantic Revival," *PMLA,* 30 (1915), 125-94; A. C. Baugh, *A Literary History of England* (New York: Appleton-Century-Crofts, 1948), pp. 178-79; Mehl, pp. 257-62; Hoops, pp. 69, 73. Arthur Johnston, *Enchanted Ground, The Study of Medieval Romance in the Eighteenth Century* (London: Athlone Press, 1964), discusses fully the scholarly recovery of the material and in an Appendix lists the MSS known to Percy, Warton, Ritson.

[12]Q. D. Leavis, *Fiction and the Reading Public* (London: Chatto & Windus, 1932), and James Hart, *The Popular Book* (Berkeley and Los Angeles: Univ. of California Press, 1961).

[13]*English Books & Readers 1475 to 1557,* 2nd ed. (Cambridge: Cambridge Univ. Press, 1969), p. 9.

[14]*Recent Middle English Scholarship,* p. 56.

[15]Mehl, pp. 17, 21.

[16]Mehl, p. 10. An Appendix, pp. 257-62, helpfully summarizes the material. See also Baugh, "Middle English Romance," p. 9; Karl Brunner, "Middle English Metrical Romances and Their Audience," in *Studies in Medieval Literature in Honor of Professor A. C. Baugh,* ed. MacEdward Leach (Philadelphia: Univ. of Pennsylvania, 1962), pp. 219-27. A handy general survey is Beverly Boyd, *Chaucer and the Medieval Book* (The Huntington Library, 1973).

[17]Mehl, p. 262. The persistence of religious interests in popular fiction is documented in two studies of eighteenth-century novels: J. M. S. Tompkins, *The Popular Novel in England 1770-1800* (1932; rpt. Lincoln: Univ. of Nebraska Press, 1961), and John J. Richetti, *Popular Fiction before Richardson* (Oxford: Clarendon Press, 1969). On the loss of idealism but use of rhetoric see Dieter Schulz, " 'Novel,' 'Romance,' and Popular Fiction in the First Half of the Eighteenth

Century," SP, 70 (1973), 77-91.

[18]Bennett, pp. 1-18. See also W. F. Bolton, "The conditions of Literary Composition in Medieval England," in *The Middle Ages,* pp. ix-xxxvi.

[19]Bennett, pp. 4-5. Schlauch, *English Medieval Literature,* p. 176, describes the expanding economics in production of romance. R. W. Ackerman, "English Rimed and Prose Romances," in *Arthurian Literature in the Middle Ages,* ed. R. S. Loomis (Oxford: Clarendon Press, 1959), p. 483, suggests that most English romances were not written at the bequest of patrons since so few dedications appear.

[20]*Anglo-Norman Literature and Its Background* (Oxford: Clarendon Press, 1963), Ch. VII, pp. 139-75.

[21]Legge, p. 175. A fuller discussion of clerical involvement appears in M. D. Legge, *Anglo-Norman in the Cloisters* (Edinburgh: Edinburgh Univ. Press, 1950). The list of manuscript locations is especially useful, pp. 113-16.

[22]"The Auchinleck Manuscript and a Possible London Bookshop of 1330-1340," *PMLA,* 57 (1942), 595-627. See Schlauch, *Medieval English Literature,* p. 176.

[23]L. H. Loomis, p. 601.

[24]Ibid., pp. 605-6.

[25]Ibid., pp. 607-8. Cf. Baugh, "Middle English Romance," pp. 1-31, who argues a semi-learned, generally clerical, origin, address not to aristocratic audience, and appeal to higher instincts.

[26]*The Medieval Library* (Chicago: Univ. of Chicago Press, 1939), p. 645.

[27]Bennett, *English Books,* pp. 7-9; H. S. Bennett, "The Production and Dissemination of Vernacular Manuscripts in the Fifteenth Century," *The Library,* Fifth Series, I (1947), 167-78; Schlauch, *English Medieval Literature,* p. 191, also admits the romances' "currency among wider groups in the population than the top layer of the aristocracy," even though her particular viewpoint forces a judgment of limited appeal for a genre intended to entertain aristocratic listeners. See Baugh, "Middle English Romance," p. 17.

[28]"Epilogue to Book III," in *The Prologues and Epilogues of William Caxton,* ed. W. J. B. Crotch, EETS, OS 176 (1928), 7-8.

[29]*English Books,* pp. 10-11; Crane, *The Vogue,* pp. 3-4.

[30]*Caxton and His World* (London: Andre Deutsch, 1969).

[31]Blake, p. 194.

[32]Ibid., p. 216.

[33]Ibid., p. 194.

[34]*Fiction and the Reading Public,* p. 69. Hart, *The Popular Book,* makes the same observation; see pp. 66, 169, 193.

[35]Crane, pp. 9-10.

[36]Bennett, *English Books,* p. 149.

[37]Ibid., pp. 149-50.

[38]Crane, *The Vogue,* pp. 13-15; Margaret Schlauch, *Antecedents of the English Novel 1400-1600 (From Chaucer to Deloney)* (London: Oxford Univ. Press for Polish Scientific Publishers, 1963).

[39]Hart, pp. 15-17.

[40]G. C. Britton, in reviewing Donald B. Sands, *Middle English Verse Romances* (New York: Holt, Rinehart & Winston, 1966), notes that he was "so careful not to claim too much for the genre, however, that some of his readers may wonder why they are bothering with the romance at all," *The Year's Work in English Studies,* 47 (1966), 82. Cf. Mehl, p. 12, for the cautionary attitude.

[41]For a typical refutation of the romantic distortion of medieval authors into 'spontaneous' and 'learned' and a case for the unified reading public, see Marc Bloch, *Feudal Society,* trans. L. A. Manyon (Chicago: Univ. of Chicago Press, 1961), I, 94-96. Richetti describes novels popular when published (1700-1734) but not admired by subsequent periods, and he notes the difficulty for "modern fastidious researchers" (p. 11) in responding to such works and the relative insignificance of style and structure in providing "the basic pleasures of fiction" (p. 176). More precisely, Schulz, pp. 87-91, distinguishes sensationalism and rhetoric of romance used to veil the excesses in exploitative 'novels.' Thus he argues more continuity than rejection of romance in the novel tradition of Defoe, Richardson, Smollett. Tompkins is dealing with similarly forgotten material in the period 1770-1800. Leavis, pp. 34 ff., gives the most fully documented account of shifting reading tastes and capacities through the nineteenth century and into modern times.

[42]E. Faral, *Recherches sur les sources latines des contes et romans courtois du moyen âge* (Paris: E. Champion, 1913), and *Les arts poétiques du XIIe et du XIIIe siécle: recherches et documents sur la technique litteraire du moyen âge* (1924; rpt. Paris: Libraire Honoré

Champion, 1962). For a summary of the arguments see Jean Misrahi in *The Medieval Literature of Western Europe,* ed. John Fisher (New York: New York Univ. Press for Modern Language Assoc. of America, 1966), pp. 154-59. The basic argument of origin in the schools was made by W. P. Ker, *Epic and Romance* (1896; rpt. New York: Dover Publications, 1957), pp. 323 ff. *Speculum Vitae* appears in *The Percy Folio MS,* ed. F. J. Furnival and J. W. Hales (London, 1867-69), II, 510, and the *Cursor Mundi,* ed. R. Morris, in EETS, OS 57 (1874; rpt. 1961), 8-13. Positive expectations appear in *Laud Troy Book,* ed. J. E. Wülfing, EETS, OS 121 (1902), ll. 11 ff.; John Gower, *Confessio Amantis,* ed. G. C. McCaulay, EETS, ES 82 (1901), VI, 875 ff.; *Barbour's Bruce,* ed. W. W. Skeat, EETS, ES 11 (1870), III, 435 ff. Incompatibility between medieval and Renaissance thinking is advanced by Rosemary Woolf, *The English Mystery Plays* (Berkeley and Los Angeles: Univ. of California Press, 1972), pp. 312-23. She advances the same argument for the decline in popularity of this great portion of Middle Enlgish literature. "The long shadow of Renaissance contempt has lain across the mystery plays almost until the present day" (p. 323).

[43]Quoted in Crane, *The Vogue,* p. 12.

[44]Chapter XXV, *Essays by Michel Lord of Montaigne,* trans. John Florio, Everyman's Library (London: S. M. Dent, 1910), I, 187. William W. Ryding, *Structure in Medieval Narrative* (The Hague: Mouton, 1971), p. 18, cites this passage as the earliest negative response in France.

[45]Ed. Edward Arber, *English Reprints* (London, 1869), p. 19.

[46]Roger Ascham, *The Scholemaster,* ed. Edward Arber (London: Constable, 1927), p. 80.

[47]Quoted in Crane, *The Vogue,* p. 13.

[48]*Literature and Pulpit in Medieval England,* rev. ed. (New York: Barnes & Noble, 1961), p. 9.

[49]Crane, *The Vogue,* p. 20.

[50]Ibid.

[51]Crane, "Vogue of *Guy,"* pp. 161-67.

[52]Arthur Dickson, *Valentine and Orson. A Study in Late Medieval Romance* (New York: Columbia Univ. Press, 1929), pp. 280-98.

[53]Blake, p. 204; Crane, "Vogue of *Guy,"* p. 187.

[54]In *John Milton Complete Poems and Major Prose,* ed. Merritt Y. Hughes (New York: Odyssey Press, 1957), p. 694. See also *Paradise*

Lost, Book IX, ll. 27-37.

[55]Helen Gardner, *The Business of Criticism* (Oxford: Oxford Univ. Press, 1959), p. vi.

[56]A classic essay is Mark Schorer, "Technique as Discovery," *Hudson Review,* 1 (1948), 67-87. The opening paragraph establishes the point of view: "Modern criticism, through its exacting scrutiny of literary tests, has demonstrated with finality that in art beauty and truth are indivisible and one. . . . Modern criticism has shown us that to speak of content as such is not to speak of art at all, but of experience; and that it is only when we speak of the *achieved* content, the form of the work of art as a work of art, that we speak as critics." An extreme development of such attitudes is epitomized by Susan Sontag, *Against Interpretation* (New York: Farrar Straus & Giroux, 1966), who praises art as an "adventure in sensation" (p. 11), prompting "something like an excitation, a phenomenon of commitment, judgment in a state of thralldom or captivation . . . an experience of the form or style of knowing something, rather than a knowledge of something (like a fact or moral judgment) in itself is what the artist is aiming at" (pp. 21-22).

[57]A neat summary of the characteristic medieval view that literature exists for its meaning, to instruct, appears in R. H. Green, "Classical Fable and English Poetry in the Fourteenth Century," in *Critical Approaches to Medieval Literature,* ed. Dorothy Bethurum (New York: Columbia Univ. Press. 1960), pp. 118 ff.; see also Schlauch, *English Medieval Literature,* pp. 120 ff.; Elizabeth Salter, *Piers Plowman, An Introduction* (Oxford: Basil Blackwell, 1962), pp. 6, 24, 28. J. W. H. Atkins, *English Literary Criticism: The Medieval Phase* (Cambridge: Cambridge Univ. Press, 1934), in discussing Geoffrey de Vinsauf and John of Salisbury notes their initial emphasis upon thought before explaining details of style (pp. 97-99), and emphasizes Chaucer's belief in the twofold function of poetry with particular attention to "the moral and didactic endings of many of his tales" (p. 157). Baugh, "Middle English Romance," pp. 6, 19-20, recognizes the combination of pleasure and profit in story. In contrast, Taylor's admission of this (pp. 175, 200, 258) is hidden amidst negative evaluations. Mehl, pp. 4-5, 17, 21, and by a choice of 'homiletic' to describe one type of narrative (analogous to Schelp's argument of 'exemplary' romances) sees this view, but is uneasy about it (e.g., pp. 253-54).

[58]Eugene Vinaver, *Form and Meaning,* The Presidential Address of

the Modern Humanities Research Association, 1966, offers an eloquent plea for reading romances without classical, humanist preconceptions. See especially pp. 10-15. This thesis is fully developed in *The Rise of the Romance* (Oxford: Oxford Univ. Press, 1971), especially Ch. V, "The Poetry of Interlace," pp. 68-98. Cf. Rosemond Tuve, *Allegorical Imagery: Some Medieval Books and Their Posterity* (Princeton: Princeton Univ. Press, 1966), pp. 369-70.

[59]*The Rise of the Novel* (Berkeley and Los Angeles: Univ. of California Press, 1957), especially pp. 11-34.

[60]M. A. Owings, *The Arts in the Middle English Romances* (New York: Bookman Associates, 1952), gives specific references. See also Schlauch, *Antecedents,* pp. 7-8; Sarah F. Barrow, *The Medieval Society Romances* (New York: Columbia Univ. Press, 1924), especially Ch. IV; Gist, passim. For discussion of the dichotomy between pictures of unreal and social worlds, see Pamela Gradon, *Form and Style in Early English Literature* (London: Methuen, 1971), pp. 214 ff.

[61]Salter, pp. 44-45. See also J. A. Burrow, *Ricardian Poetry* (New Haven: Yale Univ. Press, 1971), p. 43, on the characteristic 'long-poem style' which is "loosewoven" and has "open texture."

[62]See Hart, pp. 163-64, 262-63.

[63](Cleveland: Case Western Reserve Univ. Press, 1969).

[64]Harper, pp. 6-7, 80-81. Cf. Moorman, *A Knyght,* pp. 30 ff.; Joseph Campbell, *The Hero with a Thousand Faces* (1949; rpt. New York: World Publishing Co., 1956), pp. 245 ff.; Schlauch, English *Medieval Literature,* p. 130.

[65]Harper, p. 6, writes: "Fleming at least paid lip service to the figure of the knight, chivalric and errant."

[66]Ibid., p. 118.

[67]Ibid., p. 115.

[68](New Haven and London: Yale Univ. Press, 1953), p. 222. See also pp. 243-45. Vinaver, *The Rise of Romance,* pp. 2-3, is not convinced by the argument. Donald R. Howard, *The Three Temptations* (Princeton: Princeton Univ. Press, 1966), pp. 178, 223, 275-77, 300, offers relevant general observations about medieval doctrine of perfection and man's striving in the world. On this general point, see also Salter, pp. 67, 85. Moorman, *A Knyght,* structures his whole argument on the quest of the knight; see pp. 3, 5-6, 31 ff., 56, 73, 77, 87; he uses Campbell, *Hero with a Thousand Faces,* which treats this basic theme.

The importance of pilgrimage is stressed by Bloch, I, 63, 86, but not associated with romance; cf. I, 105-6. Another rather illuminating approach to the concept of the knight's quest is to view it in the context of the mystic's striving for perfection. See both Conrad Pepler, *The English Religious Heritage* (St. Louis: Herder, 1958), and David Knowles, *The English Mystical Tradition* (New York: Harper, 1961), recent excellent studies; Evelyn Underhill, *Mysticism* (London, 1911), for background. Key primary texts are *The Cloud of Unknowing and the Book of Privy Counselling*, ed. Phyllis Hodgson, EETS, OS 218 (1958); *Deonise hid Divinite*, ed. Phyllis Hodgson, EETS, OS 231 (1958); Walter Hilton, *The Scale of Perfection*, ed. E. Underhill (London: J. M. Watkins, 1923); Dame Julian of Norwich, *A Shewing of God's Love*, ed. A. M. Reynolds (London: Longman's, 1958), is a brief text; Clifton Walters, trans., *Revelations of Divine Love* (Baltimore: Penguin Books, 1966); *The Book of Margery Kempe*, ed. S. B. Meech and Hope Emily Allen, EETS, OS 212 (1940). *The Mediaeval Mystics of England*, ed. Eric Colledge (New York: Scribner, 1961), provides a good introduction and selections in modernized versions.

[69]See Schlauch, *English Medieval Literature*, p. 152. Morton W. Bloomfield, "Episodic Motivation and Marvels in Epic and Romance," *Essays and Explorations* (Cambridge: Harvard Univ. Press, 1970), pp. 97-128, describes the effects of Christianity, especially saints' lives, on romance structure.

[70]Mehl, pp. 4-5. Cf. Schlauch, *English Medieval Literature*, p. 176; Barrow, p. 32.

[71]Mehl, p. 12. Cf. Schlauch, *English Medieval Literature*, p. 186, on the unpopularity of Tristan and Lancelot.

[72]*Poetry and Crisis in the Age of Chaucer* (Notre Dame: Univ. of Notre Dame Press, 1972). The first lecture established the point of view, pp. 14-26. Schlauch, *English Medieval Literature*, pp. 201-7, has a detailed summary of key economic, political, social developments. For the earlier French situation with violence and insecurity, see Bloch, I, 128, 135; II. 410 ff. The nineteenth-century Leon Gautier, *Chivalry*, trans. D. C. Dunning (New York: Barnes & Noble, 1965), argues reconciliation in Christian knighthood. See also Sidney Painter, *French Chivalry* (1940; rpt. Ithaca: Cornell Univ. Press, 1957). Raymond L. Kilgour, *The Decline of Chivalry* (Cambridge: Harvard Univ. Press, 1937), discusses the "decadence" of chivalry in France through the

fifteenth century.

[73]H. S. Bennett, *Chaucer and the Fifteenth Century* (Oxford: Clarendon Press, 1947), pp. 96-104, offers a brief summary account of the age. Arthur B. Ferguson, *The Indian Summer of English Chivalry* (Durham: Duke Univ. Press, 1960), gives historical contexts, from the Burgundian court through the Tudors, with attention to literary texts as well as events. He argues the necessity for humanism, which was adjustable while chivalry was static and conservative, that could serve the emerging political state of the Renaissance (p. 11). Particularly significant to "popularity" is his argument that chivalry continued as an ideal (when the reality was so upsetting), teaching by example and inspiring patriotism that was crucial because of unusually centralized royal authority in England. Robert W. Ackerman, *Backgrounds to Medieval English Literature* (New York: Random House, 1966) provides an excellent general introduction to the entire period.

[74]M. D. Anderson, *Misericords* (Harmondsworth, Middlesex, England: Penguin Books, 1954) is a good general introduction with photographs. His *Lincoln Choir Stalls* (Lincoln: J. W. Ruddock, 1967) also has a very lucid discussion and fine illustrations.

[75]Misericords were made into the seventeenth century, but the spontaneity and independence of the earlier carvers was lost; "never again was the decoration of an important building to record the beliefs and dreams, the jests and grievances of the men whose labour has enriched our architectural heritage," in Anderson, *Misericords,* p. 30.

[76]*The Anatomy of Criticism* (Princeton: Princeton Univ. Press, 1952), p. 186. Kathryn Hume, "Romance: A Perdurable Pattern," *College English,* 36 (1974), 129-46, builds upon Frye, Campbell, and Neumann's Centroversion to describe the romance's psychological substructure which illuminates treatment of the hero.

[77]*Fiction and the Reading Public,* p. 51.

[78]Leavis, pp. 59-79.

CHAPTER II

[1]Marc Bloch, *Feudal Society,* trans. L. A. Manyon (Chicago: Univ. of Chicago Press, 1961), I, 83-84, 128, 135; II, 316-19. Cf. Leon Gautier, *Chivalry,* trans. D. C. Dunning (New York: Barnes & Noble, 1965).

[2]Q. D. Leavis, *Fiction and the Reading Public* (London: Chatto and Windus, 1932), passim, especially pp. 51-52, 58, 68, 97 ff. James Hart, *The Popular Book, A History of America's Literary Taste* (Berkeley and Los Angeles: Univ. of California Press, 1950), passim, especially pp. 128, 164, 241, 284.

[3]John J. Richetti, *Popular Fiction before Richardson, Narrative Patterns 1700-1739* (Oxford: Clarendon Press, 1969), especially pp. 11, 176, J. M. S. Tompkins, *The Popular Novel in England 1770-1800* (Lincoln: Univ. of Nebraska Press, 1961).

[4]Helpful general treatments are Willard Farnham, *The Medieval Heritage of Elizabethan Tragedy* (1935; rpt. Oxford: Basil Blackwell, 1956), especially Ch. II, pp. 30-68; J. Huizinga, *The Waning of the Middle Ages* (1924; rpt. Penguin Books, 1955), especially Ch. XI, "The Vision of Death," pp. 140-52. Cf. T. S. R. Boase, *Death in the Middle Ages* (London: Thames & Hudson, 1972), for commentary through the visual arts.

[5]N. E. Griffin, *Dares and Dictys: An Introduction to the Study of the Medieval Versions of the Story of Troy* (Baltimore: J. H. Furst, 1907).

[6]Kenneth Sisam, ed., *Fourteenth-Century Verse & Prose* (Oxford: Clarendon Press, 1950), pp 68-69. An extended analysis is Nicholas Jacobs, "Alliterative Storms: A Topos in Middle English," *Speculum,* 47 (1972), 695-719. W. P. Ker, *Medieval English Literature* (1912: rpt. Oxford: Oxford Univ. Press, 1969), p. 77, very briefly praises the poem's liveliness and alliterative style. George Kane, *Middle English Literature* (London: Methuen, 1951), notes its "virtuousity" (p. 50) and rich detail (p. 58). D. J. Williams, "Alliterative Poetry in Fourteenth and Fifteenth Centuries," in *The Middle Ages,* ed. W. F. Bolton (London: Sphere Books, 1970), p. 126, suggests greater satisfaction comes from episodic reading.

[7]George Cary, *The Medieval Alexander* (Cambridge: Cambridge Univ. Press, 1956), is the most comprehensive study. William Matthews very ably surveys the tradition, with special emphasis upon literary expression in England, in his *The Tragedy of Arthur* (Berkeley and Los Angeles: Univ. of California Press, 1960), Ch. III, pp. 68-95. Williams, pp. 123-25, stresses the theme of worldly attainment.

[8]Cary, pp. 91-95, outlines the traditions of this episode.

[9]This, of course, is a key argument of Matthews' excellent study.

Schelp, pp. 149 ff., follows the argument, focusing on *The Wars of Alexander* and *Morte Arthure.*

¹⁰Dieter Mehl, *The Middle English Romances of the Thirteenth and Fourteenth Centuries* (London: Routledge and Kegan Paul, 1969), p. 267, n. 56, calls them "rather bookish compilations and [they] cannot properly be described as romances. Undoubtedly their authors thought that they were writing true history."

¹¹Mehl, pp. 20-22; Paul Strohm, *"Storie, Spelle, Geste, Romaunce, Tragedie:* Generic Distinctions in the Middle English Troy Narratives," *Speculum,* 46 (1971), 348-59.

¹²*The 'Gest Hystoriale' of the Destruction of Troy,* ed. G. A. Panton and D. Donaldson, EETS, OS 39, 56 (1869, 1874; rpt. 1968).

¹³Siegfried Wenzel, *The Sin of Sloth: Acedia in Medieval Thought and Literature* (Chapel Hill: Univ. of North Carolina Press, 1967), is the most comprehensive study of this subject.

¹⁴"Thohaus vero sacedos quasi pro maiori parte noctis illius violenter restitit verbis anthenoris. Sed demum antequam anthenori subtraheretur de nocte libera recedendi facultas thohaus illaqueatus auri cupidine palladii subtractionem antehnori sponte concessit quod anthenor statim asportauit a templo et statim eadem nocte per nuncium suum illud transmisit ad grecos quod vlixi protinus fuit assignatum. Postea vero fama dictante publice dictum est quod vlixes sua sagacitate intercep[er]at illud a troianis. Sed odii ex quo thohaus sacerdos elegit ciuitatem suam proditorie malle perire quam aurum perdere sibi datum quis locus tutus esse poterit aut securus si sanctitas incorrumpenda corrumpitur. Sane non est in sacerdotibus nouum istud in quibus ex antiquo auaricia omnium viciorum mater suas radices affixit et ingluuiosa cupiditas suas medullas. Nullum enim scelus potest eese tam graue quod ad committendum illud sacerdotes in fulgore auri subitam non recipiant cecitatem. Sunt enim auaricie templum et cupiditatis auxilium," in *Lydgate's Troy Book,* ed., Henry Bergen, EETS, ES 126 (1935), 182.

¹⁵See Howard Patch, *The Goddess Fortuna in Medieval Literature* (1927; rpt. New York: Octagon Press, 1967), for a general survey of the subject.

¹⁶G. V. Smithers, *Kyng Alisaunder,* EETS, OS 237 (1957), 28-40. See also Mehl, pp. 229 ff. The text used is *Kyng Alisaunder,* ed. G. V. Smithers, EETS, OS 227 (1952).

[17]Smithers, EETS, OS 237 (1957), 1-2; Mehl, p. 228.

[18]M. D. Legge, *Anglo-Norman Literature and Its Background* (Oxford: Clarendon Press, 1963), pp. 105-7. See Mehl, pp. 227, 229.

[19]These characteristics are, of course, noted but systematically decried by Mehl, pp. 234-35, 238-39. Thus his final evaluation is: "By the addition of the headpieces the adapter has therefore considerably changed the character of his source and has added a new dimension. He certainly did not see Alexander's story primarily as an *exemplum*. The whole plot and the *mirabilia* he describes with such gusto, show that his interests were more varied than that and that he was more than a moralist. This is also suggested by his faithful rendering of his source, especially the more scientific and factual parts. Nevertheless, he does indicate that in the rise and fall of Alexander, as in that of some of his enemies, the same everlasting law is manifested that at all times has subjected nature and mankind to the periodic changes of days and seasons" (p. 239). For Mehl, then, the poet must be "more than a moralist," a designation which for me indicates the most praiseworthy of artistic achievement. Further, that the author of *Kyng Alisaunder* alters his source precisely to achieve a greater stress upon this moral meaning, indicates that for him it is most significant. Lumiansky, in *A Manual of the Writings in Middle English 1050-1500*, Fascicule 1, ed. J. B. Severs (New Haven: Archon, 1967), pp. 105-6, also emphasizes the 'artistic.'

[20]Smithers, EETS, OS 237 (1957), 65.

[21]Ibid., p. 70, suggests an echo of a proverb in Gower's *Confessio Amantis*, VIII, 3086, and Old French sources.

[22]The brief prayer to God (Laud, 2892-96), which follows the account of Alexander's destruction of Thebes and all its inhabitants is noteworthy. Again the poet's concern is with eternity, a life without end, away from this world. The following head-piece is a lyric about dawn and spring, other iterations of sustained existence.

[23]See my *Laments for the Dead in Medieval Narrative* (Pittsburgh: Duquesne Univ. Press, 1966), pp. 115-17.

[24]*The Prose Life of Alexander*, ed. J. S. Westlake, EETS, OS 143 (1913), is the text used. It is very helpful to find this work receiving fuller treatment in Severs, *A Manual*, where R. M. Lumiansky's evaluation is complimentary: "This prose account has been very little studied from either the historical or the interpretative point of view. A recent

critic calls it 'an uninteresting prose translation . . . with little to commend it except to a student of fifteenth-century English Prose' (Cary, p. 243). Yet—for one reader at least—the piece possesses considerable appeal as a literary accomplishment. The narrative is presented by skilful intermingling of third-person exposition with frequent and effective scenes involving pointed first-person dialogue. The development of the character of Alexander, as man of destiny possessed of human frailties, lends attractive humanity to this greatest of all conquerors. And the rather simple and matter-of-fact vocabulary and tone of the North-English writer bring even the marvels of India within the realm of possibility" (p. 110).

Interestingly, the Thornton MS is a treasure of the Library of Lincoln Cathedral, which has a misericord of Alexander's Flight. The episode comes at a crucial point in *The Prose Life,* when the author is emphasizing the futility of Alexander's activities as he moves toward death.

[25]Cf. Hanspeter Schelp, *Exemplarische Romanzen in Mittelenglische,* Palaestra, 246 (Göttingen: Vandenhoeck & Ruprecht, 1967), pp. 159 ff., on Dindimus in *Alexander-Fragment C.*

[26]I am not basically contesting the central argument of Matthews, *The Tragedy of Arthur,* pp. 94-114. Rather I want to argue the way in which the fall structure is used for this treatment of the larger theme of the relation between the temporal and eternal.

[27]John Finlayson, "Arthur and the Giant of St. Michael's Mount," *Medium AEvum,* 33 (1964), 112-20, argues this initial episode establishes Arthur as "champion of Christianity and redeemer of the people," but also a great hero not merely Fortune's victim.

[28]Note Matthews, pp. 69-71, on the heroic tradition of Alexander; pp. 95-96, for the ways in which *Morte Arthure* is not a conventional romance.

[29]Matthews, pp. 93, 118; Bloch, I, 134.

[30]Matthews, pp. 123-24; Schelp, pp. 173-74.

[31]My discussion uses *Morte Arthure, or the Death of Arthur,* ed. Edmond Brock, EETS, OS 8 (1865; rpt. 1961). The poem begins with festivities at Christmas (64, 542); further dating is indicated by religious festivals such as Epiphany (415), Lamas day (92), Easter (554), evensong (894); Saints are invoked; for example, Michael (1069) and Peter (2883). Mary is both a comfort (2867) and the device for Arthur's

fleet (3648 ff.). A specific piety and loyalty to the Papacy is also indicated in several passages (3495 ff., 2410 ff.). Many vows are made with religious references; see Matthews, p. 22.

[32]Matthews, p. 112; Schelp, pp. 171-72.

[33]Matthews, pp. 28-29.

[34]See Matthews, pp. 80-93, on war.

[35]Matthews, pp. 142 ff., regards Gawain's death as an allegory of Christ's passion.

[36]Matthews, pp. 123-24.

[37]Cf. Matthews, p. 141.

CHAPTER III

[1]Emile Mâle, *The Gothic Image* (1913; rpt. New York: Harper Torchbook, 1958), argues against symbolic interpretations of fauna and flora in medieval art and views them as decorative art. See "The Mirror of Nature," pp. 27-63. He summarizes: "The fact is that conceptions of this kind are of essentially popular origin. The gargoyles like churchyard vampires, or the dragons subdued by ancient bishops, came from the depths of the people's consciousness, and had grown out of their acient fireside tales" (p. 59). Willard Farnham, *The Shakespearean Grotesque, Its Genesis and Transformations* (Oxford: Oxford Univ. Press, 1971), in his chapter "Beautiful Deformity," pp. 1-46 begins with Mâle's interpretation and argues more comprehensively the complexity of dual attraction and aversion. Representation of the Last Judgment is discussed by Mâle, pp. 365-83. Brief comment on the clarity of narrative content in tympani appears in Erwin Panofsky, *Gothic Architecture and Scholasticism* (1951; rpt. Cleveland: World Publishing Co., 1957), pp. 40-41.

[2]Laura Hibbard, *Medieval Romance in England, A Study of the Sources and Analogues of the Non-cyclic Metrical Romances* (1924; 2nd ed. New York: Burt Franklin, 1959), pp. 49-57.

[3]Hibbard, p. 56.

[4]*The Romance of Emaré*, ed. Edith Rickert, EETS, ES 99 (1908). Hibbard, pp. 23-34, discusses versions and origins. Dieter Mehl, *The Middle English Romances of the Thirteenth and Fourteenth Centuries* (London: Routledge and Kegan Paul, 1969), p. 137, notes that the

poet's invocation shows special concern to be edifying.

[5]Rickert, p. xlviii, suggests that tales like *Emaré* demonstrate how oriental stories were adapted and transformed by the ideas of Christianity. Hibbard, pp. 30-33, notes historical possibilities and stresses the religious bias, recognizing the miraculous as the source of appeal and popularity.

[6]Margaret Schlauch, *Chaucer's Constance and Accused Queens* (New York: New York Univ. Press, 1927). See also Hibbard, pp. 23-33. An eloquent critical exposition of the duality in such stories is Morton W. Bloomfield, "The Man of Law's Tale: A Tragedy of Victimization and a Christian Comedy," *PMLA*, 87 (1972), 384-90.

[7]Ben E. Perry, *The Ancient Romances* (Berkeley and Los Angeles: Univ. of California Press, 1967), pp. 294-324, provides a summary of the events and arguments for Latin origins. Hibbard, pp. 164-73, summarizes versions and origins.

[8]Hanspeter Schelp, *Exemplarische Romanzen in Mittelenglische,* Palaestra 246 (Göttingen: Vanderhoeck & Ruprecht, 1967), pp. 105-13, explains the robe's symbolism; Mehl, pp. 139-40, summarizes his argument.

[9]Recent critical appraisals have been somewhat negative. Mehl, pp. 126-27, judges the poem an unsuccessful mixture of romance and legend; Schelp's interpretation, pp. 84-93, accepts more readily the conversion. Donovan, in *A Manual,* p. 142, suggests "deficiencies of the poem as narrative art" but notes Gowther's 'admirable struggle.'

[10]*The Breton Lays in Middle English,* ed. Thomas C. Rumble (Detroit: Wayne State Univ. Press, 1965), is the basic text used for all quotations.

[11]Karl Breul, *Sir Gowther* (Oppeln: Georg Maske, 1886), p. 115; Hibbard, pp. 52-53.

[12]Hibbard, pp. 55-56.

[13]See Jessie Weston, *The Three Days Tournament* (London: D. Nutt, 1902), pp. 21 ff.

[14]*Sir Gowther,* pp. 198-207.

[15]*Medieval Romance,* p. 49.

[16]*Robert the Deuyll,* in *Early English Prose Romances,* ed. William J. Thoms, 2nd ed. (London: Nattali and Bond, 1858), I, xvii-xxiv (Preface) and 3-56 (Text).

[17]In the metrical version this event is marked by an eclipse, a natural

portent not unlike the darkening of the heavens at his birth.

[18]"Judge not, that you be not judged. For with the judgment you pronounce you will be judged, and the measure you give will be the measure you get. Why do you see the speck that is in your brother's eye, but do not notice the log that is in your own eye?" Matt. 7:1-3. *The Oxford Annotated Bible with the Apocrypha*, ed. W. G. May and B. M. Metzger (New York: Oxford Univ. Press, 1965).

[19]A. B. Taylor, *An Introduction to Medieval Romance* (1930; rpt. New York: Barnes & Noble, 1969), pp. 169-70, argues the superior integrity of such medieval accounts over those in modern fiction.

[20]Marc Bloch, *Feudal Society*, trans. A. L. Manyon (Chicago: Univ. of Chicago Press, 1961), II, 302. A good recent discussion of the *Vie de Saint Alexis* is in William W. Ryding, *Structure in Medieval Narrative* (The Hague: Mouton), pp. 92 ff.

[21]There is a certain callous crudity in some of these antics, for example, the physical insulting of the Jew (p. 36) and the befouling of the bride (pp. 36-37). These reflect, I think, the hearty physical joking that is so characteristic of the fabliaux, or a painting of a bystander's holding his nose at the raising of Lazarus. Also we have opposition to the non-Christian and the proud Christian.

[22]In the French *Robert le Diable*, ed. E. Löseth (Paris, 1903), Robert wants to fight against the Turks, and a knight (not an angel) who is a celestial being brings the armour. The Middle English clearly emphasizes, then, the humility of Robert and his leaving his fortune to God and His Grace. Note De La Warr B. Easter, *A Study of the Magic Elements in the Romans d'Aventure and the Romans Bretons* (Baltimore: J. H. Furst, 1905), p. 35.

[23]The role of the fool is used more aggressively in *Robert of Sicily*, in *Middle English Metrical Romances*, ed. W. H. French and C. B. Hale (New York: Prentice-Hall, 1903), where a proud king is humiliated as a chastening experience. Thus the penance is not sought by Robert but compelled by an Angel who leads him away from pride so that he can become a good king. See also Lillian H. Hornstein, *"King Robert of Sicily:* Analogues and Origins," *PMLA*, 79 (1964), 13-21, for a discussion of New and Old Testament materials. Schelp, pp. 69-84, discusses the treatment of the fool.

[24]Howard R. Patch, *The Other World According to Descriptions in Medieval Literature* (1950; rpt. New York: Octagon Books, 1970),

provides a helpful general survey of this subject.

[25]Ed. A. K. Donald, EETS, ES 68 (1875).

[26]Ed. W. W. Skeat, EETS, OS 22 (1866).

[27]Wells, p. 157. Hornstein in Severs, *A Manual*, p. 166, repeats this and suggests a preference for *Melusine*. Skeat, EETS, OS 22 (1866), p. x, comments on the romance's popularity and notes that Jean d'Arras' version was one of the first books printed at Geneva.

[28]See especially the conclusion of the prologue, ll. 190-210.

[29]See my *Laments*, pp. 55-56.

[30]Hornstein, *A Manual*, p. 166, singles out this character-drawing for praise, but indicates some uncertainty by describing Geoffrey of the Great Tooth as "berserker but convincing."

CHAPTER IV

[1]Gervase Mathew, "Ideals of Friendship," in *Patterns of Love and Courtesy. Essays in Memory of C. S. Lewis*, ed. John Lawlor (Evanston: Northwestern Univ. Press, 1966), pp. 45-53, considers both classical and scholastic thought, providing helpful references and a general concept of the ideal of romantic friendship. See also William A. Stowell, "Personal Relationships in Medieval France," *PMLA*, 28 (1913), 393-95; Marc Bloch, *Feudal Society*, trans. L. A. Manyon (Chicago: Univ. of Chicago Press, 1961), II, 450, on the persistence of the idea that evolved from feudalism.

[2]A. McI. Trounce, ed., *Athelston*, EETS, OS 224 (1951), pp. 4-6, 14, 40; Dieter Mehl, *The Middle English Romances of the Thirteenth and Fourteenth Centuries* (London: Routledge and Kegan Paul, 1968), p. 149; Laura Hibbard, *Medieval Romances in England. A Study of the Non-cyclic Metrical Romances* (1924; rpt. New York: Burt Franklin, 2nd ed. 1959), pp. 143-46, after stressing the restriction to English materials, emphasizes the popular quality: "In style also, in its omission of all the elements of chivalry and romance, in its rude vigor, its occasional brutality, its liking for scenes of tumult and rapid action, in its simple motives and naive cruelty, the tale has the distinctive qualities of English popular fiction which are found in such Middle English romances as *Havelock, Richard Coer de Lion,* and *Gamelyn*" (p. 144).

[3]Trounce, pp. 41-45, has mixed feelings about the romance's

literary worth, admiring the verse form and the range of subject matter but regretting the poet's religious inspiration and lack of harmonic control. Donald Sands, *Middle English Verse Romances* (New York: Holt, Rinehart and Winston, 1966), pp. 130-31, in contrast, regrets the verse form as well as the total effect, but admires the plot and many particular details. Margaret Schlauch, *English Medieval Literature and Its Social Foundations* (Warsaw: Panstwowe Wydawnictwo Nankowe, 1956), p. 179, praises its "certain harsh and convincing reality." C. W. Dunn, in *A Manual of the Writings in Middle English 1050-1500,* ed. J. Burke Severs (New Haven: Connecticut Academy of Arts and Sciences, 1967), p. 34, notes: "The literary qualities of the romance vary in effectiveness. The plot is dramatic, the narrative swift, and the elements of the marvelous well maintained." But he finds characterization awkward and the tail-rhyme worthy of parody. Mehl, pp. 146-52, classifies it as "homiletic" and finds much to esteem in its technical skill.

⁴See my *Laments for the Dead in Medieval Narrative* (Pittsburgh: Duquesne Univ. Press, 1966), p. 36.

⁵See pp. 61-65.

⁶Trounce, pp. 31-38. See also Hibbard, *Medieval Romances,* pp. 144-46, and "Athelston, A Westminister Legend," *PMLA,* 36 (1921), 223-44.

⁷Trounce, pp. 32-33, argues deliberate borrowing and makes the further point that the historical struggle of Church and State in England inspired the ecclesiastical matter and portrayal of Alryke. The French *chansons* have no such development, not even in the figure of Turpin, of asserted rights of the Church. English translations of Charlemagne romances are few in number and not of the highest quality generally. Militant Christianity seems not to have appealed, though personal conflict—notably in Fierabras—was of interest. See Schlauch, *English Medieval Literature,* pp. 182-84, and Mehl, p. 152, and H. M. Smyser in *A Manual,* pp. 80-81.

⁸Mehl, especially pp. 151-52.

⁹*A Manual of the Writings in Middle English 1050-1400* (New Haven: Yale Univ. Press, 1916), p. 157. Hornstein in Severs, *A Manual* p. 167, maintains the classification.

¹⁰ Wells, p. 159; retained by Hornstein, p. 169. A. B. Taylor, *An Introduction to Medieval Romance* (1930: rpt. New York: Barnes &

Noble, 1969), pp. 140-41, uses the romance as a focus for attacking medieval philosophy—in contrast to classical and modern—with its exaggerations that 'hinder moral progress' because of exaltation of impossible ideals in isolation (e.g., friendship) that are beyond human possibility. Mother Mary Norbert, *The Reflection of Religion in English Medieval Verse Romances* (Bryn Mawr: Bryn Mawr Press, 1941), regards the romance as a "morally confused tale" (p. 145) and classifies *Amis and Amiloun* as one of "a few romances in which the author cannot quite reconcile the Christian principles with the deeds the story prescribes" (pp. 8, 147). Margaret A. Gist, *Love and War in the Middle English Romances* (Philadelphia: Univ. of Pennsylvania Press, 1947), pp. 37-38, views the romance as 'an example for special pleading—for the responsibilities of sworn brotherhood'—and she judges it a narrative with "a curious distortion of values." George Kane, *Middle English Literature* (London: Methuen, 1951), p. 30, repeats this idea by arguing that "absurdities of subject and faults of construction . . . are perhaps to be explained by the fact that it was first designed with a didactic intention which was wanting in later versions but still continued to affect action and motivation at cardinal points." Ojars Kratins, "The Middle English *Amis and Amiloun:* Chivalric Romance or Secular Hagiography?" *PMLA*, 81 (1966), 347-54, continues the argument to rate the poem as "a highly unsatisfactory example of the genre of romance" (p. 347). He defines the story as a legend with the theme of the testing of faith—though of a "not strictly Christian nature." Kathryn Hume argues against "secular hagiography" in "Structure and Perspective: Romance and Hagiographic Features in the Amicus and Amelius Story," *JEGP*, 69 (1970), 89-107. Just appeared—since my writing of this chapter—is Kathryn Hume, "*Amis and Amiloun* and the Aesthetics of Middle English Romance," *SP*, 70 (1973), 19-41, which sees the discrepancy but argues that the Middle English redactor recognized the problem and tried to minimize it; however, she concludes that "If you agree that a romance must be totally conformable to Christian principles, then *Amis and Amiloun* is indeed perniciously defective" (p. 38). Unfortunately, Hume seems not to have been aware of William Calin, *The Epic Quest Studies in Four Old French Chansons de Geste* (Baltimore: Johns Hopkins Univ. Press, 1966), pp. 57-117, which argues the doctrinal core in the Old French version. Hume, like Dale Kramer in "Structural Artistry in *Amis and Amiloun*," *Annuale Mediaevale,*

9 (1968), 103-22, bases her positive appraisal on the poem's stylistic excellence—the care with which details are presented, narrative economy, suitability of the story to the chosen form—rather than its thematic argument.

¹¹Dorothy Everett, "A Characterization of the English Medieval Romances," in *Essays on Middle English Literature,* ed. Patricia Kean (Oxford: Clarendon Press, 1955), p. 9, also cites the striking conclusion of the poem. She, however, uses it to illustrate a salient characteristic of romances: "On the whole the ordinary limitations of human life do not exist." The acceptability of miracles to the medieval hearer/reader is recognized and indicated by their being treated matter-of-factly and without a sense of remoteness.

¹²*Medieval Romance in England,* p. 68. The discussion of sources presents archetypal stories such as the Two Friends, Sword of Chastity, and Faithful Companion and chivalric alterations like the Jealous Seneschal, Wooing Princess, Judicial Combat, Faithful Servitor, and Recognition Tokens. The Latin "theme" is quoted in the text of *Vitas Amici et Amilii carissimorum* in Kölbing's edition. p. ciii.

¹³Ibid., p. 71.

¹⁴"Introduction," *Amis and Amiloun,* EETS, OS 211 (1937), p. xxvi.

¹⁵Leach, pp. xxv, xxviii. Delmar C. Homan, "Old Gods in New Garb: The Making of *Amis and Amiloun,*" Diss. Columbia 1964, perpetuates this view in its argument that the principal sources of the "friendship plot" are Celtic.

¹⁶Cf. Legge, pp. 119, 121.

¹⁷Leach, p. xxvii.

¹⁸Calin, p. 93, argues that *Ami et Amile* is a poem with a message far beyond friendship; a doctrinal core is evidenced by the sacramental nature manifested in the miracles. The theme he sees is renunciation, man's coming to knowledge through suffering, and ultimately accepting God's will. Some of his argument is supported by references to the Middle English version, and my analysis of this poem supports many of these conclusions.

¹⁹Legge, pp. 115-121, discusses how the Anglo-Norman *Amis e Amilun* reflects a didactic attitude, but shows how a simple legend is transformed to romance.

²⁰ See Mathew, pp. 45-46, who mentions the Anglo-Norman version.

[21]Kane, p. 30, singles out this characterization as one of the distinct virtues of the romance "which compensate for its faults of structure and expression." See also Hume, pp. 34-35.

[22]Norbert, p. 147, says that "evidently the poet accepts this wrong reasoning as a pious sentiment." The alternative I suggest not only removes the apparent failing in literary finesse, but also it is more consistent with the characterization.

[23]Amiloun's judgment is, then, not seeking revenge, retaliation (see Norbert, p. 157); he may not realize "full perfection of the virtue of charity," but he comes near.

[24]Amis' progress from church is described as "As lord & prince wiþ pride" (1890), but this formula is part of the narrative build-up of his position as a temporal lord, a position somewhat at variance with his inner nature.

[25]Ronald Crane, The Vogue of Medieval Chivalric Romance during the Renaissance (Menasha, Wis.: George Banta, 1919), p. 10.

[26]Arthur Dickson, Valentine and Orson. A Study in Late Medieval Romance (New York: Columbia Univ. Press, 1929). Appendix II, pp. 284-98, gives English editions and references to the romance through 1926.

[27]Hornstein, in Severs, A Manual, pp. 147-58, uses this designation for seven romances.

[28]Dickson, Study, p. 158.

[29]Arthur Dickson, "Introduction," Valentine and Orson, trans. from French by Henry Watson, EETS, OS 204 (1937), p. x.

[30] Dickson, Study, pp. 106 ff., has a full discussion of the sources and analogues of the French prose romance and German and Dutch versions.

[31]This quotation is the epigraph used in Dickson, Study, p. 1. He also quotes the comparison in Barnaby Rudge—"quite a Valentine and Orson Business" (p. 195). See also Valentine and Orson, p. ix.

[32]Schlauch, English Medieval Literature, p. 183.

[33]Valentine and Orson, pp. x-xi.

[34]Ibid., p. xx.

[35]Dickson, Study, pp. 217 ff.

[36]Valentine and Orson, pp. lxi-lxii.

[37]Study, p. 219.

[38]The Rise of Romance (Oxford: Oxford Univ. Press, 1971), Ch. V.

[39]Dickson, *Study*, pp. 230-31.

[40]Ibid., p. 234.

[41]See my *Laments*, pp. 113-15.

[42]Dickson, *Study*, p. 250.

[43]Ibid., pp. 191 ff., p. 216.

[44]Ibid., pp. 252-65, for detailed comparison of the two accounts.

[45]*Valentine and Orson*, pp. lxi-lxii. Evidence is also given for Shakespeare's using details for the banquet scene, the ghost of Banquo deriving from the wild Orson.

[46]*Valentine and Orson*, p. x, n. 4; cf. *Study*, p. 243.

[47]*Valentine and Orson*, pp. lxii-lxiii. For details see Harold Golder, "Bunyan and Spenser," *PMLA*, 45 (1930), 216 ff.

[48]Dickson, *Study*, p. 174.

CHAPTER V

[1]Denis de Rougemont, *Love in the Western World*, trans. Montgomery Belgion (1940; rev. ed. Garden City, N.Y.: Doubleday, 1957), is an eloquent and provocative, if somewhat Catharist, argument about essential attitudes that underlie the romantic extremes. Resulting sentimentality ignores commonplaces of human experience and emotion which is consistently exploited in popular media.

[2]Margaret Schlauch, *English Medieval Literature and Its Social Foundations* (Warsaw: Panstwowe Wydawnictwo Nankowe, 1956), pp. 144-45, 186; Dieter Mehl, *The Middle English Romances of the Thirteenth and Fourteenth Centuries* (London: Routledge and Kegan Paul, 1969), pp. 1-6, briefly surveys the differences and critical responses; Adelaide Evans Harris, *The Heroine of the Middle English Romances,* Western Reserve Univ. Bulletin No. 31 (Cleveland: Western Reserve Univ. Press, 1928), p. 6, argues for the superior morality of English versions. Misericords show a shrew sometimes, but almost never romantic lovers. Illustrations of Tristan and Iseult appear only at Lincoln and Chester, where the stalls were executed by the same craftsmen within about ten years time. The scene shows the lovers under a tree where Mark's head is to be seen peering from the branches, a dog and pool are below the main figures, and a waiting-woman and squire are seen on the supporters. The scene is much less clear than

representations of it on ivory mirrors and caskets, suggesting only a visual memory of the carver who "had no clear understanding of its significance," according to M. D. Anderson, *Lincoln Choir Stalls* (Lincoln: J. W. Ruddock, 1967), pp. 24-25.

[3]*The Meaning of Courtly Love,* ed. F. X. Newman (Albany: State Univ. of New York Press, 1968), is a diversified and comprehensive presentation of current scholarly attitudes. The outlook is "an uneasiness with the paradoxes that constitute the Paris conception of *amour courtois*" (p. viii). Applicable to Chrétien, Gottfried, and Dante in varying degrees, this is especially true of Chaucer and Wolfram von Eschenbach (as argued by D. W. Robertson, Jr., and W. T. H. Jackson), where the moral stance usually associated with "popular" literature is strong. Arguments for the usefulness of "courtly love," especially to describe a kind of poetic expression, are in Pamela Gradon, *Form and Style in Early English Literature* (London: Methuen, 1970), pp. 247 ff.

[4]Jean Frappier, *Chrétien de Troyes, l'homme et l'oeuvre* (Paris: Hatier-Boivin, 1957), is the best comprehensive study. Very useful are Frappier's chapter in *Arthurian Literature in the Middle Ages,* ed. Roger S. Loomis (Oxford: Clarendon Press, 1959), pp. 157-91, and Charles Moorman, *A Knyght Ther Was* (Lexington: Univ. of Kentucky Press, 1967), pp. 27-57. Summaries of current critical cruxes are: C. R. B. Combellack, "Yvain's Guilt," *SP*, (1971), 10-25, and Norris J. Lacy, "Yvain's Evolution and the Role of the Lion," *Rom N,* 12 (1970), 198-202. See also J. P. Collas, "The Romantic Hero of the Twelfth Century," in *Medieval Miscellany Presented to Eugene Vinaver,* ed. F. Whitehead, A. H. Diverres, and F. E. Sutcliffe (New York: Barnes & Noble, 1965), pp. 80-96. Pride of place and the most thorough annotation is given to the Middle English poem in Ritson's early collection; see Arthur Johnston, *Enchanted Ground, The Study of Medieval Romance in the Eighteenth Century* (London: Athlorre Press, 1964), p. 141.

[5]"Introduction," *Ywain and Gawain,* ed. Albert B. Friedman and Norman T. Harrington, EETS, OS 254 (1964), p. xxi. There are also helpful notes in *Ywain and Gawain,* ed. G. Schleich (Oppeln: G. Maske, 1887).

[6]Friedman and Harrington, p. xviii. Robert W. Ackerman, "English Rimed and Prose Romances," in *Arthurian Literature in the Middle Ages,* pp. 508-9, briefly comments on the differences.

See also Mehl, pp. 180-85, and Jessie L. Weston, " 'Ywain and Gawain' and 'Le Chevalier au Lion,' " *Modern Quarterly of Language and Literature,* 1 (1898), 98-107, 194-202.

[7]Friedman and Harrington, p. xv, n. 3, cite Alfred Adler, "Sovereignty in Chrétien's Yvain," *PMLA,* 62 (1947), 281-303, especially 296-99, and Julian Harris, "The Role of the Lion in Chrétien de Troyes' *Yvain,*" *PMLA,* 64 (1949), 1143-63. Combellack, pp. 23-25, argues against this reading and for an always noble Yvain who consistently resists the charms of marriageable young women and remains loyal to Laudine during the separation.

[8]See William S. Woods, "The Plot Structure in Four Romances of Chrétien de Troyes," *SP,* 50 (1953), 1-15; Moorman, *A Knyght Ther Was* pp. 31-41, 55-57.

[9]See Harris, pp. 1148-49.

[10]George Kane, *Middle English Literature* (London: Methuen, 1951), pp. 78 ff., especially admires this quality. John Speirs, *Medieval English Poetry, The Non-Chaucerian Tradition* (London: Faber & Faber, 1957), pp. 114-21, has a mythic interpretation.

[11]J. Douglas Bruce, "Introduction," *Le Morte Arthur,* EETS, ES 88 (1903), pp. xxix-xxx. Early scholars praised the poem. John E. Wells, *A Manual of the Writings in Middle English 1050-1400* (New Haven: Yale Univ. Press, 1916), pp. 50-51, calls it "one of the most notable of the Middle English romances" for form and matter and notes that "It is remarkably concise. . . . The expression is direct, and free from diffuseness. The poem is simple, unpretending, sincere. The writer lent himself to the human appeal of his material . . . earnestness and sincerity of feeling . . . make it true and real and warm." Helaine Newstead, in *A Manual of the Writings in Middle English 1050-1500,* ed. J. Burke Severs (New Haven: Connecticut Academy of Arts and Sciences, 1967), pp. 52-53, singles out the poem's "sure grasp of narrative values . . . concentration . . . well-proportioned structure" to sustain this praise. Ackerman, *Arthurian Literature,* pp. 489-91, argues the romance's distinction because "it tells a moving story vividly and swiftly" and praises the author's "humbler virtues—his good taste, his sense of proportion, and his sound ear" and his avoidance of questions or moral obloquy in his "uncomplicated retelling" of a good story. This is a slight modification of Kane, pp. 65-69, who finds the characters mildly irritable and admires the poem for purely

artistic reasons. "The many contradictions inherent in the accumulated material of the Arthur legend confuse the issues so completely in any case that no moral point of view could be consistently maintained with regard to it" (p. 69). Mehl adapts this reading: "Thus, the story is not based on an ethical conflict or Christian morality, but on a clash of loyalties which can only end in tragedy and which, with its sinister and unavoidable logic, rather suggests a Germanic and pre-Christian mentality" (p. 188). "A strictly moral presentation of the whole story from the beginning would certainly have detracted from its tragic force and from the pathetic effect of human powerlessness in the face of destiny" (p. 189). Richard A. Wertime, "The Theme and Structure of the Stanzaic *Morte Arthur*," *PMLA*, 87 (1972), 1075-82, most recently continued the arguments, suggesting reasons why the poem should not be underrated but repeating uneasiness about the total achievement.

[12]A concise summary of the controversy is provided by Wilfred L. Guerin, "The Tale of the Death of Arthur," in *Malory's Originality*, ed. Robert M. Lumiansky (Baltimore: Johns Hopkins Univ. Press, 1964), pp. 237-40.

[13]Schlauch, *Medieval English Literature*, p. 185; Wertime, pp. 1075-76, 1079.

[14]Note, for example, that Arthur and his men set out against Joyous Gard "As men that were of mykelle pryde" (2105). Lancelot, having failed to secure a reconciliation, leaves in sorrow: "Oute of the castelle gonne they fare, / Gremly teres lette they glyde; / There was dwelle and wepynge sare, / At the partynge was lytelle pryde" (2456-59).

[15]Wertime, p. 1081, dismisses the Queen summarily and charges that she treats Lancelot "as imperiously as ever." F. Whitehead, "Lancelot's Penance," in *Essays on Malory*, ed. J.A.W. Bennett (Oxford: Clarendon Press, 1963), pp. 108-10, comments on the pious Guinevere.

[16]Ch. I, pp. 6-9.

[17]MacEdward Leach, ed., *Paris and Vienne*, EETS, OS 234 (1957), p. xvii, and Caxton's text, pp. 77-78.

[18]Leach, pp. xxvi-xxxi; cf. Leon Kellner, ed., *Caxton's Blanchardyne and Eglantine*, EETS, ES 58 (1890), p. cxi.

[19]Leach, pp. xx-xxi.

[20]Leach, pp. xxx-xxxi; N. F. Blake, *Caxton and His World* (London:

Andre Deutsch, 1969), passim, especially pp. 64, 67-69, 78, 194-96.
See also Sally Shaw, "Caxton and Malory," in *Essays on Malory*.
   [21]Quotations and page references are from Leach's edition.
   [22]Blake, pp. 195ff.

CHAPTER VI

   [1]Useful studies of the popularity include: W. P. Ker, *Medieval English Literature* (1912; rpt. Oxford: Oxford Univ. Press, 1969), p. 72; Ronald S. Crane, "The Vogue of *Guy of Warwick* from the Close of the Middle Ages to the Romantic Revival," *PMLA*, 30 (1915), 125-94; Ronald S. Crane, *The Vogue of Medieval Chivalric Romance during the English Renaissance* (Menasha, Wis.: George Banta, 1919), passim; Laura Hibbard, *Medieval Romance in England* (1924; rpt. new ed. New York: Burt Franklin, 1960), 127-39; A. Ewert, ed., *Gui de Warewic* (Paris: Librairie Ancienne Edouard Champion, 1932-33), I, iii, repeats Crane's evidence; A. C. Baugh, *A Literary History of England* (New York: Appleton-Century-Crofts, 1948), pp. 178-79; M. D. Legge, *Anglo-Norman Literature and Its Background* (Oxford: Clarendon Press, 1963), p. 167; C. W. Dunn, in *A Manual of the Writings in Middle English 1050-1500*, ed. J. Burke Severs (New Haven: Connecticut Academy of Arts and Sciences, 1969), pp. 29-31; Arthur Johnston, *Enchanted Ground, The Study of Medieval Romance in the Eighteenth Century* (London: Athlone Press, 1964), passim. See Caroline Strong, "Sir Thopas and Sir Guy," *MLN*, 23 (1908), 73 ff., 102 ff., and Laura Hibbard Loomis, "Chaucer and the Auchinleck MS: 'Thopas' and 'Guy of Warwick,' in *Essays and Studies in Honor of Carleton Brown* (New York: New York Univ. Press, 1940), pp. 111-28. Note the negative judgment, p. 128; cf. *Medieval Romance*, p. 127. More sympathetic is D. S. Brewer, "The Relationship of Chaucer to the English and European Traditions," in *Chaucer and the Chaucerians*, ed. D. S. Brewer (London: Thomas Nelson & Son, 1966), pp. 11-15.
   [2]*Guy of Warwick*, ed. William B. Todd (Austin: Univ. of Texas Press, 1968). Todd, p. 168, notes Caroline Clive's fame for an early poem, "The Valley of the Morals," celebrating the past, and for *Paul Ferroll*, a novel of 1855, "one of the most sensational romances" (cf. *DNB*). The relationship between popular enthusiasm and certain elements of 'romance' thus recurs.

[3] *Gui de Warewic,* p. iii. He goes on to discuss possible historical personages involved in the creation of a tale about Warwick, pp. iv-vii. Legge, p. 162, regards the 'ancestral romance' as pure fabrication written to flatter Thomas Earl of Warwick; William Marshall is suggested as a possible model, p. 170. See also J. E. Wells, *A Manual of the Writings in Middle English 1050-1400* (New Haven: Connecticut Academy of Arts and Sciences, 1916), p. 17.

[4] See Chapter IV, pp. 87, 105ff.

[5] *Anglo-Norman Literature,* p. 175. See Chapter I, p. 5.

[6] Thomas Rumble, "The Tale of Tristram," in *Malory's Originality,* ed. R. M. Lumiansky (Baltimore: Johns Hopkins Univ. Press, 1964), pp. 118 ff.

[7] See Chapter V, pp. 119-120.

[8] Ed. Severs, p. 31. This is, of course, a reiteration of the original negative judgment of Wells, pp. 17-18, that is perpetuated by Laura Hibbard Loomis and M. D. Legge and many others. For a brief counterargument, see my *"Guy of Warwick*: A Medieval Thriller," *The South Atlantic Quarterly,* 73 (1974), 554-63. Cf. Brewer, pp. 4-7.

[9] *The Middle English Romances of the Thirteenth and Fourteenth Centuries* (London: Routledge and Kegan Paul, 1969), p. 227. Full discussion of the "novel" appears on pp. 220-27.

[10] *Exemplarische Romanzen in Mittelenglische,* Palaestra 246 (Göttingen: Vandenhoeck and Ruprecht, 1967), p. 148. For full discussion, see pp. 139-49.

[11] *Middle English Literature* (London: Methuen, 1951), pp. 41-42.

[12] *Memoirs of the Notorious Stephen Burroughs* (Hanover, N.H., 1798), argues a youthful reading of *Guy* as a reason for crime; cited by Johnston, p. 36.

[13] *The Romance of Guy of Warwick,* ed. Julius Zupitza, EETS, ES 42, 49, 59 (1883, 1887, 1891; rpt. 1966). I have favored Caius MS., which is more characteristic in structure and has greater literary excellence. It has a complete opening and concludes with Guy's death, putting the Reinbrun material in earlier (8654-9029). Mention of a son, the heir in the temporal world, is important. Thus, although the episode interrupts the Guy narrative, it is not irrelevant but a firm indication of the wholeness of man's experience. The argument about careful editing in the Auchinleck 'bookshop' is certainly fascinating and provides strong evidence for heightening popular appeal. See Laura

Hibbard Loomis, "The Auchinleck Manuscript and a Possible London Bookshop of 1330-1340," *PMLA*, 58 (1942), 595-627, for the basic points. As might be expected, Mehl, whose book is organized on the basis of the length of narrative, prefers Auchinleck. Obviously I am arguing against the irrelevance of shifting episodes about and fragmentation into parts and for *Guy* as a unified work of art. Like Schelp, I use Auchinleck when Caius lacks an episode. The notes are useful in *The Romance of Guy of Warwick, The Second or 15th Century Version*, ed. J. Zupitza, EETS, ES 25, 26 (1875-76; rpt. 1966) and in *Speculum Gy de Warewyke*, ed. Georgiana Lea Morrill, EETS, ES 75 (1898; rpt. 1973).

[14]*Literature and Pulpit in Medieval England* (New York: Barnes & Noble, rev. ed. 1961), p. 15. He quotes William of Nassington's *Speculum Vitae* (MS. Roy. 17. C. viii, fol. 26), which argues that he "will make na vayn carpynge / Of dedes of armys, ne of amours" such as are found in *Octavian, Sir Ysumbras, Bevis of Hampton*, and *Guy of Warwick* (p. 13).

[15]*The Minor Poems of John Lydgate*, Part II, *Secular Poems*, ed. H. N. MacCracken, EETS, OS 192 (1933; rpt. 1961), ll. 516-38.

[16]Cited by Johnston, p. 172. The Auchinleck MS. is used.

[17]See Mehl, pp. 226-27, 138-40.

[18]Marc Bloch, *Feudal Society*, trans. L. A. Manyon (Chicago: Univ. of Chicago Press, 1961), I, 125-30.

[19]See my *Laments for the Dead in Medieval Narrative* (Pittsburgh: Duquesne Univ. Press, 1966), pp. 107-8.

[20]Such formal indication of the development is not necessary for the perceptive reader, but its appearance does support the exemplary reading of the poem, and the three stanzas quoted suggest some differences in the two manuscripts, e.g., Auchinleck's more deliberate attempt to secure popular understanding. See L. H. Loomis, "Auchinleck MS," especially pp. 600-1, 607-8, 622-23.

[21]Auchinleck MS. is quoted here because of its heightened richness (e.g., the added detail of the changed color of hair) and as a representative passage to show the quality of the verse.

[22]Wells, p. 18, is typically negative: "The romance is a long-winded narrative of insignificant incidents, many of which might be omitted without detriment to the plot. The first episode of Sir Tirri, for example, is purely gratuitous, yet occupies over twenty-five

hundred lines."

[23]The most memorable is a display of pagan blasphemy. The Sultan elaborately abuses Apollo, Termagent, and Mahomet (Caius, 3689-3716), as epitomized by the sentiment "Thou art not worthe a mouse torde!" and climaxed by a beating and destruction of images.

[24]Precise naming of the devil is also rare in *Guy of Warwick*. There are a few exceptions: e.g., Duke Loyer, hard pressed by Guy and his cohorts, says: "þe fende hem haþ þider y-brouȝt. / To slen ous alle þai han in þouȝt" (Auchinleck, 5179-80). In this scene Triamour has attributed Guy's escape from his pursuers to the devil (Caius, 7997).

[25]Mehl, p. 224; Schelp, p. 146.

[26]Again Auchinleck MS has "To our leuedi he gan calle" (264.6); appeals to Mary are another example of 'popularization.'

[27]Schelp, pp. 146-47.

[28]See my *Laments*, pp. 61-62. Cf. also John M. Steadman, *Disembodied Laughter. 'Troilus' and the Apotheosis Tradition* (Berkeley: Univ. of California Press, 1973).

CONCLUSION

[1]*An Introduction to Medieval Romance* (1930; rpt. New York: Barnes & Noble, 1969), p. 259.

[2]*Early English Prose Romances* (London: Nattali & Bond, 1858), I, ii. The original preface is dated 1828, and italics are the author's.

[3]*Fourteenth Century Verse & Prose,* ed. Kenneth Sisam (1921; rpt. Oxford: Clarendon Press, 1950), p. 31.

[4]W. P. Ker, *Medieval English Literature* (1912: rpt. Oxford: Oxford Univ. Press, 1969), p. 69. Mortimer J. Donovan, in *A Manual of the Writings in Middle English 1050-1500,* ed. J. Burke Severs (New Haven: Connecticut Academy of Arts and Sciences, 1967), p. 136, records the poem's acceptability to modern critics, but suggests a possibility that the telling is marred by the conclusion—which reasserts the continuity of order—that distracts from "Herodis' rescue and homecoming, which should be the climax of the poem."

[5]J. R. R. Tolkien, "On Fairy-Stories," *Tree and Leaf,* in *The Tolkien Reader* (New York: Ballantine Books, 1966), pp. 68-70.

INDEX